Library of
Davidson College

GLYPH 3

Editors: Samuel Weber and Henry Sussman
Editorial Board: Alicia Borinsky, Rodolphe Gasché, Carol Jacobs, Richard Macksey, Louis Marin, Jeffrey Mehlman, Walter Benn Michaels, Eduardo Saccone, Marilyn Wyatt

JOHNS HOPKINS TEXTUAL STUDIES

3

THE JOHNS HOPKINS UNIVERSITY PRESS
Baltimore and London

COPYRIGHT © 1978 BY THE JOHNS HOPKINS UNIVERSITY PRESS
All rights reserved. No part of this book may be reproduced or transmitted in any form or by any means, electronic or mechanical, including photocopying, recording, xerography, or any information storage and retrieval system, without permission in writing from the publisher. Manufactured in the United States of America

The Johns Hopkins University Press, Baltimore, Maryland 21218
The Johns Hopkins Press Ltd., London
Library of Congress Catalog Card Number 76-47370
ISBN 0-8018-2082-0 (hardcover)   ISBN 0-8018-2083-9 (paperback)

STATEMENT TO CONTRIBUTORS

The Editors of *Glyph* welcome submissions concerned with the problems of representation and textuality, and contributing to the confrontation between American and Continental critical scenes. Contributors should send *two* copies of their manuscripts, accompanied by return postage, to Samuel Weber, Editor, *Glyph*, Humanities Center, The Johns Hopkins University, Baltimore, Maryland 21218. In preparing manuscripts, please refer to *A Manual of Style*, published by the University of Chicago Press, and *The Random House Dictionary*. The entire text, including extended citations and notes, should be double-spaced.

Copies of *Glyph*, both hardbound and paperback, may be ordered from The Johns Hopkins University Press, Baltimore, Maryland 21218.

The illustration on the cover and title page, an Egyptian crocodile from the Ptolemaic period, is reproduced through the courtesy of the Walters Art Gallery, Baltimore.

CONTENTS

ONE	An American Event on the French Stage: Notes on an Eighteenth-Century Engraving LOUIS MARIN	1
TWO	Curing Rites, Dreams, and Domestic Politics in a Sumatran Society JAMES SIEGEL	18
THREE	*The (too) Good Soldier:* "a real story" CAROL JACOBS	32
FOUR	Lingering on the Threshold PIERO PUCCI	52
FIVE	Geraldine RICHARD A. RAND	74
SIX	Pre-positional By-play ANDRZEJ WARMINSKI	98
SEVEN	Realignment: Alois Riegl's Image of Late Roman Art Industry BARBARA HARLOW	118
EIGHT	Absence, Authority, and the Text RICHARD JACOBSON	137
NINE	On the Messianic Structure of Walter Benjamin's Last Reflections IRVING WOHLFARTH	148
	Notes on Contributors	213

ACKNOWLEDGMENTS

The editors would like to express their sincere gratitude to the following individuals for their assistance in the preparation of *Glyph 3*:

To Marilyn Wyatt for her first-rate work as our editorial assistant, reading all copy and proofs and handling our correspondence. To William Arctander O'Brien for his timely help in proofreading.

GLYPH 3

The Tea Tax Tempest, by Carl Goettlieb Gutenberg, born 1743 near Nuremberg, Germany. Reproduced from the collection of the Library of Congress.

ONE
AN AMERICAN EVENT ON THE FRENCH STAGE: NOTES ON AN EIGHTEENTH-CENTURY ENGRAVING
Louis Marin

THIS PAPER is an attempt to read an eighteenth-century engraving, *The Tea Tax Tempest*,[1] by Carl Goettlieb Gutenberg.[2] It is based on the notes I took when I saw *The Tea Tax Tempest* for the first time. The paper is also part of a study I am pursuing on the semiotic and semantic features of iconic narration in the seventeenth and eighteenth centuries. I nonetheless feel that I owe the reader more explanations and justifications concerning the choice I made of this engraving for my contribution to the third issue of *Glyph*.

Indeed, my paper has two starting points: first, a set of hypotheses on historical painting that I elaborated mainly on pictorial material of the seventeenth century in France, by Ph. de Champaigne, Le Brun, Le Sueur, Coypel, Poussin, and the writings of the art theorists of the Academie Royale. Second, it is a manner of answering one of the goals of *Glyph*, that is, the critique of the notion of representation through a careful exploration of the projections of European trends of thought onto the American scene, and an analysis of the ways in which those contemporary philosopies, theories, and methodologies are provided a novel life when transplanted in a new soil, in another cultural tradition. When, in December, 1976, I visited in Paris the bicentennial exhibition,

---

This essay is a revised version of a paper read at a colloquium sponsored by Miami University, Oxford, Ohio, in April, 1977, on "The Textual Frontiers of The Enlightenment." I thank Prof. Henry Sussman for his help in the revision of my text.

America Seen From Europe, I found in one of the Grand Palais rooms *The Tea Tax Tempest*, which appeared to me particularly relevant to the *Glyph* questions, since this European engraving represents a "real" *projection* displaying the image of an American event on a screen for spectators, as well as the allegories of the four continents: Europe, Africa, Asia, and America.

But the story is even more complex: the engraver, C. G. Gutenberg, actually remade a British picture of another historical event by completely displacing its political and ideological signification,[3] and at the same time in his representation he projected to "America" the very projection of the new-born American history belonging to the European eyes and minds. I realized that *The Tea Tax Tempest* could be analyzed as a symbol of what we intend to do here, that is, to trace, within the everlasting representational frame the intricate structure of influences and counterinfluences, projections and projections of projections, between the Old and New Worlds, a structure which sometimes appears sufficiently prominent to be called "History."

Indeed, such a conjunction in a small engraving of my theoretical preoccupations with the *Glyph* project seems to me a sign sent by the Goddess Fortune, enigmatic enough to deserve a careful study. Hence it followed that I wrote the notes I present today, in which my own philosophical problems concerning historical painting are mixed up with my amazing reading of the engraving on a certain chilly morning of December, 1976.

Let us begin with the general problems of reading a picture, the operations involved in the viewing-reading process, their implications on theoretical and practical levels, and the hypotheses which guide that process. My essay can thus be considered a tentative approach to a partial history of reading in the field of visual art, a problem which has been in fact raised *as such* by the seventeenth-century art theorists and those of the eighteenth century like Du Bos, Lahgier, Grimm, La Font Saint Yenne, and Diderot. To put my undertaking in more general terms, I wish to test some notions and procedures elaborated by contemporary semiotic and semantic theories, by using an engraving, Gutenberg's *The Tea Tax Tempest*, as an experimental device or model to validate, refine, or question those notions and procedures when they are displaced into a domain for which they were not primarily constructed. Nonetheless, although the study of that particular object aims at the constitution of a theory of reading and the determination of the notion of *reader* in visual art, the final result of the enterprise *will in fact* be a description of the engraving as such, in its irreducible singularity. My aim will be to discover the system that underlies the representational text, to make it coherent and noncomparable to other representational texts, as well as to locate the viewer-reader in a position that is very specific, that is, appropriate only to this engraving. It seems to me that all studies of pictorial and literary texts made from the point of view I just described are exposed to such a tension, which may be a definition of ideology, a tension between the pole of theoretical and methodological generalization and that of unique and individual description, or an opposition I might rephrase as that of *the structure of messages* in visual art in general and that of the *system of a representational text* in particular. The concrete reading-viewing of a painting and the practical position of its reader-viewer thus have a twofold nature, a bidimensional constitution: on the one hand, *competence*, whose structure is constructed from the messages produced by codes and received by the viewer in the process of reading that particular painting as an example among many others, or as a cluster of visual "quotations" of several pictorial and extrapictorial codes; on the other hand, *performance*, whose system depends on that painting as a unique object of contemplation, which organizes it as an individual reading and is appropriate only for it in a unique situation or reception. The main problem such an approach encounters is the connection between these two dimensions, the determination of a level of analysis and, consequently, of a set of notions and relationships intermediate between competence and performance, structure and system, messages and text, codes and individual reading-viewing. In a certain sense, the analyses that follow are an attempt to construct such a level and to determine such relationships and notions.[4]

But before coming to a more precise analysis of the engraving, let me state the paradigms of my own reading and my basic presuppositions. My starting point will be the distinction made by Benveniste between discourse and narrative. As you know, the fundamental assumption of Benveniste is that in narrative, as opposed to discourse, the specific modality of its enunciation is to erase or conceal the narrator's marks in the narrative propositions. So the basic characteristic of the narrative enunciation is the exclusion of all "autobiographical" forms, such as "I–Thou," the dialogic person, "here, there, now, tomorrow, yesterday," the temporal and spatial deixis, the present tense, and the tenses of past and future connected to the present tense. On the contrary, it uses a well-defined past tense, the preterit and the third person, "he, she, they."

When this specific narrative apparatus of enunciation is translated to the iconic narrative, we have to ask difficult questions, for example: What are the level and the modalities of enunciation in this kind of representation? What is its narrative agency? How could a painting narrate a story?

In order to answer these questions, I must define a few terms characterizing the space of an iconic representation. First, the space of the icon as such, the representational screen or the representation as a window open to the world, and/or the representational mirror. I shall come back to this point. Second, the representation of space on that screen, the illusory depth created on the surface of the canvas, or the representational stage. Third, belonging to this stage, the *loci* or *topoi* where the various narrative propositions are located, propositions which basically consist in the representation of significant human actions and strong passions corresponding to the successive events of the story. The distinction between screen, stage, and loci is useful insofar as it permits a structural organization framing the narrative propositions, as well as a formal apparatus of communication or enunciation, the emission-reception process. The reading of an iconic representation would then consist in projecting the time of the story onto the stage and in putting the loci of the stage into order with respect to the temporal categories "before" and "after." In other words, the very time of the referential story regulates the spatial order of the loci and finally imposes a reading order on the viewer. As du Bos recognized, perhaps more clearly than any theorist before him, the intelligibility of the painting depends in large measure on the beholder's familiarity with the subject represented.

As you know, the so-called "classical" representation is characterized by the unity of its stage: there is only a single represented space in the space of representation, although the stage may be differentiated into, for instance, a foreground, a middle ground, and a background. These planes are the loci of the stage where the narrative propositions or sequences may be located. Now what would happen to that clear-cut organization when the painter wants to depict a narrative in which the same actors have to perform different actions successively according to the referential story? Painters have attempted to elaborate various compromises, but theoretically just one possibility is left to them: to displace the temporal diachronic sequences of the narrative into a synchronic, atemporal order or into a structural organization of space based upon the rational connection of the parts in the whole. As Charles Le Brun explained to the members of the French Academy in his lecture on Poussin's *Manna*, "the historical painter has only to represent one moment where simultaneous actions take place." Historical painting is a painting whose "tense" is present, whose time is the present moment in which it is seen. The only possible way of making the story understood or "read" by the viewer is to distribute all around this central represented moment various circumstances that are logically connected to it by implication or presupposition. This is the reason that historical painting is considered the most difficult and also the most prestigious genre of painting, because in the present presence of the pictorial representation, it has to express diachrony, temporal relationships, yet can do so only through the network of a whole which generates its parts logically or achronically by its own signifying economy. The time of the story, its succeeding parts related to the succession of events, is neutralized in the intelligible space of a model that represents only the logical relationships of elements subordinated to a center. This is the paradox of the classical painting of history. The representational process cannot "presentify" time except in terms of a model, in all senses of the term: original, paradigm, absolute presence, pure rationality. The aporia consists precisely in the fact that time is definitely not a model: it cannot be a logical or metaphysical paradigm. It always admits a "before" and an "after," a "not-yet" and an "already gone." It is this "truth" that classical painting dismisses and points out at the same time through its own process of representation. Far from being a remote application of the "classical episteme" in the domain of art, historical painting, because it necessarily presents in a spatial medium a model of time-intelligibility, is instead its ultimate paradigm.

Nevertheless, in front of the painting, the viewer tells a story to himself, he reads the painting, he understands the narrative messages. This means that he converts the iconic representational model into language, and, more precisely, into a story, thanks to the expressive power, the fascinating attraction, of human actions and passions represented by the painting he looks at. On the one hand, a moment of representation is offered to our eyes as the center or the core of the intelligible structure of the whole. On the other hand, the reader narrativizes the model into a story that gives him presence in a temporal form. Between the two poles characterizing the historical painting and its reading, a "chiasmus" is operating: the model is built in its perfect structural intelligibility just in order for a story to be told: reading-enunciation. But such a reading, such an enunciation has to be dismissed from the painting itself in order to posit the moment of representation in its objective and universal truth. In other words, the subject of enunciation-representation has to be, at one and the same time, present and absent. When it is absent, events are manifestations of being itself, pure and universal essences; when present, they exist in their actual temporal succession. The painting is, at one and the same time, an instantaneous moment of evidence in the Cartesian sense, when an eternal truth is presented, and also an ontological proof in the same Cartesian sense, when from that essence existence is analytically unfolded.

That instantaneous eclipse of the subject of enunciation can be rephrased in less metaphysical terms as the subject's negation (in the Freudian sense). It is at the same time articulated in and excluded from the representation: in Benveniste's terms, "the events seem to narrate themselves as if *nobody* was speaking."5

The way in which Gutenberg solves the aporia of the "classical" representation of time and succession is, from this point of view, very interesting, since his solution involves a contradiction that points out the aporia from which he attempts to escape. In order to give his representation its historical dimension, he projects the historical event onto a metaphorical plane: he represents an allegory of Time, projecting onto a screen (I mean, onto space) a metaphor of the historical event, and in so doing, he is obliged to duplicate the representational stage, showing spectators looking at a picture. In other words, the two- or three-times remote representation of the story *in space* is intended to give us, as viewer-readers of the engraving, the sense of a specific historical time: the outburst of a revolution and its historical meaning. We shall soon see more precisely the operations involved in such a compromise with the norms or the codes of classical representation.

Now, if this is the characteristic of the historical enunciation modality, this means that the whole deictic network has to be erased from the narrative message. Is it possible to point out in Gutenberg's engraving, for example, in its narrative content, the "negation" of the iconic deixis? Does such a question make sense in the iconic domain? My hypothesis is the following: Except for the very existence of the painting and the fact that we are looking at it, nothing in the iconic message marks it as a situation of emission and reception, and, more precisely, no figure is looking at us as viewers, nobody addresses us as representatives of the sender of the message. We are only the distant spectators of a story, separated by a spectacular distance that is the insuperable distance of the representation's narrator from the story he narrates. Moreover, what is represented on the main stage? Spectators looking at an image and commenting on it, performing the very operation that we are performing on our side, looking at a picture and transforming its model into a story. What is remarkable in *The Tea Tax Tempest* is that we find represented, set on the representational stage, a famous percept given by Alberti in his *Della Pittura*, in which he articulates very clearly the problem we have just raised: he advises the historical painter to introduce into his painting a specific figure he calls the commentator. Sometimes, Alberti says, it would be useful to make an historical painting more emotionally effective by such a character, who, by his gestures and emotional expressions, points out the important part of the story to the viewer at whom he looks and with whom he establishes a visual link. In our engraving, the fact that nobody is looking at us allows us to remark, according to our hypothesis that the represented scene operates in its propositional content, the negation of all marks of emission and reception in the narrative message. But at the same time the relationships that do not take place on the plane of representation—I mean the relationships between the sender, the viewer-reader, and the message—are precisely the main subject of the "istoria" told by the engraving: five figures on the stage are related to a picture shown on a representational screen represented in the engraving. They speak together about that picture, they look at it, they point it out. In a sense, they all perform, in front of the picture projected at the background of the engraving, the various roles that an audience would have performed at an art history lecture on *The Tea Tax Tempest*. Even the projectionist, his slide projector, and the distinguished guest lecturer commenting on the engraving are there.

Let me analyze for a moment the various positions and expressions of the five figures on the foreground. All are captivated by the picture, but in very different ways. The character on the left, seen from the back seated on a "pack," seems to be attracted by the scene projected. She is ready to stand up and join the battle. Maybe the American Princess recognizes her own image in the Indian warrior (a woman in fact) leading the insurgents in the middle of the explosions. Her raised left hand appears to grasp the image, as her double in the picture appears to grasp the Phrygian cap projected from the fire. On the extreme right, Father Time, the projectionist and the main commentator on the scene he projects, focuses the image by manipulating the machine with his left hand, while with his right he points out the scene with an open mouth: does he shout with surprise or does he enthusiastically comment on what is happening in the image? Between these two figures of America and Time are three others: two seated, Europe with a spear, a shield, and a feathered helmet and Asia with a censer on her lap, who speak together. With a serene expression and a relaxed attitude, Europe shows the image to Asia, who contemplates it calmly. Standing up, just behind Europe, is the third figure, Africa, who looks at the scene with a frightened gesture.

The matter, here and for the moment, is not the question of the meaning, but the fact that exhibited on the representational stage are actors who are the vehicles of the various functions of a communicational exchange (emission-message-reference-code), as if the Jakobsian model of communication were allegorized or metaphorized there. On the right Father Time visually emits a message that the American Princess receives on the left, while Europe, by her gesture, refers to the context of the picture, the explosion, the battle, the fight of the three animals, etc., and explains what it means to Asia. Moreover, the *expressive* subfunction is performed by Africa and America, and the conative, whose effect on America is obvious, by Father Time himself. We can go further: since the powerful rays of light coming from the magic lantern connect all figures together, even the phatic function, the channel of communication, is also represented.

A few remarks about this brief description of the engraving,[6] which metaphorizes Jakobson's model of communication, not as an explanatory sketch, but as the very subject matter of the story that the engraving tells us:

1. In a sense, the engraving is the visual representation of that model.

2. The engraver and/or the beholder occupy the meta-linguistic position of the linguist, who constructs a model about a communication process.

3. The scheme is oriented from right to left for pictorial reasons (the balance and composition of the painting), an orientation that surprisingly reverses the reading of a legible text in our culture, which implies a starting point on the left. Does it mean that a revolution is, in a certain sense, a reversal of Time? Time, is allegorized in the mythic figure of the Father reclining on the celestial globe, with his attribute, the scythe that destroys every past thing. I shall try to show that such a reading, which might be now considered an overinterpretation, can be supported by formal arguments.

4. Figures can condense several functions, as, for example, Europe, who refers to the picture and comments upon or decodes it.

5. Father Time is the sender of the message in the very precise sense that he is producing the image with the magic lantern that he handles. With his optical machine, he is the very explicit metaphor—on the stage—of the viewpoint of the engraver. On her side, the American Princess, who turns her back on us and is going to stand up and "enter" the picture, is, in a sense, our representative, the representative of the beholders, entering into the representation through our gaze.

The third step of our description concerns the circular and irradiating image projected onto the screen, that focusses gazes and gestures of the figures on the stage, an image I just alluded to simultaneously as the message and its referent (its context in Jakobson's terms). What surprises me is the fact that the focal point of the image is the teapot exploding in the middle of a glowing fire surrounded by smoke and clouds, while the historical event, the battle, is represented on the periphery of the circle behind the explosion. In other words, the historical event is the context, the circumstances of the metaphor; it is the allegory that is the message. The referent is not the story or history and the allegory, its meaning: on the contrary, the metaphor is the message, and the context, history. And if the metaphorical dimension is the code dimension, the focal point of the image signifies that the message is the code. Moreover, the center of the image is a duplicated metaphor: the exploding teapot means allegorically that the tea tax is the cause of the war between the American colonies and England, a cause whose effect is the battle. The relationship between the center and the periphery of the image is thus at the same time the relationship between the message and its context, the code and the referent, and between the cause (Before) and the effect (After). In other words, the message, thanks to that metaphorization, is constructed as the relation between code and referent on the one hand *and* between cause and effect on the other; more briefly, as a relation between intelligible synchrony and historical diachrony. But this is only the first level of the allegory: the exploding teapot in the middle of the irradiating fire surrounded by smoke and clouds is obviously a displacement of the very common representation of a theophany. It is an allegory of an allegory, but at the same time a dis-allegorization of allegory. A strange ambiguity appears here: I may read the teapot as a sign projecting a profane event pertaining to economic history onto the plane of theology and mysticism, or as a symptom of an ironic derision: God is no longer a stupefying eye, a blinding light surrounded by clouds; God is a teapot.

Before going further in my description, I have to come back to my set of hypotheses concerning classical historical painting and, more precisely, the system of the iconic deixis as it works in the classical representation. My hypothesis is the following: the formal device of enunciation in the iconic representation is defined historically as the optico-geometrical network of the legitimate perspective, as the dynamic relationship between a viewpoint and a vanishing point regulated by the laws of optics and geometry that permits the rational construction of an illusory three-dimensional space upon a flat canvas. Moreover, the structural equivalence between the viewpoint and the vanishing point has been established by an experimental device built by Brunelleschi, an optical box (something like a magic lantern) described very precisely by his biographer, Manetti. Brunelleschi's optical box shows or demonstrates the equivalence between the eye of the spectator and the vision of the painter, between the reception point and the emission point, operating through the identification of the viewpoint with the vanishing point in the panel that Brunelleschi painted and its reflection in the mirror that the spectator holds in front of it. The mirror in which the viewer's eyes looks at the reflection of the scene represented on the panel makes the painting itself into a vision: in turn, it looks at the viewer-painter as an eye. Brunelleschi's device affords us a model or an experimental analogy of the theory itself. I emphasize the fact that it is only an analogy, it refers to a specific representational structure among others equally possible. The viewer is posited in the system as a spectator; he is immobilized, caught in the apparatus as a Peeping Tom. Everything takes place as if what the viewer looked at through the small hole in the panel were the painting's vision, the mirror being the operator of that "as if."

But this function does not appear as such in Brunelleschi's device, since what the spectator will look at is a scene represented on the panel. He forgets the very fact that he is looking at a picture; he is fascinated by his own "scopic" desire (or drive).

So we may provisionally conclude that that apparatus of iconic representation constituted by the perspective network is a formal apparatus that integrates the propositional represented contents, the "discourse" of the painting presented by the painting. In a less abstract way, we may theoretically consider that in the vanishing point, in its hole, the things represented gradually disappear (reception-process), or that from the view point they gradually appear to be distributed in the represented space (emission-process). And the reversibility that constitutes that space theoretically neutralizes the temporal and successive *"parcours"* of the painting by the viewer's eye in a kind of permanent present of representation.

Before coming back to our engraving, I would like to emphasize the paradigm of the specular image in the pictorial representational model since the Renaissance. Indeed, the painting, a window opened onto the world, functions—in its theoretical and even technical constitution—as a mirror duplicating it. The actual "referent" of the picture is present on the canvas as absent, that is to say, as its image, its reflex, its shadow, scientifically built in its perceptual reality (an assumption whose universality can be questioned, as Panofsky has shown in his essay on perspective as symbolic form). More generally speaking, this is the contradictory axiom of the representational system: (1.) The representational screen is a transparent window through which the spectator, Man, contemplates the scene represented on the canvas as if he saw the real scene in the world. (2.) But at the same time, that screen, actually a surface and a material support, is also a reflecting device on which the real objects are pictured. In other words, the canvas as a support and a surface does not exist. For the first time in painting, Man encounters the real world. But the canvas as a support and a surface does exist to effect the duplication of reality. The canvas as such is simultaneously posited and neutralized. Technically and ideologically it has to be assumed transparent. Invisible and a necessary condition of visibility, reflecting transparence theoretically defines the representational screen.

Now I can redefine my working hypothesis concerning the transference of the distinction between discourse and history to the historical or narrative representation: the negation (in the Freudian sense) of the representational apparatus consists in the displacement of the vanishing point to the central moment of the story represented, and in the lateralization of the depth dimension from the level of enunciation (representation) to the level of *énoncé* (the story represented). It seems important to point out the operation implied in such a move, a ninety-degree

An American Event on the French Stage

rotation of the network of optical rays (whose poles are the view point and the vanishing point). So the plane of the represented story is built as a plane parallel to the representational screen, a plane that our gaze scans by the lateral distribution of the figures. The equivalence of the view point and the vanishing point reappears there, but on the level of the story. In the engraving, the figure of Father Time, actually a complex representation of the view point, tells the story to the American Princess and the other continents of the world—a story whose location is the transformation (by displacement) of the vanishing point into the central event, into the moment of representation which is the focus of the story.

At stake in that transformation is the making of a representation that escapes its own process of constitution, which it nevertheless requires, the positing of representation in the "objective" autonomy and adequacy that it gets, but from a subject that constitutes it in constituting himself through it.

The story set on the stage by Gutenberg in his engraving, however, the event properly speaking, is not an historical event. The actual event, indeed, is the story of enunciation (representation), even at the level of the message emitted by Father Time. What is represented is the very process of representation. Moreover, what is represented is a kind of subversion of the specific frame of the historical representation as I have just defined it, a transgression operated by the exhibition of its very production. I would like to make that point clear and more precise by a formal and historical argumentation.

First: what about the spatial structure of the engraving, what about the formal organization of the representation? It is remarkable that, although our attention is captured by the scene set on the stage and, like that of the American Princess, by the image projected on the screen, this structure is clearly marked on the floor by geometrical lines that on the left lead our gaze out of the representational frame, to a vanishing point located on the horizon line, behind two columns ranked in the back. These columns frame a relief in the shadowy background representing, as far as it is perceptible, Cain killing his brother Abel.[7] The deep visible structure is thus confined to the left superior angle of the plane, and its articulating point is expelled out of the screen according to a general movement of rejection from the left inferior angle in the foreground to the right superior part in the background. This movement of expulsion and rejection, which nevertheless structures the represented space, is counterbalanced and more than balanced, is concealed and erased by a countermovement parallel to the representational screen that is punctuated by the figures distributed along a horizontal line of the floor and is underlined by the projection from the right to the left. That movement defines the space of a stage narrowed in depth by a big curtain unfolded *before* the column on the right and drawn until the left edge of the representation. The curtain impedes any motion toward the background; it encloses and narrows the stage. The two diverging movements that I have just described define concretely, within the representation, the two processes converting the formal apparatus of enunciation into the explicit legible narrative *énoncé*. They define them, they describe them, they represent them. But they also subvert them, since the curtain enclosing the stage and completing the process of lateralization initiated on the right by the magic lantern and its light rays is illusorily open and hollowed by an image, a deep space with its central point in the teapot exploding far away on the other side of the Atlantic Ocean. This cental point is the central moment of the representation, but it plays the role of the vanishing point and is substituted for it. Moreover, a light distortion reveals the transgression, as if the artist feels the whole system escaping from his hands and still tries to recuperate and stabilize it. In effect, the curtain that seems at the first glance parallel to the representational screen is actually slightly oblique. Nevertheless, the limits (the frame) of the image projected is perfectly circular and not elliptic, a mistake in the perspective system which reveals that the image is projected for us, the "real" spectators, and not for the figures acting the role of spectators on the stage. What is mastered on the level of the stage with the two diverging movements is lost on the level of the story, for whose narration the whole operation was nonetheless planned and realized.

I may go further in my attempt to draw some iconographical inferences concerning the complex spatial structure of the engraving. I briefly alluded to one of them before. The very fact that Father Time is to the right of the starting point of the whole process, reverting and converting the deep visible structure of representation into the lateral legible organization of the *"représenté"* organization, which is completed with the image on the left and its privileged spectator, the American Princess, indicates first: an attempt to temporalize the present moment of representation, to figure such a temporalization of the representational space by that allegory, to give an historical dimension to the representation, to narrativize what is represented.

Second: that this temporal movement oriented from right to left is contrary to the reading orientation means very precisely a re-volution, an historical revolution. The fact that Time reclines upon a celestial globe that projects a circular image on the screen with the teapot in its center, signifies that this historical revolution, its initiating event, has a cosmic dimension.

Third: the symbolic significance of the relief of Cain killing Abel in the right background, the bad brother killing the good, is also reversed in the image on the left, since in the fight between the two brothers, the

An American Event on the French Stage

American and English, it is the good one, the American brother, who triumphs over the bad one.

I now come to the historical argumentation. As you know, about 1750 historical painting in France was the field of a classical revival through administrative, academic, and pedagogical circumstances, and also through a transformation of the literary and aesthetic context of creation in visual art. A main tendency can be characterized: an effort toward the ennoblement of style, a will to achieve Ideal Beauty in a closer imitation of the great masters of the sixteenth and the seventeenth centuries and in a more direct meditation of the Ancients.[8] In the classical revival, two painters of the seventeenth century, Poussin and Le Sueur, were prominent paradigms for the historical painters of the second part of the eighteenth century. In his Salon of 1761, Diderot exclaims: "O le Poussin! O Le Sueur! Where is the *Testament of Eudamidas*? Where is the *Death of Saint Bruno*?" If Poussin and Le Sueur became the models for the historical painters, these two paintings by them became the paradigms of what had to be done. The neo-Poussinist movement reached its climax in 1783 with the solemn celebration of the Master in the Pantheon, an apotheosis that provoked enthusiastic eulogies.[9]

If we consider, then, all this production in the domain of the historical painting, especially in the years preceding the publication of our engraving, we may note that the painters used devices of setting the story on the stage that are the strict application of the rules of composition and organization that I tried to formalize with my hypotheses on historical narrative in visual art: the composition is ennobled by its rarefaction, by the distribution of groups of figures on the same horizontal plane, by the closure of the stage, by avoiding great displays of perspective. Many historical paintings of that period seem to be meditations on the *Testament of Eudamidas*[10] or other related paintings by Poussin, such as the *Extreme Unction* (Chantelou) or the *Death of Germanicus*. Let us have a look at the *Extreme Unction* and the *Testament of Eudamidas*. In the first we recognize the curtain enclosing the main part of the stage, the lateralized distribution of the figures in a frieze-disposition parallel to the representational screen. We also remark, half-concealed behind the curtain, a circular shield whose center is the location of the vanishing point. It is exactly the same in the *Testament*, where the formal role of the curtain is performed here by a blind wall, while a window is open on the right hand of the painting and a door on the left. Again in the *Testament* we find the shield as the place of the vanishing point: a circular shape that is, at the same time, like a blind eye, effecting by its very shape the conversion by rotation of the deep visible structure into a clearly and logically legible lateral one.

In other words, what I intend to say is that we find in *The Tea Tax Tempest* all those representational devices, the curtain, the disposition of the figures on a horizontal plane parallel to the representational screen, the opening of the stage only in a part of the composition in order to reinforce the lateral distribution of the characters, the circular shape—but all these devices diverted, distorted. The curtain is no longer a way of closing the stage and focusing attention on the story, since it is a screen onto which is projected an image which reopens it, although illusorily. The figures are not acting, performing a story, they are only contemplating an image of it. The "actors-viewers" are not historical actors but allegories of Time or the Continents. Even the circular shape of the shield, the blinded eye of enunciation in Poussin's paintings, becomes the frame of the message reproducing the circular eye of the magic lantern. My conclusion is that, when translating or transferring the formal device of historical iconic representation from the Ancient or Sacred to contemporary history, from the level of a story where characters are the narrative vehicles of philosophical, ethical, and religious virtues to another where economic events of trade policy are the motor of human actions, the whole apparatus of representation was shaken, or, if you prefer, was self-criticizing: As if, to use an analogy we often encounter in eighteenth-century art theory texts, the representational machine was raced, pushed to its limits. It reveals that representation is ideology and ideology, representation. Allegorization and metaphorization are simultaneously a way of representing a new kind of history through the patterns of an old one, of conjuring up the disturbances created by this change, and of revealing the ideological context of such a representation.

I would like to conclude by a few observations: first, on the Indian princess twice represented in the engraving, on the stage as a figure and in the image projected on the screen. This is not the place to enter into an historical account of the Indian problem and the problem of the frontier about 1760 in North America, an historical account that would exceed my competence.[11] I'll just give a few iconographical indications.

The Indian Princess was for a long time an allegory of the fourth continent. In the engraving, we find her traditional attributes, the feather diadem, the bow and arrows, but with some interesting changes: America as an Indian woman is no longer nude, and all pejorative features are now avoided, such as the crocodiles and the beheaded corpses that usually surrounded her. But the main change concerns her seat: a pack (of furs, maybe) is substituted for the traditional tatoo we find in the drawings or engravings of the seventeenth century (in, for example, those of Stefano Della Bella, Paolo Farinati, or Martin de Voos). A natural attribute has been replaced by a cultural, or better, a commercial one.

Her duplicate image on the screen is a political allegory that displaces the geographical one located on the stage. The Indian Princess is a leader-women who guides the insurgents to freedom. The allegorized allegory is thus on the right side in the War for Independence. This is a French projection, since the leadership of the Indian woman symbolizes not only the ideal of freedom characterizing the European Enlightenment, whose representatives in America are the Boston insurgents, but also the idealized relationships of the French settlement in America to the Indians,[12] whose very existence was threatened simultaneously by the French defeat in 1763 in Canada and by the English defeat in 1783.

The distance between the political and the geographical allegories, between America as a beholder of the image and America as an actress, displays the ideological contradiction of the European vision of America. It reveals the ideological disturbances created by the American revolution on the frontiers of the Enlightenment. It discloses the French projection of the Indian problem and the political, social, and economic problems of the frontier upon the philosophical and ideological stage of the Enlightenment.

Furthermore, we may remember the famous Boston Tea Party, which is in a sense evoked in the picture on the screen by the exploding teapot and its relation to the victorious move of the insurgents: a masquerade.

Is the image of the Indian woman as a leader of the angry colonists the duplicate of the Indian Princess who contemplates the projection or of one of the disguised Bostonians at the Tea Party? The question is: what kind of representation of the Indians did the Bostonians have, when they used them as masks in order to express in that spectacular way their contest with their English brothers? A means of deciding legal authority through a process of identification with the aborigines: we are Indians and we act like savages; or a way of holding that authority in derision by deriding the Indians, by using them as masks: the derogatory English attitude is not worthy of response except by using the most deprecated figures, those of savages who we are not.

The two figures of the Indian Princess in the engraving, the "actual" allegory and its allegorized representation, seem to express such an ambiguity and, beyond the historical event itself, the ambivalence of America seen from France and Europe, the Indian America and the colonists' America.

A last word to point out in *The Tea Tax Tempest* an object which is the token and the witness of the Enlightenment, its ideology of revolution and its representation: the magic lantern.[13] A representation of the view point, it is also the source of light; an optical box more complex than Brunelleschi's optical box, which needed the natural light of the sun to work its fascination on the Florentine spectators of the Renaissance, an optical box and a cyclopean eye, a *machine* in which a transparent, preformed image, a stereotyped slide, is hidden upside down in order to be truly revealed and correctly projected to the Medused American Princess.[14] This is an Enlightenment version of the Marxian camera obscura of the *German Ideology*, and what is projected is not the real history, the history of the real life, but its allegory. But in another sense the magic lantern effects an extraordinary change when compared to Brunelleschi's box. Such a change, although only represented, is perhaps the actual revolution that happened at that time, or its anticipation. Light is no longer the universal power that makes everything visible; it is no longer, as it has been since Plato, the absolute medium of theory and representation. What happens in our engraving, through the process of projection from the magic lantern handled by Father Time to the allegorical image we see on the screen, is indeed the transformation of light, the power and means of vision, into energy, the fire that makes the teapot explode. The magic lantern, the theoretical optical box, has become the steam engine of the industrial revolution, but again displaced, diverted into the *allegorical representation* of an historical "accident" of English trade policy. Another version of the negation (in the Freudian sense) of enunciation, of the very process of representation, the viewpoint is not a living and creating eye, a thinking eye, but a mechanical one that produces and exhibits what is already produced and represented, an image of an image. But although allegorized, that eye machine ultimately is an engine, whose functioning we only contemplate in its representation.

As viewers we are within and without the allegory. Our representative in the engraving is the American Princess, who is going to stand up and join her sister who leads the insurgents to victory. But at the same time, that means that we are present within the representation only as allegories, twice removed from the battle of freedom: estranged participation, participating estrangement, whose name a century later will be alienation.[15]

NOTES

1. Catalogue of the exhibition *l'Amérique vue d'Europe*, le Grand Palais, Paris, September–December, 1976, no. 202. The date of the engraving is 1778. Its dimensions are 46 by 57.7 cm.

2. Carl Goettlieb Gutenberg, a German-French artist born in 1743 near Nuremberg. He worked there during his apprenticeship years with Preissler and Haner, then six years in Basel and afterwards in Paris, where he spent most of his life until his death in 1790. His work is principally composed of engravings after Greuze and Wille. Two of his works became famous: *Wolfe's Death*, after Benjamin West's painting, and *The Tea Tax Tempest*.

3. A satirical print by John Dixon, "The Oracle," representing Britannia,

Hibernia, and Scotia meeting together in order to consult the oracle about the present situation of Public Affairs. Father Time acts as the Great Priest. Dedicated to Concord. 1774.

Cf. M. D. George, *Catalogue of Political and Personal Satires in the British Museum*, London, 1935 t.v., pp. 298–99. For a description of John Dixon's "The Oracle," see no. 5225 in the *Catalogue*.

4. Some of the theoretical parts of this essay are included in my study on Poussin's *The Arcadian Shepherds*, a contribution to a forthcoming anthology edited by S. Suleiman on the theory of reading (Princeton University Press).

5. For bibliographical references, see my article "La dénégation de l'énonciation: à propos d'un carton de Charles Le Brun," in *Prepublications*, Center of Linguistics and Semiotics (Urbino, Italy: University of Urbino, 1976).

6. For a more detailed description of the engraving, see M. D. George, *Catalogue of Political and Personal Satires*, no. 6190.

7. In his description, M. D. George writes: "On the right, a picture or a tapestry of two nude men fighting. One lies prostrate."

8. On that point, consult, among others, Jean Locquin, *La peinture d'histoire en France de 1747 à 1785* (Paris, 1912), and R. Rosenblum, *Transformations in Late Eighteenth-Century Art* (Princeton: Princeton University Press, 1967).

9. Every year, articles, manifestos, and descriptions of Poussin's paintings were published: 1757, 1762, 1764, 1769, 1771, 1777, 1779, 1781, 1783, etc. . . . In that classical revival, the influence in Rome of Raphaël Mengs and Winckelmann on French, English, and German artists who stayed there cannot be underestimated: Gavin Hamilton, Benjamin West, James Barry, Dance Holland, Angelica Kauffmann, Salamon Gessner. Between 1765 and 1775 what has been called Raphaël Mengs's school attained greater and greater importance and gave the full measure of its originality. Among French artists, we may cite Vien, Lagrenée, Brenet, Deshays, Doyen, Greuze with his reception piece, Fragonard with Coresus and Calliroe, Challe, and soon the young David with Andromaque meditating over Hector's corpse.

10. Cf. Richard Verdi, "Poussin's Eudamidas. Eighteenth-Century Criticism and Copies," *Burlington Magazine* (1971), pp. 513–24, and also Rosenblum, *Transformations*.

11. See the catalogue of the exhibition *l'Amérique vue d'Europe*.

12. Through the French-Canadian tradition of trappers and fur tradesmen, the stereotyped idea of the "Bon Sauvage" was reinforced in France at the end of the eighteenth century. The existence of freemen's villages was known. "Freemen's villages" was a phrase designating clusters of half-bred French, Indian families, and Frenchmen living with Indian women. The idealized traits of those families were evoked a few decades later by Chateaubriand in *Natchez*.

13. One may find interesting *metaphorical* references to the magic lantern or the camera obsura in Rousseau, Seventh Promenade in *Rèveries du Promeneur Solitaire*, and in *Fragments autobiographiques* (Paris: La Pléiade, 1959), p. 1154.

14. As a matter of fact, it appears that it would have been technically impossible at that time to make a *real* slide as complex and sophisticated as that projected in Gutenberg's engraving.

15. I would like to cite here Michael Fried's superb essay published in *New Literary History* 6 (1975), "Toward a Supreme Fiction: Genre and Beholder in the Art Criticism of Diderot and His Contemporaries," pp. 543ff.

TWO
CURING RITES, DREAMS, AND DOMESTIC POLITICS IN A SUMATRAN SOCIETY
James Siegel

ONE WIDESPREAD form of curing ritual is that in which spirits in the body of the patient speak through mediums or curers. Raymond Firth has described a form of this rite in Kelantan on the West Coast of Malaysia.[1] He sees the ritual as a means of expression for the patient. In it, the patient states "issues in [her] life and behavior which relate to [her] illness." However, he also points out that the language is "stereotyped and follows conventional formula while the issues mentioned are trivial."[2] Clive Kessler has discerned the political dimension of these rites and capitalized on the cryptic quality of the language.[3] He sees the rituals as a way for women to say things that enhance their position vis-à-vis their husbands, which if expressed in everyday language would either cause trouble or be of no avail.

I want to follow Kessler's linkage of curing rites and domestic politics in a society in the same part of the world, namely, Atjeh in Sumatra. But I want to suggest that the Atjehnese ritual, similar but not identical

---

I have noted the contributions of Sandra Siegel in several places in the body of the text. Her contributions, however, exceed that. My understanding was developed partly in opposition to her own notions of Atjehnese curing and dreaming. Though she has refused to be so listed, she could rightfully claim to be coauthor of this piece.

The data in the paper were collected in 1962–64 under a Ford Foundation Foreign Area Training Fellowship and in 1969–70 under an Office of Education Area Center Faculty grant.

The orthography of Atjehnese words follows that of Hoesein Djajadiningrat in his *Atjehsch-Nederlandsch Woordenboek* (Batavia: Landsdrukkerij, 1934).

Curing Rites, Dreams, and Domestic Politics

in form to the Malay one, can best be understood not by decoding the message of the patient but by looking at the relation of language and "person."[4]

Relations between Atjehnese husbands and wives are governed by an unspoken contract; there are men's duties and women's duties, and it is the fulfillment of the contract rather than emotional attachment that is the foundation of an Atjehnese marriage. Men have the obligation to furnish money and market goods while women furnish food and their labor in raising children.[5] The delineation of exchange, however, doesn't completely describe notions of authority in the family. Men feel they have the right to tell their wives what to do—how to raise the children, what to cook for dinner and whatever else—whenever they are present, not only because they live up to their part of the contract, but because they feel they "know" better. It is certainly not experience that gives them this feeling. They spend very little time at home and their suggestions are usually impractical. The reason they feel they can command is that they sense themselves to be beings of superior rationality. This is not a quality innate to them, but is rather something they feel they have achieved through religion. They believe that reciting the five daily prayers and chanting the Koran puts them in a state of purified rationality, one in which their energies and desires are controlled and they can find solutions to whatever might arise.[6]

They have, then, a religious basis to their feeling of being authoritative. It is important to note that this religious basis is not in itself substantive. What they learn reading the Koran does not tell them anything directly about daily life and, in Atjeh at least, there is no important body of interpretation that translates God's revelations made in seventh-century Arabia into the context of twentieth-century Indonesia. Nor do they receive inspiration from God during prayer. God does not speak to them or tell them what to do. In the daily prayers what is important is to repeat the Arabic words precisely while making the appropriate gestures with hands, trunk, head, and legs absolutely accurately. In prayer one's mind and body, including one's mouth, move not as though one controlled them oneself, but as though by so moving them one becomes the tracer of sacred commands. It is not essential to understand the words that one makes with one's mouth, though most Atjehnese do know what they mean. It is important that one's mind be focused on the activities of prayer, not because one might make a mistake—after years of praying 140 times a month that is not likely—but in order to be clear of any thoughts that might result in alteration of one's gestures. Chanting the Koran is similar; most Atjehnese do not understand what they read, but it is important that they chant correctly. It is as though they make the letters of the holy book speak, not in the sense of making them understood to others or themselves, but simply by making themselves the audible correlate of the written words. These gestures are thought, if not to purify the Atjehnese Muslim from desires that arise in him, at least to put him in control of them and to leave his mind clear to function.

It is these religious gestures that are the basis of men's right to speak. For to them, what they earn in the market (and bring home with them) is derivative of the rationality gained through prayer.

It is probably not accidental that this fits very well with traditional Adjehnese notions about language. To begin with, the word for language—*basa*—refers not only to spoken language but to gestures and behavior as well. Thus one says of someone that "he has language" meaning that "he behaves well"; that his manners, his demeanor are appropriate. One uses the same phrase of someone who knows, say, Malay ("he has Malay language"). If someone is crude, one says "he has no language," which we would have to translate as "he doesn't know how to act." But this would be a mistranslation in the same way that translating the sentence about Malay as "knowing" rather than "having" Malay would be wrong. For one *has* language, not when one can understand the meaning of linguistic signs or can vocalize it, but rather when one "brings" or "bears," perhaps "suffers," language. There is another word for "understand," derived from Arabic, that usually means to "grasp the meaning of." The word that means to "have" a language is not to "understand" it, but to "get a fix on it"—*toepeuë*; the root of the word means "what," "how," "where." It is a question of location, because linguistic signs to Atjehnese are as visible as audible signs—thus behavior is included. There is even a unique verbal form of the word for "language" (b*asa*) which means "to make a gesture." The correlate of this is that the word usually translated as "voice" means not "voice" but "noise" and is applied in phrases such as the "noise of the tree." A human (or animal) "voice" is "the noise of the mouth." It is the gesture of the moving mouth as well as the sound that issues from it that is involved in the relation of voice to language.[7]

Thus one who prays "has" God's language, not when he "understands" God's word (when he can put the Arabic into Atjehnese), but when his own body *reproduces* God's words. It is essential to note that this happens in relation to writing. Mohammed is the seal of prophecy. No one alive on earth will hear God's voice or should try to do so. To pray is not to recover God's meaning but to trace or conform oneself to God's writings. One thus "becomes" the signs. These written graphs are reproduced or carried in visible or audible gestures. It is thus that men become rational, become authoritative.

When one listens to the speech of Atjehnese it is easy to tell men from women, and not simply by the quality of their voices. Men seldom speak. This is not because they value silence, but because they think they should speak only when they have something of significance to say. Their speech expresses their rationality; it must therefore be substantive. The result is that it is usually portentious in tone but banal or absurd in content. Limiting oneself to saying only what is so limits one to the obvious or nearly obvious. Conversations with men tend to be confined to subjects such as what bus passed by, prices of various commodities, and other matters of fact. When they speak to their wives men are freed from the constraints of experience, which does nothing to lighten their tone, but rather allows them to utter an order for duck for dinner or to have a child washed up and make it sound highly important. Women, on the other hand, chatter continuously. Their activities are always filled with sounds, illustrating the Indonesian concept of *ramai*—or noise-making activity. What they say is only occasionally outrageous, but they feel, nonetheless, that they can say anything. Unlike men, they feel no constraint to be rational, but neither do they conceive of themselves as irrational. Rather their speech to them has authority which comes from a different source. In their struggle with their husbands they win not simply by subverting men's belief in themselves as rational, but by feeling no hesitation to speak. It is my contention that they find a source analogous to the Koran for the resultant authoritative tone in curing rites and dreams.

Atjehnese curing rituals are similar to those of Kelantan but somewhat simpler. There is no music and no dancing. They differ also in that the curer—or medium—is always a woman, while the patients are mostly women or children and occasionally an old man (in the last case, usually someone unusual in that he has spent his life in the village farming rather than out of the village trading).

The rites themselves involve two sets of spirits: the djinns, or the spirits who have caused the illness, and the spirits who "belong" to the medium—the *pòtjoets*—who enter the body of the sick person to drive out the djinn's.

In the curing rites themselves, the sick person usually lies on a mat on the floor while the medium sits with her legs crossed Indian fashion next to her. There are ordinarily one or two other women of the house present as well and neighbors may occasionally drop in if they hear the noises of the ceremony. (I have the impression that more people than usual were present at the rites we witnessed, as people were ordinarily anxious to talk with us.) The rites begin when the medium rubs scent on her hand, neck, and face to summon the *pòtjoets*. Often in the initial stages she mumbles unintelligible verses in Atjehnese. After a few minutes her knees begin to flap like wings, beating on the floor, as the first *pòtjoet* enters her. The beating increases in tempo till, when it is very rapid, the medium half rises and then collapses on the floor, usually landing on her side. She then sits up again and the *pòtjoet* speaks through her. The sound of the voice is no longer the sound of the everyday voice of the medium. Generally what is said is similar to these words taken down as at a performance in 1963:

Assalamualeichum. I am Pòtjoet Gloempang Pajōng. Who are you? [Addressing the djinn.] What do you want? Where do you live? Why have you come? What do you want? Go home. Don't bother us here. Leave the body of . . .

The women in the audience can ask both the djinn and the *pòtjoets* questions and they will answer. They usually ask the djinn how many of his friends are in the body. Sometimes the djinn will tell them why he is there. The reason is always trivial. It is often because the sick person urinated on the (invisible) spirit. As one person told my wife, "Wouldn't you be angry if someone urinated on you?" Or it may be that the patient stepped on the djinn. Sometimes too the djinn may want something simple like a glass of water and they promise to give it to him.[8]

After the *pòtjoet* has told the djinn to go away, the djinn leaves and then also the *pòtjoet* herself. As this happens, the medium's body trembles again. The medium rubs scent on herself and another *pòtjoet* enters through her and speaks to the djinns remaining in the sick person. The *pòtjoet* goes away and another djinn passes through the medium on its way back to the mountains. In the course of a single session, lasting about two hours, more or less, a dozen *pòtjoets* and a dozen djinns appear. Very sick people have more djinns in them than those with minor ailments, but every patient seems to have at least a dozen. In some cases the djinns refuse to come out and the *pòtjoets* become angry. The medium is forced to leap at the sick person as the *pòtjoet* tries to get the djinn to leave and must be restrained by those watching. At the end of the session the servants of the *pòtjoets*, who cook rice for them in the mountains, come and through the medium make jokes and rub oil on the patient. When they have left, the medium, who from the time the first *pòtjoet* entered her has not spoken a word in her everyday voice, awakens. Before she leaves she is given a small gift of money.

Throughout the ceremony the patient lies quietly. If she is not too sick she can act like any other person watching, asking questions of the djinns and *pòtjoets*, though this is not usual, and chatting with the other women. Her attention, like that of everyone else, is directed to the medium. The medium is the stage upon which the drama of the *pòtjoets* and the djinns takes place. The drama itself, however, is not elaborate. If the djinn is stubborn and does not want to leave the body of the sick person, the *pòtjoet* can become angry. But the cause of the djinn's stubbornness is never of importance to anyone. Sometimes it is just the nature of the djinn. There was one woman who was temporarily out of her wits—she had thrown her baby against the wall and had herself jumped into the well. Several different mediums had tried to drive the djinns out without success. When the djinns finally began to leave they took the form of animals—goats, dogs, snakes, and others. I did not myself witness this, but it is important that the person who told my wife about it never mentioned why the djinns had entered the woman in the first place. One never comes across stories of the guilt of the woman involved, for instance, or, for that matter, stories of social relationships in the tales told by the djinns and *pòtjoets*. Sickness is only a matter of the djinns entering the person; if there is a reason it is unimportant.

Nor is it usually the case that djinns image pain or parts of the body of the sick person, as is often the case in such rites in other cultures. The animal forms that left the body of the uncontrolled woman perhaps come closest to representing the illness itself, but the case was quite exceptional. Most rites involve persons with physical complaints where the complaint is not reflected in the story of the djinn; the djinn, who happened to be thirsty or to have been stepped on by the patient, just entered her.

Identification of the spirits does not take us much further in understanding the rite. Belief in djinns is an article of faith for Muslims, and men, therefore, do not deny that they exist. They do deny ever having experiences involving djinns, however, and they also deny that djinns make people ill, bring dreams, or in any way affect behavior. Women believe all of these things. Djinns, like the rest of the spirit-world creatures, are vague beings. They live in the mountains and forests. They can also be found in the inhabited world and particularly in the rice fields and in privies. However, in Atjeh there are no longer beliefs in spirits, djinns, or otherwise, who regularly inhabit specific places, as is believed in many other Southeast Asian cultures.[9] Similarly, while during curing rites djinns will sometimes give their names, there are no djinns with whom people are familiar from a context other than curing rites.[10] They have no identifiable shape. As one woman said, "They are like the wind; if you can see the wind, you can see the djinns." People's knowledge of djinns comes almost exclusively from curing rites when djinns speak through the mediums. When people are ill and the djinns causing the illness speak, it nearly always is the case that they want something. Djinns are themselves vaguely believed to be unfulfilled desires. Here is a portion of my wife's notes:

[B. said that] her father was sick before he died and they called K [a medium] who asked the djinn what it wanted. It answered that its name was . . . from Rambòng [a village nearby]. It said . . . that it wanted to drink and that was why it had come. That before it died it wanted to drink and could not because it was killed before it found water. Now it wandered all over looking for water. [B. said that] when she was giving birth the same djinn bothered her; she was very sick and K. came again and identified the djinn as the same one. [B. said and the others agreed] that whatever you want when you die, that's what you go wandering about for trying to satisfy after death.

There are no developed myths about the origin of djinns, nor, for that matter, are there any tales or stories that explain what they are or what they do. The *pòtjoets*, the other set of spirits, also live in the mountains and are usually believed to be the spirits of wives of nobles, though some women deny this. *Pòtjoet* is, in fact, the term used to address women of the Atjehnese nobility and also men of the sultan's family. Not all such women become spirits, however. Ordinarily they are women who died in childbirth without some desire being fulfilled. Each *pòtjoet* has a name and each curer has a series of *pòtjoets* who speak through her in the curing rites. The stories about the *pòtjoets*, naturally, are not uniform and the same stories are sometimes told about different *pòtjoets* while the same *pòtjoets* are described in conflicting ways. One such story is about the spirit often called Pòtjoet Gleumpang Pajōng. She is believed to have been the wife of the ruler of a nearby place called Gleumpang Pajōng and to have died in childbirth. Her husband and father argued about where to bury her, and the body remained in the house till people began to die from the smell. Finally she was buried under her own house and the house was burned. Since that time she has gone from place to place asking for things that are hard to find—a green duck and multi-colored goats, for instance. Her wants are sometimes made known during the curing rites. This story is an unusually detailed one. Most tales are confined to saying merely that the woman died in childbirth or died wanting something or other.

Insofar as spirits have identities, then, it is not as the remains of particular historical personages. Though they may be identified as being from a particular place or even as being the shade of a particular person, this is never someone known to the medium or the audience. So far as they stand for anything at all, spirits are a generalized expression of women's desires that are unfulfilled and therefore perpetually adrift. The biographies of spirits are really a means of indicating not that they were someone in particular but that they once had a body and now no longer do so; that they are now "like the wind" in being incorporeal. The source of the trouble djinns cause, in fact, is that in being incorporeal they therefore lodge in other people's bodies.

While spirits do not have bodies, they do, however, have voices. It would perhaps be safer to say not that they have voices, but that they have language. They speak only through the medium. When she gives them voice, it is with the physical apparatus of her own body. There is no dissembling involved in this. She is not a ventriloquist and in no way hides that they speak via her larynx, her tongue, and her mouth. The sounds of their voices differ from the sound of the medium's everyday voice and from each other. This, however, is not meant to indicate that the sound is produced or controlled by the djinns. They are simply without bodies and can produce sound only through the body of the medium.

What one sees in the rite, then, is the medium giving voice to a series of creatures. What is said is always insignificant. The cause of the trouble, the reason the djinn lodged in the body of the sick person, does not reflect the intentions or the character of the sick person or, even in a coded way, her dealings with others. Firth notes that in Kelantan such an occasion is important because it furnishes the means of dealing with the spirit. That which the spirit is known to want can be given to it. What was "fate" is then "manageable." But if it is manageable, it is not because the djinn can be satisfied, but because of the presence of the other spirits—the *pòtjoets*, who sometimes drive out djinns simply by threatening or struggling with them. The desires of the spirits are thus not a means of articulating djinns with patients or curers. The spirit's intersection with the patient's experience is most tangential. The djinn's desires are important only for giving the spirits as much identity as they have—that is, as desire itself, without the body necessary to slake that desire. Though the djinns are promised whatever they ask for, no one sees any point in trying to give it to them.[11]

These desires of the spirits, though trivial or unsatisfiable, could be the basis for dramatic narration. However, what one sees watching the rite is not a drama with a moral or, indeed, with any other kind of significance, but a series of entrances and exits with little connection between them. It is as though one were to go to a theater and, instead of a play, see twenty-six people walk across the stage, one by one. Half of them would never have been seen before; the other half would be significant only because one knew that as they left a stranger would appear. Whatever potential there is for developing the imaging of wishes and thus connecting it to experience is in no way developed.

The whole event is so undramatic, in fact, that one can attribute nothing cathartic to the scenes of departure. The patient is presumably cured when the last djinn is driven out. But the last is very like the first and little different has happened between their appearances. If one were to think in such terms as "completion" or narrative development, one would have to say that the ritual ends arbitrarily. There is neither conclusion nor change but only cessation.

In what way, then, could such a ritual image the experience of the patient as Firth and others say it does? If it does not do so, why is it believed to be effective? Is it not simply a series of practically meaningless images arranged in the skimpiest of ways? To answer these questions we have to move to the other major manifestation of spirits, that is, dreams.

The Atjehnese recognize three separate events which we class as dreams, two of which are said to be "brought" by djinns. There is no general word for dream that includes all three of these events. A *wèn-wèn* is a remembrance that occurs while one is asleep. Here is an example, told to me at the time I returned to Atjeh after an absence of four years, by the woman in whose house my wife and I had lived:

Two nights ago there was a *wèn-wèn*. It's not important. It was as though you and Sandra [my wife] came here without your child. I asked, "Why didn't you bring the baby?" "Because it was still small." That is a *wèn-wèn* because I always think of you coming back home in the afternoons.

One notes that it is not only events, but memories that can be remembered in *wèn-wèn*.

A *rabeuë* is distinguished from a *wèn-wèn* in that it does not refer to anything that happened in the past in one's own experience. That is, it is not an emergence into dream of something one was aware of earlier. Another meaning of *rabeuë* is "chaotic" or "disordered." *Rabeuë* are always said to have an odd quality to them. Here is an example told by the same woman to my wife:

I dreamt Djalil was selling fish on the path by the edge of the stream. Usually people put their money into a basket or a box, but he put his into a big can.

I bought a fish for fifty rupiah because the fish were still fresh. Then I went home and sat on the porch. I ate some betel. After that I didn't feel well and my teeth were all red. My mouth didn't feel pleasant and I did not sleep well.

What makes this a *rabeuë* is that, in addition to not really happening, the events are odd. The facts that the man is using a can instead of a basket for his money and that she bought only one fish instead of several, even though they were fresh, makes the dream odd, although the sequence of events is very much as it might have been in reality.

The third category is *loempòë* or *rahasia* ("secret"). A *loempòë* also refers to events that one has not experienced, but it is distinguished from a rabeuë insofar as it is "true" (*keubit*) and complete (*lengkap*). A *loempòë*, it turns out, has no reference at all to what is thought to have happened any more than the other two. It is true, however, because it contains a message. It is a sign of what will happen. Moreover, it is sent not by djinns but by God. It is therefore coveted. When women have to make a decision, they may await the sending of a sign in a dream.

The connection of dreams to curing rites, aside from the first two categories of dreams being "brought" by djinns, is made through the attitudes of men and women toward them. Men and women agree about the definition of the various categories of dreams. They agreed that *loempòë*, for instance, are "true," and that the other sorts are not. They differ, however, in what one might call their cultivation of dreaming. During the time we did field work my wife and I went about every morning asking people if they had dreamed and we recorded their answers. Women nearly always had done so but men almost never. In four months we had hundreds of women's dreams and only two from men. It is not surprising that men reject their dreams. *Loempòë*, true dreams, are brought by God, and God, they believe, no longer speaks directly to man. Men either claim that they do not remember their dreams or that they did not dream. Women, on the other hand, remember not only their true dreams but also *wèn-wèn* and *rabeuë*; in particular they remember the latter. (We have, in fact, only a couple of examples of "true" dreams.)

Curing rites, taken as a set of signs, are much like untrue dreams. The content of untrue dreams is dismissed. They have no "message" for women and make no "sense" to them. Insofar as they represent what happened, they are false. One is left with a set of signs devoid of content and yet remembered, even, it appears, dwelt upon. The appearance of the spirits in curing rites is likewise empty of content. The two sets of spirits may be identified as "desires," yet this is not elaborated into a narrative. Furthermore, the division of spirits into good and bad, the chasers and the chased, is unconnected with what it is that either set of spirits wants. The "content" or meaning of spirits is thus marginalized. Nor are the biographies of spirits significant. The dismissal of possible meanings of the spirits, then, is similar to the dismissal of the content of dreams.

We can put all these facts together by turning back to the central figure of the ritual—the medium. A woman becomes a medium by being "summoned" by the *pòtjoets*. She falls ill and until she agrees to "receive" the *pòtjoets* she cannot get well. Here is an account one medium gave to my wife:

I asked her how long she had been with the *pòtjoets* and she said 25 years. In the beginning she was sick and ate a handful of rice during a month's time and just lay flat thinking about nothing. And her hair was down to her thighs and there was not another person in the village who had hair as long as hers and it all fell out. Tjualima [an old medium] came to heal her and said that the *pòtjoets* wanted to be received by her and that until she received them she would remain very ill. She said she did not want to become a medium and when she said that her mouth became all twisted on one side for a whole week. Everyone said to receive them. Finally she agreed and they killed a black goat and the men were summoned to read the Koran at night and they had a *chanduri* (feast). She was "cooled" (a ritual) by Tjualima [the medium mentioned above] and from that time on she has received *pòtjoets*.

On another occasion she said that the *pòtjoets* had asked for a black umbrella when she agreed to become a medium. She went to the market and bought one and, she said, she still uses it when it rains.[12]

The initiation of the sick person as a curer depends on her willingness to let the bodyless djinns use her own body as their "voice." They are language without a means of expression until this happens. She, in exchange, is released from their power when she agrees to become their voice. Initially, the spirits chose her and occupied her body. Once she agreed to let them speak through her, however, they became her set of spirits whom she summons when she has need of them. To have their language come out through her gestures is thus not to be possessed but to escape possession and, as it turns out, to possess those whose language it initially is.

One's language is one's own, we believe, to the extent that we speak in our own voice. For Atjehnese women this is not the case. For the curer in particular, all the voices are hers not because they speak in the sound of her everyday voice—they do not—but because they speak through her body, including the physical apparatus of her voice. The spirits—language without body—have found a voice in her. This does not mean that they must speak with the characteristic sound of that voice, because the curer, named "Katidjah," is identified by neither the character of her thoughts—as men would be—nor by the sound of her voice—but by her body plus the language that comes out of her. There is a voice that is "Katidjah's"—in the sense that it is her everyday voice—and there are other voices with other names—but she is the scene of all these manifestations of language and that makes them "hers." She is not one voice but many; that does not make her divided, because it is not the sound of the voice that is the sign of unity, but the body as it produces noises and gestures.

What the curer knows about her trance when she awakens is that there was a recent period, initiated by herself, during which spirits "entered" (*sandrōng*) her, but whose sense is unknown to her. She does not know "what happened," which amounts to what she said, during that time. What she agreed to in her compact with the djinns is to be their sounding box and set of props. She has escaped illness by converting their language into her speech.

The patient sees the twitches of the curer's body and hears the messages. Nothing that she feels in her own body is an indication of what is happening there. The twitches of the curer are her only signs of what is going on within herself. But there are two ways of reading these signs. The first is that the twitches are signs of the djinn; that is, indications of what is going on within the body of the patient. In this interpretation, the signs would be produced in the body of the medium, but they would indicate what would currently be happening to the patient. It would be as though the curer were a fluoroscopic image of the patient's body. The other possibility is that the noises and gestures of the curer are the curer's own; they exist in the medium's body not merely as automatic reactions to the movements of the spirits, but as a conversion of the spirits' desires into the speech of the medium. In the second case, the reading of the medium's gestures is a reading of what has already happened within the patient. For the patient to read these gestures as the curer's is thus to read them as deferred from a time inside her to a time outside, in the medium. To recognize the language of the djinn as the speech of the medium is for the patient to be released from that language. The efficacy of the rite depends on the second assumption.

We might note that just as curing rites say nothing of significance about the past of the patient, neither do they speak of her pain. To listen to the messages of the spirits is not to speak of the woman's experience or of anything substantive. The important operation in reading the signs of the spirits is not to apprehend "what they say" about anything whatsoever, but rather to attribute the signs to the curer and thus to escape from their language. To think of the djinns is not to develop an image of them or of the patient but to put them out of mind.

Dreams, aside from "true" dreams (*loempòë*), function like curing rites. It is remarkable that Atjehnese divide dreams so many ways and yet have no word for "nightmare." This is because all dreams, or at least all false dreams, are unpleasant while they are being dreamed. Dreams, like illness, are thought to be brought by djinns. There is a curse that says "may a djinn weigh you down" (by sitting on your chest), which it is customary to translate as "may a djinn bring you nightmares."[13] However the dream is known only after the djinn is gone. While the djinn sits on the chest of the dreamer he or she is simply in their grasp. If one sees someone tossing about in their sleep, one must not waken them. They are in the possession of the djinn who may carry them away. (One tries instead to scare away the djinn.) The dream itself is known only after the time that it occurs.

For women to "remember" the dream or to "put it into speech" is not to recover what occurred to them while they slept. What happened was that the djinn visited them, but they do not speak of this event. Rather, to "remember" the dream is to transform the visit of the djinn into a set of signs that are theirs since they exist in their bodies. It is thus to move out of the grip of the djinns. The djinns, language without a means of expression, do in dreams what they do in curing rites; they make women their means of speech. By accepting the demands of the djinn for expression, women, in thinking of their dreams, think not of the dream as the visitation of the djinn, but of what only in retrospect is conceived to have happened at that time: the dream itself. It is not, then, the "meaning" of the dream or its phenomonological immediacy that is important to them. In remembering their dreams women give the djinns expression; but in signs which, since they are women's own, celebrate not what the djinn says but their release from the djinn's grasp.

All dreams brought by djinns have unserious messages, as we have seen. We can now understand why this is so. Were the message serious, what would be celebrated would be the content and the bringer of the content. The dream would then be a *loempòë*, a message brought by God. To say that the message of a dream is trivial and yet to dwell on it is to celebrate not the dream or its occurrence, but one's own possession of a set of signs. To discard content is at the same time to salute one's own control of language.

Women only seldom engage in curing rituals. They seem to dream nightly, however. Their commemorations of these occasions are parallel to their husbands' self-constitution in prayer and make understandable the authority of their trivial words.

NOTES

1. Raymond Firth, "Ritual and Drama in Malay Spirit Mediumship," *Comparative Studies in Society and History* 9 (1967).
2. Ibid.
3. Clive Kessler, "Conflict and Sovereignty in Kelantanese Malay Spirit Mediumship," in *Case Studies in Malay Spirit Possession*, ed. V. Crapanzano and V. Garrison (New York: Wiley-Interscience, 1977).
4. The chief difference between the Atjehnese and Malay rituals are noted later. It is, however, important that the Atjehnese ritual lacks the metaphor of the body as a state which Kessler has brilliantly demonstrated for the Kelantanese rite.
5. See Chandra Jayawardena, "Women and Kinship in Acheh Besar," *Ethnology* 16 (1977), and his "Achehnese Marriage Customs," *Indonesia*, April 1977, as well as J. T. Siegel, *The Rope of God* (Berkeley: University of California Press, 1969), chapter 7, and Snouck Hurgronje, *The Achehnese* (Leiden: E. J. Brill, 1906).
6. This has been described by Siegel, *The Rope of God*, chapters 6 and 9.
7. In traditional Atjehnese literature, however, sound is privileged not because the sound of the voice contains one's ideas in closest proximity to oneself, but because sound is believed to be continuous and thus to obliterate all distinctions. See Siegel, *Shadow and Sound: The Historical Thought of a Sumantran Kingdom* (Chicago: University of Chicago Press, forthcoming), chapter 1.
8. I use "him" for djinns, but they are of indeterminate gender. *Pòtjoets*, however, are always female.
9. This is true, at least, of Pidie, the section of Atjeh where the data presented were collected.
10. There is one exception, which is noted below.

Curing Rites, Dreams, and Domestic Politics

11. Women say that they give djinns what they ask for during feasts. However, though we inquired on several occasions, we never saw or learned of anything being specially set out for djinns. The feasts are given for various purposes, none of which have to do with djinns. See Siegel, *The Rope of God*, pp. 52, 116, 159, and 161.

12. This may be connected with the name of the first spirit she summons, Pòtjoet Gloempang Pajōng or Ptjoet/a kind of large shade tree (gloempang)/ umbrella (Pajong). If so, what is involved is simply the transfer of a signifier. The place name is Gloempang Pajōng. The "umbrella" of the title is transferred as the black umbrella used when it rains. The other association is with shadow and social position. Umbrellas are used for shade as well as protection from rain. They were traditionally reserved for nobility, including those labeled "pòtjoet" and royalty. Shadow is associated with royal writing while the djinn who brings dreams is also associated with shadows. See below and Siegel, *Shadow and Sound*.

13. I have myself mistranslated this phrase in "Si Meuseukins's Wedding," *Indonesia* 22 (Autumn, 1977). Djajadiningrat translates it the same way. See *beunò* in Djajadiningrat, *Atjehesch-Nederlandsche Woordenboek* (Batavia: Landsdrukkerij, 1934). *Beunò* is the name of the particular spirit who brings dreams. It is interesting that the spirit is associated with shadows, since shadow is a term used by Atjehnese to speak of writing. See note 12.

THREE
THE (TOO) GOOD SOLDIER: "A REAL STORY"
Carol Jacobs

> For a lie is a figurative truth—and it is the poet
> who is master of these illusions.
> "The Nature of a Crime"[1]

THIS IS as I had hoped and expected—a more intimate setting than the one in which I spoke of *Wuthering Heights*.[2] It is quite proper that it should be so. For if in the novel of Emily Brontë it was continually a question of locking people out, here it is a question of taking them in—into one's confidence, that is. But can I reasonably hope to inspire the same trust in my auditors as John Dowell, the narrator of *The Good Soldier*, inspires in his? I offer you his bid to the reader's imagination:

So I shall just imagine myself for a fortnight or so at one side of the fireplace of a country cottage, with a sympathetic soul opposite me. And I shall go on talking, in a low voice while the sea sounds in the distance and overhead the great black flood of wind polishes the bright stars. From time to time we shall get up to go to the door and look out at the great moon and say: "Why, it is nearly as bright as in Provence!" (12)[3]

You see, don't you, what it would take to have a heart to heart talk—about this text, itself so concerned with affairs of the heart. In order to have confidence in what I am about to say—you see—it is merely a matter of closing your eyes to the reality at hand. It is perhaps not too soon to admit that this room resembles a country cottage as little as Texas resembles Provence. And it is only fair to remind you—for I want to be as honest as "the situation" permits now that we are on intimate terms—that whereas you have known me for two short days, nine years of extreme intimacy with the Ashburnhams left John Dowell as blind to what they were about as anyone could be. This is the way he opens his story:

> This is the saddest story I have ever heard. We had known the Ashburnhams for nine seasons of the town of Nauheim with an extreme intimacy—or, rather, with an acquaintanceship as loose and easy and yet as close as a good glove's with your hand. My wife and I knew Captain and Mrs. Ashburnham as well as it was possible to know anybody, and yet, in another sense, we knew nothing at all about them. This is, I believe, a state of things only possible with English people of whom, till today, when I sit down to puzzle out what I know of this sad affair, I knew nothing whatever. (3)

To be sure Dowell is the most straightforward character of the novel and past ignorance offers no ground for present mistrust. No narrative could be more insistent on "puzzling out" (3), as Dowell puts it, what must have been, on "piec[ing] together afterwards" (109), just as I hope to piece together for you the broken threads of the text at hand. And if that text forgets to put the pieces in their proper places, if it now and again creates false impressions, if the path of the narrative which ultimately promises to bring us out of the labyrinth occasionally seems less than straightforward, doesn't this paradoxically authenticate the reality of the tale?

> I have, I am aware, told this story in a very rambling way so that it may be difficult for anyone to find his path through what may be a sort of maze. I cannot help it. I have stuck to my idea of being in a country cottage with a silent listener, hearing between the gusts of the wind and amidst the noises of the distant sea the story as it comes. And, when one discusses an affair—a long, sad affair—one goes back, one goes forward. One remembers points that one has forgotten and one explains them all the more minutely since one recognizes that one has forgotten to mention them in their proper places and that one may have given, by omitting them, a false impression. I console myself with thinking that this is a real story and that, after all, real stories are probably told best in the way a person telling a story would tell them. They will then seem most real. (183)

There would seem to be nothing amazing in taking this line of argumentation. Certainly Dowell's roundabout way of saying things approximates the involuted ramblings of human thought far better than a linear narration. What we have before us is the impressionistic experiencing of Dowell's past and therefore not only a "real story" but one that justly "seems most real" (183).[4] Isn't that the point Dowell is making? Perhaps. But the other point he immediately gets to is Maisie

Maidan's death. This point, at least, has found its proper place. The passage continues as follows:

> At any rate, I think I have brought my story up to the date of Maisie Maidan's death. I mean that I have explained everything that went before it from the several points of view that were necessary—from Leonora's, from Edward's, and, to some extent, from my own. You have the facts for the trouble of finding them; you have the points of view as far as I could ascertain or put them. (183-84)

We are compelled to be amazed after all. For just after Dowell admits "that it may be difficult for anyone to find his path through what may be a sort of maze," we arrive at Maisie Maidan's death, the death of the maiden of the maze. Are we not, as readers of the text, very much like Maisie lost in a labyrinth from which we can never escape? Are we not brought to a country cottage far away from all that is familiar—just as Maisie was brought to Germany all the way from Chitral—in order to be entangled in a maze of illusions and conjecture? At the last moment, in fact, Maisie finally reads the scene correctly. In this, her triumphant moment of interpretation, when she has finally gotten to the heart of the matter,[5] when she has understood the intrigues of Nauheim, just as she is packing her portmanteau and preparing her exit, she finally succumbs to her heart and dies:

> She [Leonora] had not cared to look round Maisie's rooms at first. Now, as soon as she came in, she perceived, sticking out from beyond the bed, a small pair of feet in high-heeled shoes. Maisie had died in the effort to strap up a great portmanteau. She had died so grotesquely that her little body had fallen forward into the trunk, and it had closed upon her, like the jaws of a gigantic alligator. The key was in her hand. (75-76)

"The key was in her hand." Could this be our key to the interpretation of the text? If so it remains closed within that which it would presume to open. How could it be otherwise? For if Dowell's narrative promises "the facts for the trouble of finding them," it nonetheless lures us into the comfort of blind alleys:

> Somewhere between Nice and Bordighera provided yearly winter quarters for us, and Nauheim always received us from July to September. You will gather from this statement that one of us had, as the saying is, a "heart," and, from the statement that my wife is dead, that she was the sufferer.
> Captain Ashburnham also had a heart. . . . The reason for his heart was, approximately, polo, or too much hard sportsmanship in his youth. The reason for poor Florence's broken years was a storm at sea upon our first crossing to Europe. . . . (4)

The facts are indeed troublesome to find here since what we "will gather" can only be what Dowell strews in our path—the misinformation that Florence had heart trouble and died of it—that Edward too had a heart. To be sure, both Florence and Edward committed suicide because they "had, as the saying is, a 'heart' "[6] in another sense, but this play on words renders Dowell's statement accurate only at the price of questioning the univocity of his tale.

And question it one should.[7] Not only does the narrative mislead us, but as it "goes forward" (183) it doubles back on itself with a violence usually camouflaged in better circles. If the intimacy of the Ashburnhams and Dowells is like a tranquil "minuet de la cour" (6), one page later "it was a prison—a prison full of screaming hysterics, tied down so that they might not outsound the rolling of our carriage wheels . . ." (7). If Edward and Leonora are the "model couple" (8), "perfectly wealthy" (9), "honest" (8), "the real thing" (8–9), perfectly devoted, one page later they are endlessly poor, endlessly acting, and (in a scene that recalls *Madame Bovary*), we find Leonora ready to commit adultery in the back of a carriage. As the narrative rolls along in this manner, we begin to suspect that the text itself is a kind of adulterer, continually turning from the straight line of narration in which it might remain true to what it said before. It promiscuously betrays not only itself, but also us, its intimates,[8] enticed as we are to a two-week honeymoon in a country cottage only to find that our own text is unfaithful.

This proves all the more amazing since the reader has taken it for granted that Dowell was one of the "good people." It was a given proposition. "Indeed, you may take it that what characterized our relationship was an atmosphere of taking everything for granted. The given proposition was that we were all 'good people' " (34). What does it signify to be among this elite? "You meet a man or a woman and, from tiny and intimate sounds, from the slightest of movements, you know at once whether you are concerned with good people or with those who won't do. You know, that is to say, whether they will go rigidly through the whole programme from the underdone beef to the Anglicanism" (37). As the concept is introduced, it appears an appropriate subject for epistemological and semiological ecstasy. "Good people" are immediately recognizable, immediately predictable, and the two-word rubric is permanently linked to a fixed catalogue of significations. Yet as Dowell continues, the phrase becomes less a vehicle for intimate understanding than a guarantee of mere acquaintance, indeed less a guarantee of acquaintance than an aggressive refusal of comprehension.[9] "But the inconvenient—well hang it all, I will say it—the damnable nuisance of the whole thing is, that with all the taking for granted, you never really get an inch deeper than the things I have catalogued" (37).

The moral of the story is that the "good people" are those who are "too good to be true" (9). Or is this saying too much, for the narrative as we have cited it spoke not of falsehood but only of a resistance to penetration? Yet how else can one explain that Florence's maiden aunts are unable to warn Dowell that their niece, as they thought, was a harlot? Unable to speak directly, their most impassioned pleas are a wide deviation from the truth:

> You see, the two poor maiden ladies were in agonies—and they could not say one single thing direct. They would almost wring their hands and ask if I had considered such a thing as different temperaments. I assure you they were almost affectionate, concerned for me even, as if Florence were too bright for my solid and serious virtues. (81)

And they carried their protests to extraordinary lengths, for them. . . .

> They even, almost, said that marriage was a sacrament; but neither Miss Florence nor Miss Emily could quite bring herself to utter the word. And they almost brought themselves to say that Florence's early life had been characterized by flirtations—something of that sort. (81)

They were too good to be truthful. Perhaps even this is saying too little. With each definition one gives to the phrase "good people," it's as though the text retorts "that's too good to be true." It retaliates with an abrupt escalation of the term, always radically shifting its definition. Consider for example that other event that occurs on the date of Maisie Maidan's death. The Dowells and the Ashburnhams have traveled to Marburg where Florence has staged her first open assault on Edward's heart by insulting Leonora's religion and nationality. Leonora, who reads the scene immediately, reacts with an impassioned horror that even Dowell does not fail to sense. Being one of the "good people," however, she displaces the crux of the matter, the question of the impending affair, with the same figural language that Florence has used. She voices her warning to Dowell as follows: "'Don't you know,' she said, in her clear hard voice, 'don't you know that I'm an Irish Catholic?'" (46). The blank whiteness of a chapter break marks the end of this phrase and also marks the obliteration of its meaning that Dowell, himself one of the "good people," performs. As Chapter V opens he writes, "Those words gave me the greatest relief that I have ever had in my life" (46). And, as if even this denunciation from Leonora is too violent to take at face value, Dowell goes on to displace her meaning yet further:

> Yes, I remember thinking at the time that it was almost as if Leonora were saying, through me, to Florence:
> "You may outrage me as you will; you may take all that I personally possess, but do not you dare to say one single thing in view of the situation that that will set up—against the faith that makes me become the doormat for your feet."

The (too) Good Soldier

But obviously, as I saw it, that could not be her meaning. Good people, be they ever so diverse in creed, do not threaten each other. So that I read Leonora's words to mean just no more than:

"It would be better if Florence said nothing at all against my co-religionists, because it is a point that I am touchy about." (68–69)

"Good people," then, not only deviate from the truth like the aunts Hurlbird, they camouflage its violence with metaphor, saying something utterly different from what they mean, like Leonora, or purposely disfigure it, like Dowell.[10]

Even systematic distortion and misinterpretation may not be the text's final word on the "good people." It nevertheless explains why one of the key passages in the novel should be the moment when Florence rounds a screen in the hotel corridor to find a certain scene of entanglement. It is a scene in which language has been silenced: "There was not a single word spoken" (53), a scene in which violence has left only the barest of traces, the red mark on Maisie Maidan's cheek where Leonora has slapped her. In this, the only instance of literal violence in the text, Leonora has forgotten to act with the repressive decorum of a good person. She immediately attempts to cover her tracks.

> And there was not a word spoken. You see, under those four eyes—her own and Mrs. Maidan's—Leonora could just let herself go as far as to box Mrs. Maidan's ears. But the moment a stranger came along she pulled herself wonderfully up. She was at first silent and then, the moment the key was disengaged by Florence, she was in a state to say: "So awkward of me . . . I was just trying to put the comb straight in Mrs. Maidan's hair. . . ." (53)

Dowell marks this scene as a pivotal point, for it was at this moment that Florence became intimate with Leonora and began to gain control. "Leonora behaved better in a sense. She just boxed Mrs. Maidan's ears—yes, she hit her, in an uncontrollable access of rage, a hard blow on the side of the cheek, in the corridor of the hotel, outside Edward's room. It was that, you know, that accounted for the sudden, odd intimacy that sprang up between Florence and Mrs. Ashburnham" (52). "At any rate that was how Florence got to know her" (53).

Florence knows to interpret the signs just as we as "good" readers of the text must learn to read its traces. Let us begin by reading one that is left there specifically for us. What is it after all that entangled Leonora in Maisie's hair but the gold key that hung from her wrist and about which Dowell has already written:

Certain women's lines guide your eyes to their necks, their eyelashes, their lips, their breasts. But Leonora's seemed to conduct your gaze always to her wrist. And the wrist was at its best in black or a dogskin glove and there was always a small gold circlet with a little chain supporting a very small golden key to a dispatch box. Perhaps it was that in which she locked up her heart and her feelings. (32)

Like Maisie's (and our) key, it is caught within the very labyrinth from which it would hope to provide an escape. For it is, of course, precisely by disengaging it as she does, that Florence becomes the next point of entanglement.

As I am sure you see, then, this scene entangles more than meets the eye. The violence here is demarcated by the silent trace, that almost perfect expression which expresses almost nothing.[11] The silence quickly gives way first to the rhetorical screen of the "good people" and then to that fateful moment of Leonora's compromise when she openly begins to indulge herself in intercourse.

> She opened the door of Ashburnham's room quite ostentatiously, so that Florence should hear her address Edward in terms of intimacy and liking. "Edward," she called. But there was no Edward there.
> You understand that there was no Edward there. It was then, for the only time of her career, that Leonora really compromised herself—she exclaimed: "How frightful! . . . Poor little Maisie! . . ." (53)

This movement from silence to talk will prove significant for the text as a whole. The lapse into communication takes place at the juncture marked by the scene in the corridor and the trip to Marburg:

> If there was a fine point about Leonora it was that she was proud and that she was silent. But that pride and that silence broke when she made that extraordinary outburst, in the shadowy room that contained the Protest. . . . (184)
>
> That was really a calamity for Leonora, because, once started, there was no stopping the talking. She tried to stop—but it was not to be done. (192)
>
> I don't in the least blame Leonora for her coarseness to Florence. . . . But I do blame her for giving way to what was in the end a desire for communicativeness. (192)

As Dowell would have it, however, these "nine years of uninterrupted tranquility" from the death of Maisie Maidan to the death of Florence "were characterized by an extraordinary want of any communicativeness" (34) between the Ashburnhams and the Dowells, between "Edward and Leonora [who] never spoke a word to each other in private" (8), and of course between Dowell and Florence. Dowell's entire role as nurse to Florence was, as he understood it, to restrain her intercourse because she "had, as the saying is, a 'heart' " (4).

> For do you understand my whole attentions, my whole endeavors were to keep poor dear Florence on to topics like the finds at Gnossos and the mental spirituality of Walter Pater. I had to keep her at it, you understand, or she might die. For I was solemnly informed that if she became excited over anything or if her emotions were really stirred her little heart might cease to beat. For twelve years I had to watch every word that any person uttered in

any conversation and I had to head it off what the English call "things"—off love, poverty, crime, religion, and the rest of it. (15–16)

It is strange that the only function of the novel's narrator is to silence all reference to love, poverty, crime, and religion, the very subject matter of the text; for what is *The Good Soldier* about if not love, the poverty of the Ashburnhams, the crime of adultery, and questions of Protestant and Catholic religion. One wonders if Dowell's habit of "heading off" rhetorical violence, the violence of rhetoric, hasn't been difficult to break. "You cannot, you see, have acted as a nurse to a person for twelve years without wishing to go on nursing her" (70–71).

Dowell's imposition of censorship functions as something of a joke, of course: silence does not repress Florence's emotions but merely deforms her discourse. There is perhaps a certain shrewdness in the gesture after all, however, for the violence of *The Good Soldier* takes place, not in the outburst of sexual passion, but in that of talk. Language operates in this tale less by way of expressing passion than by creating it. It creates the greatest passion of Dowell's life, for example, and the only real passion of Edward's.

> The odd thing is that what sticks out in my recollection of the rest of that evening was Leonora's saying:
> "Of course you might marry her," and when I asked whom, she answered: "The girl."
> Now that is to me a very amazing thing—amazing for the light of possibilities that it casts into the human heart. For I had never had the slightest conscious idea of marrying the girl; I never had the slightest idea even of caring for her. (103)

> And in speaking to her [Nancy] on that night, he [Edward] wasn't, I am convinced, committing a baseness. It was as if his passion for her hadn't existed; as if the very words that he spoke, without knowing that he spoke them, created the passion as they went along. Before he spoke, there was nothing; afterwards, it was the integral fact of his life. (116)

Language, the talk of desire, does not mediate an already existing passion but rather generates it. And it's not simply that language generates passion: the fatal driving passion of the tale becomes this desire for talk, the "desire for communicativeness" (192). However Dowell may condemn it in Leonora, it is certainly his single passion, determined as he is to create the text as a space for a fortnight of intimate conversation. Isn't it Edward's talk that drives Maisie to her death and Florence to suicide, and isn't it the talk at Branshaw Teleragh that ultimately brings Edward to suicide and drives Nancy to madness? Before we reach this point, let us make a detour by way of Marburg to retrace the path of this lapse into talk.

This journey, you understand, turns the relationship of the four completely on its end. The upheaval is not merely the result of Leonora's outburst (her displaced announcement that she is Irish Catholic). Dowell writes of this entire day: "I was aware of something treacherous, something frightful, something evil in the day. I can't define it and can't find a simile for it" (44). What is it on this journey that is treacherous and indefinable, treacherous perhaps because it is that for which no simile can be found? If we can offer no definitive answer to this question, we might begin by noting that the entire journey rides on Florence's seemingly insignificant chatter. And not only Florence's, for Dowell, in turn, chooses this moment of his story to ramble on rather aimlessly, to interject the single gay, descriptive, and apparently irrelevant interlude of the novel. It is here when we are most thrown off guard that Dowell's narrative operates as an inexorably precise, almost mechanical, if ultimately problematic, allegory.

Why, I remember on that afternoon I saw a brown cow hitch its horns under the stomach of a black and white animal and the black and white one was thrown right into the middle of a narrow stream. I burst out laughing. But Florence was imparting information so hard and Leonora was listening so intently that no one noticed me. As for me, I was pleased to be off duty; I was pleased to think that Florence for the moment was indubitably out of mischief—because she was talking about Ludwig the Courageous (I think it was Ludwig the Courageous but I am not an historian), about Ludwig the Courageous of Hessen who wanted to have three wives at once and patronized Luther—something like that!—I was so relieved to be off duty, because she couldn't possibly be doing anything to excite herself or set her poor heart a-fluttering—that the incident of the cow was a real joy to me. . . . [I]t does look very funny, you know, to see a black and white cow land on its back in the middle of a stream. It is so just exactly what one doesn't expect of a cow. (42)

This is exactly what one doesn't expect of a text; and yet it is there for us in black and white.[12] Three times, we are told, it is the "black and white" that is turned on its end. This passage that talks of Florence imparting information and history, that itself appears an informative if pointless moment of personal history, has a certain hitch. It is just about this time, while the narrator is "off duty," that Maisie Maidan is thrown into the middle of a portmanteau, with her feet in the air, like the black and white cow. It is the same moment in which Florence is maneuvering to toss Leonora aside:

And we went up winding corkscrew staircases and through the Rittersaal, the great painted hall where the Reformer and his friends met for the first time under the protection of the gentleman that had three wives at once and formed an alliance with the gentleman that had six wives, one after the other (I'm not really interested in these facts but they have a bearing on my story). (43)

These facts *are* Dowell's story. For who is the "gentleman that had six wives, one after another" if not Edward Ashburnham whose love affairs and flirtations (you have the facts for the trouble of finding them), are just about to number six at this point in the tale: Leonora, the servant girl of the Kilsyte case, the Grand Duke's mistress, Mrs. Basil, Maisie, and Florence. And who is "the gentleman that had three wives at once," under whose protection the Reformer and the man with six wives meet, if not the protective Dowell who in the course of the novel admits to having loved Leonora (32), Maisie Maidan (51), and Nancy Rufford at one and the same time.[13] And who is the Reformer, if not Florence, who, we have just been told, "was at that time engaged in educating Captain Ashburnham" (39).

Her method of education is by way of a certain text: "You see, in the archives of the Schloss in that city there was a document which Florence thought would finally give her the chance to educate the whole lot of us together" (40). This text which holds such promise of enlightenment documents the entire problematic of the trip to Marburg—Florence's coded monologue, Dowell's narration of that monologue, and the lapse into talk in general. It does this less by way of what it says than by way of its unlikely appearance. "She was pointing at a piece of paper, like the half-sheet of a letter with some faint pencil scrawls that might have been a jotting of the amounts we were spending during the day. . . . 'There it is—the Protest'. . . . 'Don't you know that is why we were all called Protestants? That is the pencil draft of the Protest they drew up'" (44). Florence points the finger at a scrap of paper, the original draft of the Protest, the point of rupture between Catholics and Protestants, and between Leonora and Edward of course. She never bothers to elaborate on its content. It resembles the "half-sheet of a letter with some faint pencil scrawls" and thereby claims the same insignificant innocence as the chatter of Florence and the conversational recordings of Dowell. Unlike the all too clear letter Maisie presently writes, the Protest is a study in illegibility. It forewarns us that the shift into talk will not fulfill a promise of revelation but will produce a text all the more demanding of interpretation.

All the more demanding of interpretation because Protestantism functions in *The Good Soldier* as the destruction of an established code, the moral code of the marriage sacrament. This is the maddening lesson that Nancy will learn at Branshaw Teleragh:

"I thought," Nancy said, "I never imagined. . . . Aren't marriages sacraments? Aren't they indissoluble? I thought you were married . . . and . . ." She was sobbing. "I thought you were married as you are alive or dead."

"That," Leonora said, "is the law of the church. It is not the law of the land. . . ."

"Oh, yes," Nancy said, "the Brands are Protestants."

She felt a sudden safeness descend upon her, and for an hour or so her mind was at rest. It seemed to her idiotic not to have remembered Henry VIII and the basis upon which Protestantism rests. (220–21)

The Protest makes possible polygamy and divorce, having three wives at once or six wives one after another. It challenges the law of the church which insists on the indissoluble one-to-one relationship between man and wife and implicitly between sacramental text and meaning.[14]

It is this challenge that takes place as they enter the "large old chamber full of presses" in which that document is to be found. Florence

> told the tired, bored custodian what shutters to open; so that the bright sunlight streamed in palpable shafts into the dim old chamber. She explained that this was Luther's bedroom and that just where the sunlight fell had stood his bed. As a matter of fact, I believe that she was wrong and that Luther only stopped, as it were, for lunch, in order to evade pursuit. But, no doubt, it would have been his bedroom if he could have been persuaded to stop the night. (43–44)

It is the sunlight of course that is palpable, and not the bed of Luther that Florence passionately strives to evoke. Unlike her reformer counterpart, Florence has no desire to "evade pursuit." She could well—this is her point—she could well be "persuaded to stop the night." "And then," the passage continues, "in spite of the protest of the custodian, she threw open another shutter and came tripping back to a large glass case" (44). The custodian, who was tired and bored only a few lines back, seems to recognize the potency of those "palpable shafts" of sunlight that create beds where only printing presses stood before. He raises a "protest" as a reminder of the significance of the term, for Florence is about to illuminate *the* Protest, which is to say, as we have seen, that Florence is out to re-form it. "She continued, looking up into Captain Ashburnham's eyes: 'It's because of that piece of paper that you're honest, sober, industrious, provident, and clean-lived. If it weren't for that piece of paper you'd be like the Irish or the Italians or the Poles, but particularly the Irish. . . .' And she laid one finger upon Captain Ashburnham's wrist" (44).

It is indeed hard to put one's finger on what is happening here. As Dowell puts it two lines later, "I can't define it and can't find a simile for it," and it is now, you remember, that Leonora is driven to her "desire for communicativeness." The indefinability and the lapse into communication both revolve around Florence's reading of "the Protest" by means of a certain mode of discourse in which literal and figural language prove mutually exclusive. It is because of that piece of paper, she insists, that Edward is sober, industrious, provident, and clean-lived. Edward, of course, is none of these: he nearly drinks himself to death, is indolent, cannot control his excessive expenditures, and is heading rapidly for his sixth affair. If Florence inverts each of his characteristics, she does so, it would seem, out of ignorance. What she means by saying that Edward is clean-lived is that she wishes he weren't,[15] for the reformer wishes to go to bed with the "gentleman that had six wives one after another." She lays her hand on Edward's wrist then by way of saying—"This is my body."

What does it mean to say "This is my body" in the Castle of Marburg while pointing at a manuscript signed, we are told, by Martin Luther, Martin Bucer, and Zwingli (44)? Dowell and Florence have been "imparting information so hard" (42) that one is tempted to remain "off duty" (42). In rejecting a literal reading of their narrations one is tempted, that is, simply to fix upon the limited mechanical allegory of Dowell's black and white cow as Maisie Maidan or Leonora[16] and of Florence's Reformer, Henry VIII, and Ludwig the Courageous as figures for Florence, Edward and Dowell. But let us shuttle back from the figurative to the historical as the document in question demands in order to restore to it its proper name. It is thus, paradoxically enough, that the black and white is turned truly on its end.

The fact of the matter is that the "piece of paper" Florence insists on calling "'the Protest" can be none other than the Articles of Marburg signed in the Castle of Marburg, October 1529, by Luther, Bucer, Zwingli, and seven others.[17] "I don't really deal in facts;—[you understand. Along with Ford Madox Ford] I have for facts a most profound contempt."[18] It's not that "I'm . . . really interested in these facts but they have a bearing on my story" (43). Those Articles, you will remember, are the result of several days of vertiginous argument between Luther and Zwingli[19] as to the reading of the phrase "This is my body." Throughout the talks on the interpretation of these words, Luther insists that he "cannot understand them in any other way than according to their literal meaning."[20] For him, the proper interpretation of the sacrament means "The body is present in the bread" (LW 30). Zwingli and Oecolampadius, however, regard the bread of the sacrament only as a spiritual remembrance of the body of Christ. They read the phrase "This is my body" as figurative speech: "In such cases [Oecolampadius explains], words have a different meaning from what they say" (LW 37). It is precisely this difference that Luther will not accept. "A metaphor," he says, "abolishes the content altogether: e.g., as when you understand 'body' as 'the figure of a body.' . . . Your figure of speech does away with the kernel and leaves the shell" (LW 30–31).

In this shell and kernel game of the colloquy one wonders indeed where the kernel is to be found. The critical problem at hand, it would seem, continually shifts from the question of the phrase "This is my body" to the status of the sacramental bread as either literally or figuratively the body of Christ, as equivalent to the body or merely a sign for it. The shift permits a repeated repression of the role of the phrase itself in the context of the argument.[21] Significantly enough, none of the interlocutors at Marburg pronounces the phrase, presupposing it to function *either* literally *or* figuratively *in that context*. When Luther writes "Hoc est corpus meum" on the table top, he does not expect "the body [to be] present bodily in the word" (LW 25) nor does the Swiss contingent read here a figural representation. "This is my body" is rather the verbal contrivance that fabricates the discord between the literal and the figurative: it is the locus of rupture and operates altogether differently from the linguistic machines that Luther and Zwingli attempt to construct. These latter would guarantee the presence of Christ's body, the one literally or immediately, the other figuratively or mediately. Their complicity, you will perceive, is all but manifest. The phrase "This is my body," however, is the kernel that cracks the shell: it generates days (and even years) of unending talk in which neither language as literal nor as figurative expression can gain the upper hand. "This is my body" generates the disparity between the two and their ultimate indecidability: "And talk!" (201), the passion for talk.

"Is all this digression or isn't it digression?" (14). I have given you the historical fact necessary for the interpretation of this passage: I regret it provides "no current to draw things along to a swift and desirable end" (164). For if I earlier gave the impression that Dowell might be deciphered by shuttling from a literal to a figural reading, you will gather that this is no longer possible. His narration is governed by the same passion for talk as the Marburg Colloquy, in which the literal and figurative remain perpetually in conflict.

We begin at least to have some sense of why this scene takes place coincident with the shift into talk and why it is precisely this for which Dowell can find no definition and no simile. The talk in which Florence, Leonora, Edward, and later Nancy are about to indulge themselves is language denying the operations both of literal and figural adequation. It is not the answer to the camouflage of silence. It does not release those once repressed passions in a violent wave of ex-pression. The violence is not on the side of that which is expressed but is the force of language itself, language as the force of refusal:

> What had happened was just hell. Leonora had spoken to Nancy; Nancy had spoken to Edward; Edward had spoken to Leonora—and they had talked and talked. And talked. . . . You have to imagine my beautiful Nancy appearing suddenly to Edward, rising up at the foot of his bed. . . . You have to imagine her, a silent, a no doubt agonized figure, like a spectre, suddenly offering herself to him—to save his reason! And you have to imagine his refusal—and talk. And talk! (201)

The more they talk the worse it gets. As the orgiastic exchanges become increasingly exaggerated, Dowell's narrative searches more and more desperately for the appropriate simile, for the key that will enable him to ground this violence in a "real world" counterpart:

Those two women pursued that poor devil and flayed the skin off him *as if* they had done it with whips. I tell you his mind bled almost visibly. I seem to see him stand, naked to the waist, his forearms shielding his eyes, and flesh hanging from him in rags. I tell you that is *no exaggeration* of what I feel. It was *as if* Leonora and Nancy banded themselves together to do execution, for the sake of humanity, upon the body of a man who was at their disposal. They were *like* a couple of Sioux who had got hold of an Apache and had him well tied to a stake. I tell you there was no end to the tortures they inflicted upon him.

Night after night he would hear them talking; talking; maddened, sweating, seeking oblivion in drink, he would lie there and hear the voices going on and on. (239, italics mine)

But what if "the situation" excludes the possibility of tying it down? What if the flaying, whipping, bleeding, and execution are inadequate to fix that which takes place—in a figure that is "as if," that is "like," that is "no exaggeration"? What if there is indeed "no end," if the voices will insist on "going on and on"? Isn't that what Dowell must finally concede? Isn't this the unimaginable hell of a narrator who can no longer say that he wishes except through the oblique admission that it exceeds his powers of definition and simile, except by a comparative that renounces finding an equivalent violent enough to express the state of affairs? "It was a most amazing business, and I think it would have been *better* in the eyes of God if they had all attempted to gouge out each other's eyes with carving knives. But they were 'good people'" (249, italics mine).

You will forgive me if I have made another detour, if I have shuttlecocked once again to the question of the narrative. This going back and forth cannot be avoided, for it is not only the so-called "Protest," Florence's description of it, and the shift to talk, but also storytelling, and especially Dowell's, that is at stake here. The fidelity between narrative text and its signification is menaced at the very moment when the language of its characters becomes most frenzied. The violence generated by the repressive force of their talk is carried over into Dowell's attempts at description where the same refusal of definitional similitude takes place. From the very beginning, Dowell has more or less intimated to us that it could not be otherwise. Just a few pages into his tale, he writes about the relationship between stories told and the reality behind them.

For, as I've said, what do I know even of the smoking-room? Fellows come in and tell the most extraordinary gross stories—so gross that they will positively give you a pain. And yet they'd be offended if you suggested that they weren't the sort of person you could trust your wife alone with. And very likely they'd be quite properly offended—. . . . Then, if they so delight in the narration, how is it possible that they can be offended—and properly offended—at the suggestion that they might make attempts upon your wife's honour? Or again: Edward Ashburnham was the cleanest-looking sort of chap. . . . And

> he never more than once or twice in all the nine years of my knowing him told a story that couldn't have gone into the columns of the *Field*. . . . You would have said that he was exactly the sort of chap that you could have trusted your wife with. And I trusted mine—and it was madness. (10–11)

As paradoxical as the situation may seem here, we are provided with a rather simple key to interpretation. Those who tell gross stories are unlikely to live them: those who are offended by gross stories are not to be trusted. The relationship between textual statement and meaning is merely a matter of inversion. But there is a noncoherence added to the notation of this hermeneutic formula, and that noncoherence is Dowell.

> And yet again you have me. If poor Edward was dangerous because of the chastity of his expressions—and they say that is always the hallmark of a libertine—what about myself? For I solemnly avow that not only have I never so much as hinted at an impropriety in my conversation in the whole of my days; and more than that, I will vouch for the cleanness of my thoughts and the absolute chastity of my life. At what, then, does it all work out? Is the whole thing a folly and a mockery? (11–12)

Dowell insists on the coherence between his textual and sexual chastities and with that gesture indeed makes a mockery of all hermeneutic consistency.[22]

It is here—and certainly it is no coincidence—that Dowell invites us to a fortnight of conversation in the country cottage of his imagination. It is just here after the insistence on a coherence between story and history has disrupted the formula for exegesis that Dowell will set the scene for his narration as one in which the intimacy between storyteller and auditor should guarantee its historical validity. Of these two passages, "I can't make out which of them is right. I leave it to you" (246).

You will understand, no doubt, that I have to leave all critical judgment to you. For if the talk of the "good people"—Edward, Leonora and Nancy—was more violent than the gouging of each other's eyes because it refused the expression of passion, if Dowell's talk in turn is invaded by the violent force of nonadequation, if Dowell repeatedly admits his own ignorance, how am I to find the facts? "I don't know; I don't know" (9). How successfully can I piece together the fragments from a narrator who never noticed that his wife was living with her lover in his own apartment, who was thirteen years a devoted nurse to a heart patient—who didn't have a heart, from a narrator for whom all memories are fragments to begin with?

> . . . Florence got all she wanted out of one look at a place. She had the seeing eye.
>
> I haven't, unfortunately, so that the world is full of places to which I want to return. . . . Not one of them did we see more than once, so that the

The (too) Good Soldier

whole world for me is like spots of colour in an immense canvas. Perhaps if it weren't so I should have something to catch hold of now.

Is all this digression or isn't it digression? Again I don't know. You, the listener, sit opposite me. But you are so silent. You don't tell me anything. (14)

Perhaps this is because you are "good people." "Good people," if you remember, are always silent, even when they talk. No, doubtless you have your reason. Silence is the the logical response to a call for critical judgment in the context of this novel. Yours is certainly the silence of perfectly normal reason.

Indeed the novel leaves us, the living, with only two alternatives between which we are "tossed backwards and forwards" (283)—the perfectly normal reason you have chosen and madness:

Nancy was a splendid creature but she had about her a touch of madness. Society does not need individuals with touches of madness about them. So Edward and Nancy found themselves steam-rolled out and Leonora survives, the perfectly normal type. . . . (238)

Well, that is the end of the story. . . . The villains—for obviously Edward and the girl were villains—have been punished by suicide and madness. The heroine—the perfectly normal virtuous, and slightly deceitful heroine—has become the happy wife of a perfectly normal, virtuous and slightly deceitful husband. (252)

But not only the perfectly normal, also the mad—you see, don't you—can be quite reasonable. As Dowell comes upon her in Ceylon, Nancy is uttering the most reasonable words of the entire novel. This is at least the single moment when Dowell will insist on the category of reason.

I have visited Asia, to see, in Ceylon, in a darkened room, my poor girl, sitting motionless, with her wonderful hair about her, looking at me with eyes that did not see me, and saying distinctly: *Credo in unum Deum Omnipotentum. . . . Credo in unum Deum Omnipotentum.*" Those are the only reasonable words she uttered; those are the only words, it appears, that she ever will utter. I suppose that they are reasonable words; it must be extraordinarily reasonable for her, if she can say she believes in an Omnipotent Deity. (234)

There is, however, her other declaration, and it is that other assertion, surely, that is the sign of her hopeless condition; for rather than a grounding in theological stability, it concerns the perpetual shift between possibilities.

Well, yesterday at lunch she said suddenly:
"Shuttlecocks!"
And she repeated the word "shuttlecocks" three times. I know what was passing in her mind, if she can be said to have a mind, for Leonora has told me that, once, the poor girl said she felt like a shuttlecock being tossed backwards and forwards between the violent personalities of Edward and his wife. . . . And the odd thing was that Edward himself considered that those two women used *him* like a shuttlecock. . . . And Leonora also imagined that

Edward and Nancy picked her up and threw her down as suited their purely vagrant moods. So there you have the pretty picture. (252–53)

If the same word passed in the mind of the perfectly normal Leonora, it cannot simply be "shuttlecocks" that marks the madness of Nancy but rather the endless back and forth between "shuttlecocks" and the Omnipotent Deity. This is what robs the pretty picture of its meaning.

Then she will say that she believes in an Omnipotent Deity or she will utter the one word "shuttlecocks," perhaps. It is very extraordinary to see the perfect flush of health on her cheeks, to see the lustre of her coiled black hair, the poise of the head upon the neck, the grace of the white hand—and to think that it all means nothing—that it is a picture without a meaning. (254)

And now I'm sure you finally have a clear insight into our amazing predicament. I have played the role of the omnipotent narrator, for according to our epigraph, this figure is promised the mastery of the illusions of figurative truth, and who can resist the illusion of mastery. And yet, since we are now on intimate terms, I felt obligated to make clear to you my auditors just where we stand, to shuttle back to my role as reader and to make you see that the reader of *The Good Soldier* is tossed back and forth between possibilities. For if we started with Maisie Maidan as the figure of Dowell's auditor—caught as she is at the very center of the text just at the moment of perfect understanding, the other figure of the listener is, of course, Nancy. "[T]hey haven't restored her reason. She is, I am aware, sitting in this hall, ten paces from where I am now . . ." (p. 236).

NOTES

1. Joseph Conrad and Ford Madox Hueffer, *The Nature of a Crime* (London: Duckworth and Co., 1924), p. 66.
2. This paper was first presented at the University of Texas at Austin as the second in a series of three lectures on *Wuthering Heights*, *The Good Soldier*, and Artaud's *Héliogabale*.
3. All citations are from Ford Madox Ford, *The Good Soldier* (New York: Vintage, 1961). Page numbers are given in the body of the text.
4. Ford wrote of this theory of impressionism: "We accepted without much protest the stigma 'Impressionists' that was thrown at us. . . . [W]e saw that Life did not narrate, but made impressions on our brains. We in turn, if we wished to produce on you an effect of life, must not narrate but render impressions." Ford Madox Ford, *Joseph Conrad* (Boston: Little, Brown, and Co., 1924), pp. 194–95. "It seems to me that one is an Impressionist because one tries to produce an illusion of reality—or rather the business of Impressionism is to produce that illusion." Ford Madox Hueffer, "On Impressionism," *Poetry and Drama* 8: 323.
5. See Hugh Kenner: "If one seeks for a centre, one is driven through ironic mirror-lined corridors of viewpoint reflecting viewpoint and this is the

book's essence, an optical illusion of infinite recession. . . . The gap between presentation and 'values' is never bridged" ("Conrad and Ford: The Artistic Conscience," *Shenandoah* 3 [1952]: 54).

6. An obvious pun, noted repeatedly in readings of *The Good Soldier*. See, for example, Mark Schorer, preface to *The Good Soldier* (New York: Vintage, 1961), p. xv; T. J. Henigan, *"The Desirable Alien:* A Source for Ford Madox Ford's *The Good Soldier," Twentieth Century Literature* 11 (1965–66): 27; and T. A. Hanzo, "Downward to Darkness," *Sewanee Review* 74 (1966): 838.

7. The argument about the reliability of the narrator in *The Good Soldier* has become a given proposition, not to say a commonplace, in Ford Madox Ford criticism. See, among many others, Samuel Hynes, "The Epistemology of *The Good Soldier," Sewanee Review* 69: 225–235; James Hafley, "The Moral Structure of *The Good Soldier," Modern Fiction Studies* 5 (1959–60): 121–128; Mark Schorer's preface (in many respects the most subtle of these essays); and Grover Smith, *Ford Madox Ford* (New York and London: Columbia University Press, 1972). A simple questioning of narrative "truth" is not the point of this essay, for even an apparently complete renunciation of epistemological certainty such as one finds in the essay of Joseph Weisenfarth ("Criticism and the Semiosis of *The Good Soldier," Modern Fiction Studies* 9 (1963–64): 39–49) does not begin to take up the ultimate critical problematic. Here it is not a matter of once again reforming the same question, but of per-forming the method of its textual madness.

8. I use the term according to the text's own double definition of "intimacy," or at least according to that of Nancy's mind—which ultimately may be the best figure we have for the text. "Intimacy" is at the same time the telling of secrets and the act of adultery. "So these matters presented themselves to Nancy's mind. But later in the case she found that Mr. Brand had to confess to a 'guilty intimacy' with someone or other. Nancy imagined that he must have been telling someone his wife's secrets. . . ." (218)

9. This is certainly the movement of the opening paragraph of the novel cited on p. 2.

10. Just as Dowell misreads Leonora's words in order to repress the violence they camouflage, so Leonora, Edward, and Nancy will render the cruelty of their daily scenes as illegible as Dowell could wish in his first weeks at Branshaw Teleragh.

> Still there it is. And there it is also that all those three presented to the world the spectacle of being the best of good people. I assure you that during my stay for that fortnight in that fine old house, I never so much as noticed a single thing that could have affected that good opinion. (246)

11. His face hitherto had, in the wonderful English fashion, expressed nothing whatever. Nothing. There was in it neither joy nor despair; neither hope nor fear; neither boredom nor satisfaction. . . . I never came across such a perfect expression before and I never shall again. (25)

12. This interpretation is less scandalous than it seems. Elsewhere in the novel the "black and white" specifically refers to a written text. As Nancy reads of the Brand divorce case we read: "That was incredible. Yet there it was—in black and white" (219).

13. "I suppose that I should really like to be a polygamist; with Nancy,

and with Leonora, and with Maisie Maiden, and possibly even with Florence" (237).

14. It is the comprehension of this relationship between the sacramental text of the marriage service and its meaning that defines reason.

> I should marry Nancy if her reason were ever sufficiently restored to let her appreciate the meaning of the Anglican marriage service. But it is probable that her reason will never be sufficiently restored to let her appreciate the meaning of the Anglican marriage service. Therefore I cannot marry her, according to the law of the land. (236)

15. Thus Florence's mode of discourse in interpreting the significance of the "Protest" renders literal and figural language mutually exclusive. She uses a figural language of inversion whereby she claims Edward to be clean-lived in order to say she wishes he weren't. Yet the literal truth of the matter (the fact that Edward is not clean-lived) renders Florence's attempt at figural inversion senseless. The historical facts behind the scene will explain the significance of this mutual exclusion.

16. This scene of the cows has often been mentioned as a hint of the action to come, but the brief readings always remain at the level of limited allegory. See for example Jo-Ann Baernstein, "Image, Identity, and Insight in *The Good Soldier*," in *Ford Madox Ford, Modern Judgments*, ed. Richard A. Cassell (London: Macmillan, 1972), p. 129; John A. Meixner, *Ford Madox Ford's Novels*, (Minneapolis: University of Minnesota Press, 1962), p. 168; Richard Cassell, *Ford Madox Ford, A Study of His Novels* (Baltimore: The Johns Hopkins University Press, 1961), p. 187; and R. W. Lid, *Ford Madox Ford, The Essence of His Art* (Berkley: University of California Press, 1964), p. 57.

17. The good literary historian might well protest at this point. As Violet Hunt relates the *real source* of this passage (*The Desirable Alien at Home in Germany* [London: Chatto and Windus, 1913], as cited in T. J. Henigan, *The Desirable Alien*), it was none other than Ford himself who called the piece of paper "the Protest." As Hunt, Ford, and Ford's mother toured the castle at Marburg, it was Ford who played the role of Florence, saying:

> "There, that is what I have brought you to see. The Protest of Zwingli, Luther and Bucer. That bit of paper *is* Protestantism. It all began with the signing of that bit of paper." And turning to me: "That is what you mean when you say you are a Protestant!" pp. 159–60

If I have rejected this bit of literary history in favor of actual history, it is partly because of the decade Ford spent preparing a biography of Henry VIII. He knew his Protestant history, then, better than he here lets on. Moreover, who at this point could have confidence in the word of Ford filtered through that of Violet Hunt, through that of Florence, and that of the novel's narrator once again?

18. Ford Madox Hueffer, *Memories and Impressions* (New York and London: Harper and Brothers, 1911), p. xviii.

19. This took place, incidentally, "under the protection of" Philip of Hesse (not Ludwig the Courageous) who (much later) wished to have two (not three) wives at once.

20. Martin Luther, *Luther's Works* (Philadelphia: Fortress Press, 1971),

p. 37. References to this work in the body of the text will hereafter appear as LW followed by the page number.

21. This is not to say that the status of the words "This is my body" is not repeatedly questioned (LW 19, 22, 24, 27, 41, 56). But the question is always immediately shifted beyond the confines of the colloquy: their role as language in the text of the argument is all but forgotten. Nevertheless, the discussion of the phrase puts the defender of a literal reading into something of a predicament. Once Luther insists on the bodily presence of Christ in the bread, he is forced to depend on a series of backup mechanisms to guarantee that presence. The words "This is my body" must be added to bring the body into the bread, and the words are in turn meaningless unless guaranteed by the authority of God. The problematic of literal versus figurative language thus becomes far more complex than we are able to indicate clearly in the body of the text.

22. This is the same logical double-bind as Florence's discourse on the Protest, in which a figural language that operates by inversion and a literal language of truth are mutually exclusive. See note 15.

LINGERING ON THE THRESHOLD
Piero Pucci

IN THE EIGHTH elegy of Propertius's first book, Cynthia threatens to leave Rome and Propertius: we understand from this poem that she is lured by rich offers, and we may surmise from another poem that the rival is a Roman governor going to take his office in Illyria. In the first part of the poem, the lover (Propertius) tries to persuade Cynthia not to leave. The text begins *in medias res*, reproducing, as it were, the last or conclusive part of a peroration, or appeal:

Are you then [*igitur*] out of your mind? Doesn't the thought of me [*mea cura*] detain you [*MORATUR*]? (1.8.1)

The title alludes to the classical motif of the lover who sits on his mistress's threshold (*LIMEN*) calling her up, complaining of his exclusion, hoping to be admitted to her house, and finally being refused, which has been studied in its thematic form and history. The standard work on the subject is: F. O. Copley, *Exclusus Amator. A Study in Latin Love Poetry* (Oxford: 1956). For more recent bibliography see L. E. Rossi, "Il Ciclope di Euripide," *Maia*, 1971, M. Leroy πΑρΑκΛΑγΣιθγρση "Mélanges de Linguistique, de philologie, et de méthodologie de l'enseignement des langues anciennes," *Offerts à M. René Fohalle* (Gembloux: 1969).

On the obscene connotations of door, *LIMEN*, etc., see J. Taillardat, *Les Images d'Aristophane*, (Paris p. 70 f. and 77. L. E. Rossi, p. 19 n. 26). On the use of the LIMEN in philosophical writings, see M. Leroy. *LIMEN* was felt connected by popular etymology with *limis*, "oblique." The Latins felt also a semantic relationship to *limes*, "limit" (Ernout-Meillet).

Lingering on the Threshold

Sililoquy or address? As later in the poem we are told that Cynthia has been persuaded by his prayers, the fiction of the poem is that she is actually there, present, listening to his words. And, coherently, his words repeat the teaching/warning with which the poet concluded his first programmatic poem:

Let loving care [*cura*] detain [*MORETUR*] each lover and not change place [*mutet . . . locum*] once love has become a familiar habit. (1.1.35–36)

This teaching is couched in an impressive text and it is elicited by a powerful rhetoric. For Propertius ends his first programmatic poem with a non sequitur. Despite the representation of his own unhappy affair, despite the assertion that love (*Amor*) is slow to help him,[1] and despite the recognition that nothing can rescue him, the lover ends by assuming the role of a teacher, and by admonishing even the successful lovers.[2] The knowledge that allows him to assume such a role comes to the lover from poetry, as we shall discover.

The powerful rhetoric of the teaching, on the other hand, resides more in the felicitous cluster of images than in concrete advice or practical know-how. By advising the lovers to allow their love to *detain* them, the text suggests a conceptual connection between *AMOR* and *MORA*—anagrams of each other[3]—and by rephrasing this principle by the notion of "not moving house" (*mutet . . . locum*)[4] the text suggests the idea of not crossing back across the threshold once the lovers are at home and their love has become a familiar habit (*assueto . . . amore*).[5] Though not explicitly, the idea of *MORA*, *LIMEN* (threshold), and *AMOR* are here interconnected. A sort of "detention" within the house assures the continuation of happy love.

It is this cluster of interrelated notions that the poet evokes with dismay at the beginning of 1.8, when he questions Cynthia:

Are you then [*igitur*] out of your mind and doesn't the thought of me [*mea cura*] detain you [*MORATUR*]? (1.8.1)

Cynthia's *dementia* (insanity) consists in her neglect of such notions as they are packed in the poet's teaching. Obviously neither *MORA* nor *LIMEN* constitute such a defense and protection of love for one who, like Cynthia, is ready to leave Rome (*ROMA*, 8.31, and *MORA* are anagrams)[6] for cold Illyria (8.2), who is willing to stand the fury of the sea (8.5), the unfamiliar snow (*insolitas . . . nives*, 8.8), etc., in order to follow the rich lover.

The fact that *MORA* and *LIMEN* do not constitute any defense and protection against rivals does not depend simply on Cynthia's transgression and unfaithfulness; more importantly and in principle, they are not a *defense* at all. For *LIMEN* indicates the threshold, an open space, and *MORA* designates an odd temporality, implying a sort of *lingering* in view of a future thing or a detention from something.⁷ If, then, *MORA* and *LIMEN* play in Propertius's teaching the roles of detention and custody, these roles transgress to some extent the unstable and open meaning of *MORA* and *LIMEN*. And since Propertius's representation of happy and unhappy love affairs is produced by a series of erotic placements and displacements around the *LIMEN*, it is possible that this representation is always the result of some rhetorical transgression and violence. Propertius's desire for transgressing Cynthia's *LIMEN* would be always parallel to a rhetorical transgression.

Let us analyze how Propertius imagines his own loyalty and faithfulness to Cynthia, while she will be far away in Illyria (8.21 ff.):

For no girl shall tempt me and detain me from uttering words of complaint about you *on your threshold* [*tuo LIMINE*] nor shall I cease to question sailors as they hurry by: "Tell me what harbor *holds fast* my girl [*clausa est*]?" and say: "Though she is in Atrax, though she is where the Hylaei dwell, *she shall be mine.*"

The most curious feature of Propertius's own loyalty is his promise to complain about Cynthia at her threshold, if she leaves. In her absence, he reverts to court her as an *exclusus amator*. The *exclusus amator* complains outside the threshold of the girl in order to be heard and to persuade her. But Propertius promises to do the same while she is away. This gesture reaches the peak of sublime pathos and of farcical nonsense, a paradoxical mode found not infrequently in the best Propertian conceits and inventions.⁸ To have Cynthia's lover complaining at her *LIMEN*, while she is far away, is a flippant touch that mocks a conventional theme; but it derives its force also from another source, since it coexists with a textual necessity by which Cynthia's absence is really never total and absolute. And in fact the dynamics of desire about the *LIMEN* teaches us just this point.

It is too well known how the *LIMEN*, by separating ritually sacred from profane, becomes symbolical of a suspension between these two states, a suspension that accordingly is called *liminal*. I do not intend to elaborate these general problems, nor the ritual function of the *LIMEN* in marriage and in particular, in Roman marriage,⁹ but simply to call the attention to the paradoxical force of this separating line. For the *LIMEN*, whether or not surmounted by a door, is indeed crossable and must be crossed: accordingly sacred and profane are in continuous communication, contiguity, and interdependence. The *LIMEN* therefore outlines an undecidable line that opens the possibility of both outside, profane, absence, etc., and inside, sacred, presence, etc., and that therefore holds, so to speak, in its grip both possibilities. In Latin, no word represents so well this Janus-like force of the *LIMEN* as the word *ianus*, from which the word for "door," *ianus*, is derived.¹⁰

In erotic poetry, *LIMEN*, by metonymy, may indicate also "the house" and, by extension, the sweetheart. By this metonymical force, *LIMEN* becomes synonymous with an inside, with a presence, with a fulfillment. Here again the transgression is evident: the line that opens the possibility of the inside and outside, of presence and absence, etc., becomes synonymous with one set of the opposites.

Let us notice that the transgression ensues as a result of a domestication of the Janus-like force of the word *LIMEN*: the process of domestication is visible in another word for "door," *fores*, that tends to becomes synonymous with the "outside," both in Latin and in Greek.[11]

In Latin erotic language, the metonymy whereby *LIMEN* means the sweetheart, the object of desire, implies that the pursuit and fulfillment of desire take on the connotations of a crossing of the *LIMEN*. Accordingly, crossing the *LIMEN* and possessing the mistress become the same thing.[12] To what extent the metaphorical use of "door" for female sex may have contributed to this identification is difficult to say: the metaphor, at any rate, is alien to the style of elegy.[13] Since the identification of the *LIMEN* with the inside and the beloved constitutes a rhetorical transgression, the lover's desire for transgression is simultaneously inscribed in this precise rhetoric. In accordance with this inscriptional quality of the transgression, the poet's representation of his love affairs emerges as the production brought forth by endless transgressions and detours aiming at coming closer and closer to the presence and fulfillment. But this line, as *LIMEN*, withdraws ceaselessly, for it always retraces its ambivalent, undecidable track.[14]

For the line emerges as a line (*limen*) insofar as it is drawn in the place of a trace. In the process of this drawing that which is polysemic and differential on the track of the trace becomes distinguished, separated, and opposite. The line so drawn does not coincide with anything in particular (it is a "threshold") and remains Janus-like, i.e., a simple mark of separation. Yet the advantages that sustain the emergence of this straightened line are obvious. The protective "inside" of the house is a most eloquent example. By the simple step of crossing the line, the possibility arises to reach an univocal, enclosed, and preserved entity or meaning, a "presence." Moreover the crossing of the line can be ascribed to the volition, power, privilege, and skill of a specific agent, lover, or poet. Finally, the metonymical or figural force of language may attempt to destroy the last element of discomfort haunting the line, i.e., its structure of contiguity between opposite terms.

These are the points I intend to analyze in the wake of Propertius' elegy 1.8 and 2.15.

The lover's promise to visit Cynthia's *LIMEN* while she is far away (1.8.22) recalls the equally pathetic devotion of Penelope and the analogous expression *VIRI LIMEN AMARE* (to love the husband's threshold) that Propertius uses in order to describe such kind of devout love:

Felix Admeti coniunx et lectus Ulixis et quacumque viri femina LIMEN amat. (2.6.23–24)[15]

Happy Admetus' wife and the bed of Ulixes and every woman who loves her man's threshold!

One intention of this text is to identify the threshold of the husband's house with him, and therefore to connote the husband with all the protective and pleasurable aspects of the inside and of the presence. But the text sounds ambiguous and ironical, since Ulixes was absent from his threshold for twenty years, and Alcestis, the wife of Admetus, chose to die for him.[16]

Just as Penelope loves her husband's threshold in the absence of her husband Ulixes, so Propertius promises that he will visit Cynthia's *LIMEN* during her absence. This means that he will continue to love and nag her, just as if her *LIMEN*, metonymically meant herself, and therefore implied her presence. The fact that the mistress is absolutely absent endows this gesture with a paradoxical pathos, but because of the possibly metonymical meaning of *LIMEN*, this foolish gesture parallels the celebrated love of Penelope.

Yet because Propertius will nag and complain on Cynthia's *LIMEN*, his gesture seems that of an *exclusus amator*.[17] In this convention, the *LIMEN* and the door (*ianua* or *fores*) separate the lover from the sweetheart, but by the same metonymy the *ianua* and the *LIMEN* become both the image of her refusal (her absence) and the personification of her denied presence. Accordingly, the lover addresses the door and the *LIMEN*, and insults, cajoles, kisses, curses them.[18]

As a result of the implications in the image of *LIMEN*, Cynthia in 1.8.21 plays either the role of the absent consort or that of the mistress whose absence/presence is symbolized by the *LIMEN*, and by *ianua*. In both cases the image of the *LIMEN* reduces Cynthia's outsideness, unfaithfulness, and absence to a mere separation, a separation due to time, or the separation of a door. The *LIMEN* reactivates her presence; we see immediately that the effects of this domestication reverberate in the next lines:

nor shall I cease to question sailors as they hurry by "tell me what harbor holds fast my girl [*clausa est*]?" and say: "though she is in Atrax, though she is where the Hylaei dwell, she shall be mine." (1.8.23–26)

Though Cynthia is determined to leave, and—as we will learn in the next section of the poem—to leave with a rich man, the representation of her leaving and of her becoming absent is constantly displaced by the hidden emergence of her presence and of her being there. As the text mentions her *LIMEN*, suddenly a protective curtain descends over her, excludes her from Propertius's rivals, and detains her for himself: "She shall be mine!" For the text imagines Cynthia held fast, detained, closed up (*clausa est*) in some harbor, as if some sort of *LIMEN* were suddenly surrounding Cynthia and preventing him, indeed, from reaching her, but also his rivals. Because of this protective *custodia*, Cynthia appears not at all lost and gone forever, but close, separated only by a fraction of time ("She shall be mine") or by a line (the *LIMEN*) that also marks her tremendous closeness, her metonymical presence. Accordingly, at the end of the reading, we realize that notwithstanding Cynthia's projected trip far away from Rome, she is really not much farther than if she were behind the door of her house listening to Propertius's complaint.

In fact, according to the fictional reference of the poem, Cynthia is not much more distant: for, as we have already implied, she is imagined to be there, listening to Propertius's words. As we begin to read the second part of the poem,[19] we are immediately told that Cynthia has decided to remain. In shocking contrast to the poet's imagination that has represented Cynthia already in Atrax or Scythia, the text begins by saying that she has been here where the poet is, namely, that she has never left, or, if we choose to read *erit*, that she will be here and not leave at all:

Here she was! Here she remains loyal to her oaths. Let our enemies burst with envy. I won. She could not stand my persistent prayers [*assiduas preces*]. Cynthia has ceased to go on new roads [*novas vias*]. She says that I am dear to her, that for my sake Rome is the dearest city, and without me no kingdom is sweet. She has preferred to rest with me [*requiescere*] on a narrow bed and to be mine in whatever way [*quocumque modo*] rather than obtain the old kingdom, dowry of Hippodamia, and all the wealth that Elis has gathered by its horses. Though he was giving great gifts and though he promised more she did not flee greedily from my embrace. Not by means of gold, not by means of Indian pearls, I could deflect [*deflectere*] her, but by the devoted service of my beguiling song. The Muses then exist nor is Apollo slow to aid the lover; on their trust I love. Rare Cynthia is mine. (1.8.27–42).

In commenting on these lines, let me first discuss the question of Propertius's claim that Cynthia is his own, and then the question of his poetic success. By repeating excitedly, "Cynthia is mine" (30, 34, 42, 44), the text suggests that Propertius has succeeded not only in having the *LIMEN* crossed but also in achieving some permanence, such as that of an *assuetus amor*. Indeed, we see that this is the case: she refuses the riches of a kingdom and she prefers to rest on a narrow bed with him. The *LIMEN* has been crossed and the lovers are united in the intimacy and familiarity of resting together (*mecum requiescere*). Propertius's possession of and intimate familiarity with Cynthia is emphasized by the domestic qualities of the narrow bed that is pitted against the unfamiliar remoteness of the riches of Elis: the mention of this mythical wealth makes the togetherness of Propertius and Cynthia just as splendid as a mythical event, and yet just as familiar and domestic as the narrow bed of a real and poor lover. Moreover, if the narrow bed is Propertius's bed, and not Cynthia's, the crossing of the *LIMEN* has occurred almost *more uxorio*, namely from her house into his own. Cynthia therefore belongs to him almost as a wife belongs to a husband. The reversal from the first part of the poem in which Propertius promised to be loyal to her *LIMEN*, just as a wife would be loyal to her husband's *LIMEN*, is here complete. The *LIMEN*, the *lectus* detain her: it has become a protective fence.[20]

Finally, the permanence of this possession is strongly emphasized in the last lines of the poem:

. . . rare Cynthia is mine. Now I can set my feet on the highest stars: night or day she is mine. No rival steals my sure love [*certos . . . amores*]: this glory will last to my old age.

The *assuetus amor* of 1.1.36 is paraphrased by *certi . . . amores*, if the text is sound,[21] and the success of Propertius's victory is emblematized by the glory which will accompany the poet-lover forever. The hyperbolic images of the last lines point at an equally permanent success in literary and erotic terms. The images of setting the feet on the highest stars, the total defeat of rivals, her readiness to be his night and day make clear that Propertius outruns all rivals and reaches the peak of happiness alone with her.

Such a reading would then strengthen the elements in the first part of the elegy that bespeak Cynthia's absence: accordingly, the whole poem could be read as a contrast between a lover's quarrel and their final idyll. But such a reading is made possible by the fascination that Propertius's thematic representation exercises on the reader, and therefore by some degree of complicity that the reader entertains with the idyllic imagery. For in fact, the process whereby such a representation is produced contests the representation itself, and dislocates the center of the representation from the comforting contrast between initial absence and final presence into an unresolved and rhythmical tension. This process is writing and it marks this representation with its own transgression and violence. We have only to assess in this elegy, the bending power of writing, and the superior force that the poet attributes to it, even in comparison with royal gifts.

The particular transgression and violence of writing is akin to that of the lover in his pursuit and crossing of the *LIMEN*: in fact the inscriptional transgression contains the lover's. But before we focus on this point we read again the last part of 1.8 and we look for the traces and marks of this transgression and violence.

We become aware that the text is now explicitly significant on two levels, that which suits a conventional lover and that which suits an elegiac poet. Thus, for instance, Cynthia is said to have been bent by the "devotion of a beguiling song" (*blandi carminis obsequio*). This expression may designate simply the blandishments that a lover addresses to his sweetheart, especially when he is excluded and chants before her door as in 1.16.16,[22] or as the lover promised to do in 1.8.22, but here it must also refer to the poetic song we are reading among the others of Propertius's first book.[23]

These beguiling utterances take on a pressing, besieging tone already in the transparence of the adjective *assiduas*[24] attributed to the lover's begging (*assiduas . . . preces*, 28), and they receive further power as they are pitted against the corrupting power of the king's gifts (of the murderous king Pelops)[25] and against the conventional riches of India.

The fact that a comparison between the king's and writing's violence is possible makes clear that writing aims at substituting the king. By assuming the humble form of *obsequium* the song really aims at usurping the power of the king. We do not have to look too far to realize that Propertius usurps *verbatim* and explicitly royal prestige and *insignia*. The narrow bed on which he has persuaded Cynthia to remain appears in 4.7.6 as "the cool kingdom of my bed," (*cool*, because it is now deserted by Cynthia). Analogously, the humble song that detains Cynthia is defined finally in the same poem as the kingdom in which Cynthia has been for a long time a queen (4.7.50): "long did I reign—she says—in your books." The narrow bed on which the elegiac lover wins his battle and his sophisticated song have royal prerogative and *insignia*. It is therefore understandable that Propertius pits them against the splendid gifts and seduction of the king.

The hyperbolic extolling of his own art and song does not result in an innocent self-aggrandizement. The allusion to the royal power of Pelops is pertinent and significant, since Propertius's rhetoric proves to be violent: it embraces Cynthia with a kiss of death. Cynthia indeed remains in Rome, yet not simply as the powerful woman she is, but as the image of Propertius's poetry. For in the last part of the poem, just where Propertius sings of her loyalty, Cynthia's concrete erotic personality melts with a mere rhetorical image, and becomes a "theme" of the poet's song:

She has preferred to rest with me on a narrow bed and to be mine in whatever way rather than obtain the old kingdom, dowry of Hippodamia . . . Though he was giving great gifts and though he promised more, she did not flee. Not by means of gold, not by means of Indian pearls could I deflect her, but by the devote homage of my beguiling song. The Muses then exist nor is Apollo slow [*tardus*] to aid the lover. . . .

Notice: the narrow bed—an unambiguous reference to Propertius's model, Callimachus[26]—the Muses, and Apollo. In particular, the expression "Apollo is not slow" by referring to Amor, who in 1.1 was slow (*tardus*) in helping the lover, proves that the erotic success is contained and inscribed in the rhetorical and poetical one. Propertius's love affair with Cynthia is inscribed on the poetic page, kingdom of Apollo: "and trusting in them (Apollo and the Muses) I love: rare Cynthia is mine" (1.8.42). But if so, what Propertius aims at is not simply the presence and beauty of Cynthia, but through her he glances at the beauty and the permanence of his own artistic product:

Lucky she whom my book celebrates! My songs will be so many monuments of your beauty . . . A fame [*nomen*] gained by talent [*ingenio*] shall never perish: for beauty [*decus*] that talent achieves endures deathless. (3.2.17ff.)

Consequently at the end of 1.8 the lover-poet does not look any longer simply at Cynthia and at her threshold, but he looks at his own poetry and aims at transgressing a new threshold: "Now I can tread the highest stars with my feet . . . This glory will last to my old age." Line 43, in particular, seems to echo Horace's last line of his introductory *carmen* (1.1.35–36):

If you (Maecenas) place me among the lyric poets, I'll hit the stars with my extolled head.

The Propertian line therefore alludes to a text where it is a question only of literary glory. It is clear now that Propertius's conquest of Cynthia and his possession of her on his "narrow bed" doubles the retrieving of poetic presence under the force of Apollo's inspiration. And we realize immediately that "Now I can tread the highest stars with my feet" (1.8.43) not only continues the metaphor of walking (1.1 and 1.8.30), but also points to the crossing of *coeli LIMINA*, the threshold of heaven. The threshold of Cynthia is left behind notwithstanding the text's assurance that she is his night and day.

As a result of this reading, elegy 1.1 cannot be interpreted in the light of a contrast between a menace of absence and a retrieving of presence. Too many elements contest this simple conclusion. On the one hand, the object of the lover's desire, Cynthia, is represented with an ambivalent focus that removes her when she is imagined to be present and makes her close when she is imagined to be absent. This ambivalence that is set along the lines of distance and closeness, power and weakness, reveals the odd dynamics of the *LIMEN* in its undomesticated force as that which holds in its grip—so to speak—the opposite terms. For the *LIMEN* functions as that line that the poet draws and crosses in order to retrieve permanence and beauty in his own representation. But, as this rhetorical manipulation marks the idyll, it contests the carefully constructed contrast between the two parts of the poem and dislocates the balance of this contrast into an imbalance, a tension of various terms. Both moments coexist in the spectrum of the poem's significations, and the texture that allows and allays this coexistence is what makes up the poem.

But what specific territory or line is intended by the *LIMEN* when we think of it as the *LIMEN* of writing? We have seen that Cynthia crosses Propertius's *LIMEN* and rests on Propertius's narrow bed. Already the adjective "narrow" attributed to the bed shows that the line of the bed must signify also a special literary territory, i.e., the territory of imitation of and competition with Callimachus. Finally, but "touching the highest stars with 'his' feet," the poet alludes to the heavenly *LIMEN* (of immortal fame) and points to his imitation of and competition with Horace. There is no doubt then that the *LIMEN* of writing points to the oblique line—and open space—that outlines the contacts between Propertius's own language and that of the poetic tradition and of the contemporary masters. In fact, poetic rivals and masters alike are imagined in a setting that reproduces again the line of the *LIMEN*. Take for instance, the opening lines of 3.1:

Shade of Callimachus and sacredness of Coan Philitas, allow me, I pray, to enter your grove [*in vestrum, quaeso, me sinite ire nemus*].

The masters are in this case inside the sacred place—where the Muses or Apollo are perhaps imagined to inspire them—and Propertius asks for the permission to go inside, to have access to the same privilege. The line that separates Propertius from the excellence of his masters is drawn between a grove and an unspecified space, but it is the drawing of the line that places the grove on one side of the line.

This setting reproduces that of the lovers and rivals on the *LIMEN* of the mistress. The either-way and Janus-like trace of the *LIMEN* is made to signify a steady line that insures and protects an inside and an excellence. By locating the excellence of the masters and the permanence of their creations behind a certain line, the text gives them a status of being that relies only on rhetorical transgressions, namely, on the straightening of the line and on the metonymy which does violence to the Janus-like *LIMEN*. By the first transgression, mastery and excellence are not only located in the Callimachean grove of the Muses to which a viable access exists, but are also separated from their opposites and preserved uncontaminated by special guardians, Callimachus and Philitas. So that as the poet obtains access to the Muses' grove he accedes to pure forms of excellence.

It is important to notice that he must ask for the permission to *cross* the line: for the line, notwithstanding and because of its rhetorical status, is unavoidable. No lifting or vanishing of the line would be possible—for this would reinstate the trace—and the poet must walk and cross the line. As he does, he would possess the territory of pure excellence. He would then also leave behind himself, Callimachus, and Philitas, just as he leaves behind himself, Cynthia and her threshold: the *LIMEN*, just as the guardians on the *LIMEN*, are necessary *only* to insure the establishment and recovery of pure forms of excellence. As the poet masters the uncontaminated form of excellence and leaves behind the masters, he obtains a victory over his rivals and over the masters themselves.

Finally, the "grove" of the Muses is placed at the point of the only possible entrance: the *LIMEN* opens to the grove of the Muses. This proves that the straightening of the line ends with a domestication of the Janus-like quality of the *LIMEN*: the line tends to coincide with an "entrance" or an "exit," then with one or the other side of the line, and to lose therefore its threatening force.

It is clear already from what precedes that the drawing and the crossing of the line correspond to the transgressions and violence that arise in the process of writing. The polysemic, differential, and deferring nature of language corresponds to the "trace"; the control over the difference and the displacements of the "trace" emerges with the straightening of the trace into a line; and finally the figural violence of metonymy reveals the paradox of writing itself as the metonymy displaces meaning while promising to retrieve a univocal meaning. As presence, then, emerges textually in the mode of rhetorical displacement and transgression, presence is forever unreachable unless in the mode of transgression.

The notions of imitation and competition (Greek $\zeta\hat{\eta}\lambda o\varsigma$, Latin *imitatio, aemulatio*) are deprived of their most troubling aspects if a clear-cut line insures the univocal status of the self, originality, and mastery. Only the closing up of the open *LIMEN* allows this reassuring, metaphysical possibility, and allays ambivalence, difference, dislocation, and complicity, properties of the *LIMEN*. Notice, for instance, that Propertius asserts his own victory over the rivals, i.e., his own excellence and originality by imitating a line of Horace (1.8.43). But what can originality and imitation mean in this context? The critic cannot simply dismiss Propertius's intention of proclaiming his own originality, for this intention is conveyed by this line through typical Propertian imagery—of walking, crossing thresholds, etc.—nor can he forget the passivity of this line that is Horatian only in the sense that Horace is probably the closest poet to Propertius to use this otherwise most conventional motif.[27]

No doubt elegy 1.8 is the scene of a pervasive and subtle *aemulatio* (competition) with innumerable other texts that makes it what it is: a weaving of threads that connect the poem at each moment to a "source," to the passivity of the genre, and that simultaneously point at an active self-awareness. But this formulation is already metaphysical because it introduces a neat separation between model and copy, as if the model and the copy were connected by a set of univocal and one-way relationships. This would simplify the terms greatly, as though the act of copying the copy would not also assume the quality of "model" belonging to the model. Inversely, the model is itself also a "copy." It must not have escaped Propertius that his "models" were themselves working in the same way that he was working, and that by imitating his "models," he was in fact imitating their "imitations" of their models. Rather, we should consider Propertius's propensity to indicate his "models" and to praise them as an attempt to control the bottomless play of differences and displacements that intervenes in the act of writing. For by indicating poetic models as the final terms with which to enter into competition, the author circumscribes a territory and reproduces the situation of the rivals lingering on the *LIMEN*. The images in 3.1.1 ff. textually prove this point. By this control he would of course be able always to define his position in relation to them, the clear-cut quality of values (originality, sophistication, etc.) and a certain ease in achieving these values.

Yet this situation obeys the metaphysics of the *LIMEN* as effacement of contiguity, displacement, and difference. In reality, the difference of the model is at once declared and denied in accordance with the dynamics of the *LIMEN* as contiguity. It may be interesting and amusing to trace at least another tiny moment of this ambivalence. As we have seen (note 26), the "narrow bed" refers to Callimachus's precepts and prescriptions. They outline a type of poetry that bases its success on polishing, erudition, and originality of conceits and concepts, and therefore in careful elaboration of short compositions. Callimachus describes all this by the metaphors of the narrow roads and untrodden paths. Propertius enthusiastically subscribes to this poetics and imagery.

Cynthia, as the erotic image of Propertian poetry, the symbol of its success, is a blatant contradiction of that precept. Erotically, she is promiscuous and literarily, she is a "common place":

Varro too played on these themes, when his Jason was finished, Varro the greatest flame of his love, Leucadia. Such were the songs written by tender Catullus whose Lesbia is better known than Helen. Such, too, were the utterances on the pages of the learned Calvus when he sang the death of wretched Quintilia. How many wounds that fair Lycoris inflicted on Gallus, dead of late, does he wash in the infernal waters! Now Cynthia, too, has been praised by Propertius' poems if Fama shall grant to place him among these poets. (2.34.85–94)

Yes, a commonplace, though an exclusive one too.

All this shows that the terms that are installed around the line of the *LIMEN* are continuously dislocated and never retrieved by representation. Even the *augustus lectus* (the "narrow bed") on which Propertius should possess Cynthia displaces Cynthia not only from a real bed into a book page, but also from Propertius's page into Callimachus's book. This process seems endless.

If the *LIMEN* is thus a signifier that opens polysemic significations and simultaneously is forced to function as the object of desire (mistress, Muses' grove, presence, etc.), nothing can prevent the object of desire from always being also in the mode of ambivalence and from betraying the troubling force of an open signifier. This explains why the object of desire is unretrievable and why this desire must keep on transgressing. Therefore Propertius may well have Cynthia crossing his *LIMEN* and resting on his bed: he will gaze at the heavenly *LIMEN*. Or he may cross the *LIMEN* of Cynthia's house but then he may find other *limina* he does not dare to cross, her bed, for instance. Or he may succeed to enter her bed, but then he may find that something still prevents him from possessing her fully.

Elegy 2.15 is most instructive in this regard. The lover has obtained full access to Cynthia's house and bed.

O happy me! O shining night for me [*o nox mihi candida*]. And you my bed [*lectule*] blessed by my delight! How many words did we change while the lamp was on! And what a struggle [*rixa*] when the lamp was off. For now she wrestled against me with her bare breasts [*nudates . . . papillis*] and now she delayed me [*duxit MORAM*], with her tunic buttoned up. (1–6)[28]

Notice the presence of the lamp that, already announced by the oxymoron *nox candida*, continues to be a leading theme in the elegy. The oxymoron reveals a sharp illogicity, a transgression of some kind, which points to the transgression of Cynthia's nakedness by the eye.

When the light is on, the lovers speak; when the light is off, they engage in amatory struggle and Cynthia seems to lead the battle, now unveiling herself and provoking her partner, now covering herself and allaying the partner's assault. No mention of words in this phase, but of struggle (*rixa, luctata*) and of deferment (*MORA*). Is it a sheer chance that *rixa* simultaneously means the erotic struggle on the bed and the struggle of the rivals on the *domina*'s *LIMEN*?[29] We must wait a little for an answer.

As Cynthia delays him—is she teasing him?—Propertius falls asleep, but Cynthia wakes him up by kissing his eyes and scolds him gently: "Are you lying in this way? So sluggard?" The important detail here is the mention of the eyes, for Propertius's pleasure lies, as he will say in an instant, in looking at Cynthia's naked body. When he is woken up, the lovers begin to embrace and kiss each other: "How often we shifted arms and we varied our embrace. How long my kisses lingered [*MORATA*] on your lips!" (2.15.9–10). But suddenly the playful scene is interrupted by Propertius's admonishment to Cynthia: whether this admonishment is delivered to her during this night of love, or must be considered as an afterthought of the poet can be disputed; but the content of the admonishment is not controversial: Propertius dislikes embracing, kissing, and making love when the light is off. If he does not see her naked he does not enjoy love:

There is no pleasure [*non iuvat*] in corrupting love [*venerem*] with blind movement: let me tell you, eyes are guides of love [*in amore duces*], Paris himself is said to have perished for love as he saw the Spartan naked when she rose from Menelaos' bed. (2.15.11–14)

The eyes are *duces*, i.e. leaders in love; they alone guide and lead forward the whole force of desire and transgression.

This transgression involves the transgression of a certain interdiction, which is, to begin with, a mode of violence in itself. For the norm that establishes what is unexposable and unfathomable implies the drawing of the line between what can be spoken about and what is unspeakable, between public and private, etc., in order to protect that which, once it is immersed in the chain of language, can no longer be unspeakable, private, and closed up. This drawing of the line is therefore itself a transgression of the trace of the *LIMEN*.

Propertius's desire for Cynthia's nakedness, therefore, means desire to transgress a given norm and line. But since only the drawing of that line insures the status of nakedness as nakedness, the vanishing or lifting of that line would dissolve nakedness as such. The lover must then cross the line between being covered and nakedness. Accordingly, nakedness is an "uncoveredness" in which the act of uncovering is always active and the "cover" of "un*cover*edness" is in principle undefinable. Desire for nakedness implies desire to transgress the line on whose drawing nakedness emerges as separated from being covered and that establishes nakedness by some extent of arbitrariness and gratuitousness. As in the case of the *LIMEN*, therefore, desire for nakedness is desire for transgressing transgression and must trigger only more desire for uncovering, possessing, and mastering.

Without this desire, nakedness becomes invisible, as Propertius knows well. In 4.8 the poet has organized a little orgy in his house while Cynthia is away: two girls entertain him with erotic enticements. But Propertius is thinking of Cynthia and he does not hear the songs of the girls nor perceive their nakedness: "They were unveiling [*nudabant*] their bosoms for a blind man (caeco)" (4.8.47). The eyes see nothing at all. Nakedness, in this case, does not emerge as exposure: it is nothing, just as a *LIMEN* that would not be trangressed. Only the act of transgression bestows a precise meaning on these signifiers, for meaning and desire arise, so to speak, after the fact, on the wake of that transgression.

There are specific ways of speaking about nakedness: reticence, for instance, or obscene language. In Propertius we find both the expressions *reticere* (e.g., 1.10.13) and *obscena carmina* (1.16.10), but the *obscena carmina* are simply mentioned reticently and not reported. Both expressions imply exposure by the act of covering: *reticentia* in its etymological and rhetorical usage,[30] obscene language in its practice. Generally such language needs constant new coverings in order to provoke newer and bolder exposures. This situation corresponds to the rhetorical stance in which the poet finds himself in relationship to the reader. Through Cynthia's reticence, the text gives us a reticent exposure of her beauty and nakedness and controls the amount and degree of her exposure.

For Cynthia gives herself to Propertius but controls her self-exposure: when she is exposed to light, she veils herself; whereas, under the cover of darkness, she unveils herself or delays Propertius's assault by covering herself. She is in control of her self-exposure and her pleasure must therefore also consist in being able to provoke and allay his desire for her nakedness. This situation corresponds to the rhetorical stance in which the poet finds himself in relationship to the reader. Through Cynthia's reticence, the text gives us a reticent exposure of her beauty and nakedness and controls the amount and degree of her exposure. This rhetorical stance is described by Propertius in 1.4 where, among other enticing attributes of Cynthia, he mentions (14): "joys of which I am glad to speak [*dicere . . . libet*] under silent veil [*sub tacita . . . veste*]." The meaning of this line is disputed, but clearly the joys here mentioned are the same as 2.15.[31] Propertius's pleasure (*libet*) lies in the rhetorical stance he occupies: in retorting to his audience (in this case, Bassus), he entices him and gains mastery over him by revealing joys which he will not speak about, and are therefore mentioned and left unspoken. Propertius uses Cynthia's beauty and enticements to master his own audience by a shrewd balance of exposing and covering. The emphasis, therefore, does not fall on the joys themselves, but on the rhetorical process of unveiling and covering which simultaneously puts Propertius in the position of the master and the audience in the need of asking for more.

This reticence then creates the same effect on the audience that Cynthia's reticence provokes on Propertius in 2.15. For she remains in control of her self-exposure, derives pleasure obviously for her mastering game, and excites Propertius's desire for her nakedness. From Propertius's point of view her nakedness is in fact an uncoveredness that is always somehow covered by his desire to keep uncovering. As a result, though Propertius, the lover, loses control of Cynthia, Propertius the poet remains in control of her exposure. Accordingly, for the reader too Cynthia's nakedness remains an uncoveredness that is always somehow covered by the reader's desire for longer and deeper exposure.

The lover of 2.15 finally resents Cynthia's reticence:

But if you persist in lying clothed, you shall have your garment ripped by my hands. Even more, if anger (*ira*) carries me further you will show your mother how your arms are bruised. Your breasts are not yet drooping as to forbid you to make merry. (2.15.17–21)

We are reminded of the rivals who at night besiege the *LIMEN* of their mistress and threaten to break through unless she opens the door: the *rixa* on the *LIMEN* and that of love share the same desire of transgression.

The lover's wrath for Cynthia's reticence implies also the reader's bafflement with a rhetorical reticence that covers just as it exposes and vice versa. If, then, the language that should focus on Cynthia's shining beauty and expose her pure, naked forms, can present that beauty only through reticence, there is no chance that writing may fully expose Cynthia's nakedness. The predicament of this language of exposure is correlative to the inability of language of desire when it tries to represent the crossing into the realm of the presence. The Janus-like line of the *LIMEN* and the silence of a reticent language contest forever the possibility of full possession and exposure. As the *LIMEN* signifies both a structure of differences (ambivalence, contiguity) and a presence, so reticence implies the paradox of speaking and silence at once: both the image of the *LIMEN* and reticence point at the paradoxical force that removes language from the realm of presence.

As Propertius's frustration mounts to the point of wrath and as we see in the transparence of this scene the violence of the *exclusus amator*, we recognize concretely the setting of the *LIMEN*. Not even the rival is absent: Paris falls in love with Helen as he sees her rising naked from Menelaos's bed. The text conjures up a triangle, as though without some additional transgression (of the husband's *lectus* and *LIMEN*) there would be no desire. We might then surmise that Helen's naked beauty would not have appeared so appealing to Paris had not Helen risen from Menelaos's bed.

The poetic rivals and competitors are here too, peeking through this poem; the most dangerous rival is Tibullus whose lines are literally evoked, to such an extent that Jachmann was ready to bracket a part of the elegy as the work of an interpolator.[32]

Finally here, too, as in 1.8, Cynthia's beauty seems only an askance aim in order to pass to a more inspiring contemplation—that of immortality (2.15.37 ff.):

But if she consents to grant me such nights, one year will be a long life for me. If she gives me many such nights, I'll grow immortal in them; one such night might make any man a god. If all men desired to spend their life in such a way and lie with their limbs weighed down by large drinking of wine, no cruel weapon would exist nor ship of war, nor would our bones be tossed in the Actium Sea, nor would Rome, so often beset on every hand by her victories over her own people, be weary of untying her hair.

Situations may be similar but are never the same: the immortality of the lover on the bed of his ungirt mistress seems here to have a jocular ring.[33] Yet, as this theme is pitted against the catastrophe of war, it seems to allude to the *topos* of *recusatio* and even raise objections to Augustus's propaganda and policy.

The contrast between immortal lover and death of Roman soldiers, especially in civil wars, represents a typical trait of Propertian pacifism and a theme of his counter-culture—to use Sullivan's definition. Yet, despite the pathos of the impersonation of Rome as a mourning mother, the contrast fails to be convincing in its tone. On the one hand, the poem destroys or dulls the contrast between the immortality of lovers and the doom of soldiers by ending with the recognition that lovers—despite everything—may die tomorrow (2.15.51–54). On the other hand, the contrast entails a jarring note between the purely fictional language that jokes about lovers' immortality and the referential language that evokes the all-too-real mourning of mothers for their sons. The "ideological" contrast therefore lacks rhetorical consistency: it is, in fact, impertinent and frivolous.

The analysis of two Propertian elegies has allowed us to witness the force of transgression that is operating in his writing. We have chosen such images as LIMEN (and *lectus*) because they occasionally display the direction and force of this transgression. LIMEN, for instance, holds in its grip several opposite significations, but writing tries to impose one or the other as if the trace and the Janus-like ambivalence of the image could be mastered. The transgression by writing therefore produces representations in which conceptual and tonal aspects seem to occupy a fixed stance; but this transgression leaves marks in the representation that point to the open signifier and connote the poem with troubling, unsettled tensions. Such tensions constitute irony, i.e., contrasts that contest all logic and are operative in specific rhetorical modes, as reticence, for instance. The combination of Propertius's *ars amatoria* and his *ars poetandi* create a texture of subtle and complex inventions, Eros helping the Muses and vice versa in the incessant and most shrewd attempts to transgress the LIMEN and at fully mastering the language of exposure.

Lingering on the Threshold

But these attempts lead back to a certain lingering on the Janus-like line of the threshold, to the troubling mixture of passion and frivolity, and to the uneven rhetoric of exposing through reticence.

NOTES

1. For me, slow Amor [*tardus amor*] does not devise any craft and does not remember [*meminit*] to tread the well-known paths as of old. (17–18)

2. Any one slow to turn his ears [*tardas aures*] to my warnings [*monitis*], alas with what pain will repeat my words! (1, 1, 37–38)

3. The explicit connection of Amor and MORA (in some declined forms) occurs in 1.3.44: IN AMORE MORAS; 1.13.6: *in nullo* . . . AMORE MORAM.
   In 2.2.3 AMOR is connected with a form of MOROR (see also Ovid Met. 2.846) while *cura* and MOROR appear explicitly connected in 1.1.35 and 1.8.1.
   The etymology of MORA is uncertain. Ernout and Meillet connect MORA with Irish *maraim* (I remain) and define the connection with Lat. *memor* ("mindful," "remembering") adventurous.

4. Though neither LIMEN nor *door* appear *verbatim* in the poem, the expression: *neque . . . mutet . . . locum* ("which Plautus uses as equivalent of 'to move house,'" Ahl, p. 95) insures the correctness of any interpretation.

5. *Assuetus*; from *assuesco*. The verb is connected with the group of the reflexive *suus*, *sui* which indicates what is proper of an individual or of a group of men (Ernout-Meillet).

6. An explicit example of such anagrams is: 1.12.2; and one of ROMA and AMOR: 2.6.22.

7. MORA conveys the ideas of 1) delay or belatedness; 2) obstruction, detention; 3) lingering, staying. Analogously, MORARI, used intransitively, means to linger, to dwell; used transitively, it means to detain someone, or make him late. MORA represents a notion of time that is connected with the present and at the same time disjointed from the present.
   In this paper I do not pursue the semantic force of MORA, MORARI in relation to Propertius's attempt at retrieving the immediacy of a possession and presence.

8. A very similar paradoxical invention is in poem 1.3 where the lover (Propertius), coming late to visit his mistress, finds her already asleep. His first stimulus would be that of satisfying his sexual desire, but imagining Cynthia's reaction and being afraid of it, he represses his desire, and begins to accomplish the usual gestures of a courting lover: he unloosens the crowns from his hair and places them on Cynthia's, amuses himself by shaping a lock of hair, gives her apples . . . All these gentle gestures of homage and courting are acted while she sleeps and obviously all these gifts "roll down from the slope of her lap!" With an allusion to a very bitter Catullan line, the poet is even able to find Cynthia's sleep thankless!

9. As the bride reached the husband's house, she adorned the threshold with wool fillets and anointed it with lard or oil. After a short ritual exchange of words between husband and wife, the bride was raised up and taken inside

the house so that she might not touch the threshold with her feet (Serv. Aen. IV. 458, Isid. IX. 7. 12, Festus s.v. *rapi*, etc.).

10. *Ianus*: "archway," "gateway," *transitiones perviae iani nominantur* Cic. N.D., 2.27.67; "gallery" where bankers and money exchangers held their business; personified, *"Ianus,"* "God of gates and doorways," frequently represented with two-faced head; subsequently god of beginning to whom the month *Januarius* was consecrated—the month between the old and the new year. The etymology of *ianus* is disputed.

11. *Fores -ium* or *foris -is:* the door of a building, room, etc.; *foras, foris,* "outside." The notion of "outside" is often expressed by words which signify "at the door," in Latin, Greek, etc., see Ernout and Meillet, s.v. *fores.*

12. See, for instance, 2.2023–24, where Propertius mentions the period of seven moons for a love affair described by the following couplet:

> and all this time not seldom the door (*ianua*) has been compliant (*mollis*), not seldom I have had access to your bed.

Mollis ranges from "soft" to "wanton" "through *voluptuous, sensuous, languishing, erotic,* etc." (Camps): it gives to *ianua*, "door," almost the metaphorical signification of "mistress." On the other hand, "to your bed" obviously means "to you." For examples with *LIMEN*, see 1.4.22, 1.13.34, where *LIMEN* means the sweetheart, or 2.6.23–24, where it means the house of the husband and the husband himself. See Copley, p. 78: "Propertius reaches the extreme point in the symbolic use of the *LIMEN* when he makes the term (or one of its substitutes such as *fores* or *ianua*) a synonym for *amor.* . . ."

13. See Rossi.

14. *LIMEN* must be thought of in the light of a deconstruction of the line, limit, etc.

Unfortunately, terms such as ambivalence, contiguity, opposition, etc., that should help to deconstruct the line, are still compromised by the metaphysics that supports this line. What matters is that *LIMEN* retrieves its open power play in several texts despite the textual—and in general, linguistic—tendency to close it up. It traces back its *anceps* quality and force: the necessity of this retracing constitutes the starting point of recent criticism.

15. *Coniunx* (wife) and *lectus* (bed) are here in a chiastic position while being synonymous with each other and with *femina* (woman). On the other hand, Admetus, Ulixes, and the man's threshold constitute the synonymous counterpart. In this connection the man's *LIMEN* means his house, bed, himself, while also marking the limit that detains the wife inside his house, absolutely loyal to her husband.

This passage shows that *lectus* (bed) undergoes a semantic displacement analogous to that of *LIMEN:* it designates the piece of furniture we call "bed," a place to lie, and metonymically the wife, the mistress, the woman. It is the place of a certain indifference and simultaneously the object of desire. This metonymic meaning is implicit also in 2.20.23–24 (see n. 12).

16. For another example in which Propertius plays on the ambiguous meaning of *LIMEN*, see 1.13.34–35:

> Since you will once die by love, take her: you were worthy of no other threshold (*non alio limine dignus eras*).

Copley, p. 79: "Complete abstraction . . . may be seen in 1.13 . . . The figure of the *LIMEN* does far more than to imply that Gallus has performed vigilations at the doors of other, less worthy women, or that he will in all probability find himself some day excluded by his present mistress. It represents in itself the total experience of the lover, all that he does and feels in the name of love."

17. Because of the relative awkwardness of *verba querar* ("to lament words," 1.8.22), many editors prefer to change the text into arbitrary conjectures.

18. See, for instance, 1.16.15–17.

19. Critics and editors from Lipsius on have often denied unity to the elegy and broken it into two parts. Yet recent criticism has made justice of the unity of the poem: Tränkle, p. 145 (with bibliography) and Cairns, p. 150, among recent scholars, accept the unity of the elegy. So, with some uncertainty, also Hubbard, p. 46. Tränkle finds the evidence for the unity of the poem in the echoes and inner references that bind and even "fuse together" the two parts, and in other arguments as well.

20. Our concise paraphrase fails to point to the extraordinary allusiveness of the passage; since its construction relies on the repetition of special words, tag words, as it were, and almost formulae. The image of the road, so important in 1.1 (see in particular 1.1.18) and suitable to describe the movement of crossing, transgressing, etc., is repeated here (1.8.30) with a clear echo of the above-mentioned line. *Caru*(s) is an anagram of *CURA*(S) and *CURA* detains (*MORA*) Cynthia in Rome (*ROMA*, 1.8.31 is an anagram of *MORA*), etc.

In particular, the images of the first poem are repeated but contrariwise in order to show the success of a unique remedy, *i.e.*, of the poetic song (*carmen*). In the first poem the wretched love had invoked the help of the magicians whose *carmina* supposedly pulled down the moon, the help of medicine and friendship (25ff.), but to no avail.

The motif, "the power of the song," develops throughout the first book, see, for instance, besides 1.8, also 1.9.5–6 and 1.10.18 (for which see H. Akbar Khan, *Class. Philology* 1965, p. 131ff.: the success of Gallus's affair depends on Propertius's *carmen*.)

21. *certos . . . amores* in 1.8.45 is contended by *summos . . . amores* of other MSS and by scholarly conjectures as *firmos*. Recent editors accept *certos* which is supported by 2.29.19. In both contexts *certus* means "proved," "sure," and therefore "faithful."

22. In 1.16, a door (*ianua*) is imagined to complain about the shameful behavior of her mistress and the disconcerting behavior of the lovers on the *ianua*'s LIMEN. One of these lovers—the *ianua* goes on—"repeats songs with shrilling beguilement" (*arguta . . . carmina blanditia*). Yet these beguilements do not succeed in bending the mistress's mind.

Blanditia characterizes especially the voice (Th. L. L. II. 2083, 79ff.) and emphasizes, rather than the articulation of words and thoughts, the musical power.

Obsequium (from *sequi*, "to follow") is *hapax* in Propertius: it has many different connotations as it hints at several social obligations, the obedience of a servant, the kindness (or flattery) of clients, friends, the waiting upon a corpse at the burial, etc.

23. On the tight and explicit correspondence that Propertius's text intimates between erotic desire and the literary writing, see the illuminating paper by Steele Commager, especially pp. 3–12.

24. The *obsidio* (besieging) of the lover on the *LIMEN* is mentioned in Ovid *Ars Am.* 2.526.

25. As it is known, Pelops gained both the hand of Hippodamia (daughter of Oenomaus) and the kingdom of Elis by cheating in the chariot race against Oenomaus himself. Pelops had a pinchpin removed from the wheel of Oenomaus's chariot: the king died in the race and Pelops took over the kingdom and Hippodamia.

26. The "narrow bed" (*angustus lectus*) is an allusion to the poetics of the Callimachean school. In 2.1.44, Propertius extols his love poetry and pits it against epic: "We, on the contrary, tell and wage fights on the narrow bed" (*angusto . . . lecto*). This line follows a praise of Callimachus, who never thundered forth the battles of Jove from his "narrow breast" (*angusto pectore*). See S. Commager, p. 8. Let me also recall that the "narrow bed" is the kingdom (*regna*) of Propertius just as his page is: in both Cynthia is queen.

27. On the proverbial quality of the expression see the Horace commentary by Nisbet and Hubbard and on its popularity in classical literature, see Hunziger, *Die Figur der Hyperbel in den Gedichten Vergils* (1896), pp. 115–119.

28. In line 3, *narramus* and in line 9, *mutamus* raise the question whether we deal with present tenses or with contracted perfect tenses. The questions is not idle, for the present forms mingled with historical perfects would represent the events as though they were appearing under the eyes of the writer and reader. Enk (see also Camps) finally accepts these forms as present tenses on the ground that this construction is frequent in Propertius.

The point of this note is to show the temporal ambivalence of this representation of the lovers' full love. To call attention to the possibility that *narramus* and *mutamus* are not present forms means to call attention to the past time of the events. This, of course, to the extent that a Roman reader would feel the same uncertainty we feel today.

29. In Propertius, *rixa*, "fight," "brawl," occurs five times: of these occurrences three times it indicates the strife and brawl of rival lovers before the *LIMEN* (1.16.5) or the windows (2.19.5), or in a tavern (4.8.19); one time it indicates the brawl and rage of the mistress against the poet (3.8.1). Only in our instance (2.15.4) the struggle or the wrestling has erotic overtones. But it is still wrestling. Curiously K. Flower Smith (*The Elegies of Tibullus*, 1913, p. 204) understands this *rixa* as "strenuous attentions."

30. Reticence derives from Latin *re-ticere*, "be silent." *Reticentia* is a rhetorical figure implying the interruption by which an argument already hinted at is suddenly and *explicitly* dropped, so as to leave it to the imagination, suspicion, etc., of the audience.

31. See Camps, who defends the meaning here upheld, by quoting other examples of aposiopesis (*reticentia*) in Propertius, and by quoting phrases that could justify the meaning here attributed to *tacita veste*.

32. See *Rh. Mus.* N.F. 84 (1935), 193ff.

33. The theme is found in light epigrams, see *AP.* 5.55.94, etc.

BIBLIOGRAPHY

Ahl, F. "Propertius 1.1." *Wiener Studien* 37 (1974): 80ff.
Butler, H. E., trans. *Propertius*. London: Loeb Classical Library, 1924.
Cairns, F. J. *Generic Composition in Greek and Roman Poetry*. Edinburgh: Edinburgh University Press, 1972.

Camps, W. A. *Propertius Elegies, Books I–IV*. New York: Cambridge University Press, 1961–.
Commager, S. *A Prolegomenon to Propertius*. Lectures in memory of Louise Taft Semple, vol. 3. Cincinnati: The University of Cincinnati, 1974.
Enk, P. J. *Sex. Propertii Elegiarum liber primus*. Leyden: E. G. Brill, 1945; *Liber secundus*. Leyden: A. W. Sythoff, 1962.
Ernout, A. and A. Meillet, *Dictionnaire Etymologique de la langue Latine*. 4th ed. Paris: Klinksieck, 1967.
Hubbard, M. *Propertius*. London: Duckworth, 1974.
Sullivan, J. P. *Propertius. A Critical Introduction*. New York: Cambridge University Press, 1976.
Tränkle, H. *Die Sprachkunst des Properz und die Tradition der lateinischen Dichtersprache*. Wiesbaden: Steiner, 1960.

FIVE
GERALDINE
Richard A. Rand

The reason of my not finishing "Christabel" is not that I don't know how to do it—for I have, as I always had, the whole plan entire from beginning to end in my mind; but I fear I could not carry on with equal success the execution of the idea, an extremely subtle and difficult one.
  S. T. Coleridge, *Table Talk*, July 6, 1833

I

LEAVING HER father's hall at midnight, by a "gate that was ironed within and without,"[1] and kneeling in prayer, in a forest, beneath a huge oak tree, the lady Christabel hears a low sound of moaning. She springs to her feet, listens again, then steals around the tree for a look at the other side:

> There she sees a damsel bright
> Drest in a silken robe of white,
> That shadowy in the moonlight shone:
> The neck that made that white robe wan,
> Her stately neck and arms were bare;
> Her blue-veined feet unsandal'd were,
> And wildly glittered here and there,
> The gems entangled in her hair.
>   (58–65)

What follows is a taking in: Christabel questions this remarkable figure ("and who art thou?," 70), and takes in the answer ("My sire is of

Geraldine

a noble line / And my name is Geraldine," 79–80); takes in as well the tale of forcible kidnapping; and takes in, finally, the person of Geraldine herself, into the safety of her father's hall. Once there, however, she does not take in some absolutely suspicious signs, such as Geraldine's too brief seizure of pain at the threshold (129ff.), her refusal to join in prayer (141ff.), the "angry moan" of the mastiff (145ff.), or the strange flaring of the brand 156ff.). Is it Christabel's turn to be taken in by Geraldine? Ignoring these portents and others like them, she draws closer to her quest, close to the point of lying at Geraldine's side, naked, and in bed.

There it is that a shock occurs, shocking first of all to Geraldine ("Ah! what a stricken look was hers!," 70): Christabel, reclining on her elbow and watching Geraldine, takes in something she was never meant to see, the sight of Geraldine's horrible "bosom and half her side" (231). In her closeness, Christabel suffers an irreversible moment of *accuracy*, confirmed by Geraldine's defiant embrace:

> Yet Geraldine nor speaks nor stirs:
> Ah! what a stricken look was hers!
> Deep from within she seems half-way
> To lift some weight with sick assay,
> And eyes the maid and seeks delay;
> Then suddenly, as one defied,
> Collects herself in scorn and pride.
> And lay down by the Maiden's side!—
> And in her arms the maid she took,
>   Ah wel-a-day!
>   (255–64)

What is the import of this embrace? If the shock of accuracy does not prevent the women from drawing closer still, does it not change, at least, the character of that closeness? Geraldine continues with a speech that is often read as a malediction but also serves as a statement of fact:

> And with low voice and doleful look
> These words did say:
> 'In the touch of this bosom there worketh a spell,
> Which is lord of thy utterance, Christabel!'
> Thou knowest to-night, and wilt know to-morrow,
> This mark of my shame, this seal of my sorrow;
>   But vainly thou warrest,
>   For this is alone in
>   Thy power to declare,
>   That in the dim forest
>   Thou heard'st a low moaning,
> And found'st a bright lady, surpassingly fair;

And didst bring her home with thee in love and in charity,
To shield her and shelter her from the damp air.'
(265–78)

A strange turn: Christabel, taking in Geraldine, draws so close that she sees the "mark," a sight that is like a dream, vivid and unforgettable, but not to be put into words, "a sight to dream of, not to tell!" (253). The mark is thus a "seal" in two senses of that word—a hallmark or signature, but one that also "seals" up or encrypts the fact of its own existence, of its meaning (if it has one), and of its history (which is never revealed). And this seal, by sight and by touch, also seals up Christabel, and so becomes her seal and signature as well. Christabel, who cannot forget the mark, nor openly and articulately "declare" it, must live henceforth as Geraldine lives, bearing, even as she dissembles, the sealing up of the seal, concealing the mark of her difference, saying one thing and meaning, knowing, and being something else.

The consequences of this moment are spelled out in part 2, but before we pursue them, we should remark that Coleridge is treating something of interest to readers of poetry. For Geraldine, who dissembles, is a kind of poem, and the story of Christabel is the story of one of her readers. In writing the poem, Coleridge tells about the process of reading, the process, indeed, of reading the poem known as *Christabel*. The poem exhibits a number of mirroring tendencies, or specular properties: it begins, for example, with a prosodic and phonemic symphony of bell tones, cock crows, and owl hoots, interspersed with the regular responses of the mastiff—"sixteen short howls, not over loud" (12)—which happen to mime the loose octosyllabic couplet of the poem. Christabel's bed chamber, also like a poem, is a place of intellectual delights, figured and sensuous, and not to be grasped by the light of nature alone:

> The moon shines dim in the open air,
> And not a moonbeam enters here.
> But they without its light can see
> The chamber carved so curiously,
> Carved with figures strange and sweet,
> All made out of the carver's brain,
> For a lady's chamber meet:
> The lamp with twofold silver chain
> Is fastened to an angel's feet.
> (175–83)

Taking, then, the poem named *Christabel* as a meditation on itself, with the figure named "Geraldine" as its own interior mirror image; and taking the figure named "Christabel" as one of her readers, perhaps a naive one, or perhaps an exemplary one, whose openness to Geraldine is a kind of willing suspension of disbelief; we begin to feel that the poem

Geraldine

extends a particular question to the reader: what is the "seal" or "mark" of the poem called *Christabel*, and if we should happen to see it, would we, like the lady Christabel, also lack the "power to declare" it, and therefore carry it, cryptically, within?

It remains to *see* the mark, a situation anticipated in the second part of the poem. There, we encounter two readings of Geraldine that miss the mark completely: Sir Leoline's and Bard Bracy's.

Unlike his daughter, Sir Leoline does not simply take in Geraldine's story, but puts it to the test as he hears it. He verifies it in terms of an earlier story, the story of his own life. Posing his own life as the known truth, he hears the tale of Geraldine as a more or less credible figure, or trope, of that truth. The trope is complex in structure. It is first of all a metonymy:

> But when he heard the lady's tale,
> And when she told her father's name,
> Why waxed Sir Leoline so pale,
> Murmuring o'er the name again,
> Lord Roland de Vaux of Tryermaine?
> (403–30)

For Sir Leoline, the name of his erstwhile friend Lord Roland is a memory-trace or "scar" (421), and "neither heat, nor frost, nor thunder / Shall wholly do away, I ween, / The marks of that which once hath been" (424–26). Sir Leoline thus verifies the story of Geraldine by association or metonymy, by the connection of one name to another. He then goes on to read by analogy, or metaphor, comparing two faces:

> Sir Leoline, a moment's space,
> Stood gazing on the damsel's face:
> And the youthful Lord of Tryermaine
> Came back upon his heart again.
> (427–30)

Validating the tale in this manner, Sir Leoline accepts it without further challenge. In other words, having refused to take in Geraldine's tale as Christabel did, with no questions asked, he does take it in with a very slight degree of rhetorical circumspection. He never suspects that her tale differs from her condition as a figure differs from its meaning; and he never suspects that his own true thoughts are cast in the form of figures, that they are the figures furnished by Geraldine herself, Geraldine being the first to utter the name of Lord Roland de Vaux of Tryermaine.

Unlike his master Sir Leoline, the servant Bard Bracy also misses the mark, but with the highest degree of rhetorical understanding. His reading is oblique: he never says anything to or about Geraldine, at least explicitly, but speaks only to his master, in the context of his master's commands. His reading comes in the midst of a speech about "Clearing yon wood from thing unblest" (529), where its pertinence to Geraldine is bound to be lost on the master. The reading itself is also offered up in the form of a "dream" or "vision," an allegory in the medieval style: the Bard, a paragon of rhetorical lucidity, does not present his reading as a truth, but as a fiction or veiled hypothesis, which may or may not be true:

> '... in my sleep I saw that dove,
> That gentle bird, whom thou dost love,
> And call'st by thy own daughter's name—
> Sir Leoline! I saw the same
> Fluttering, and uttering fearful moan,
> Among the green herbs in the forest alone.
> Which when I saw and when I heard,
> I wonder'd what might ail the bird;
> For nothing near it could I see,
> Save the grass and green herbs underneath the old tree.
>
> 'And in my dream methought I went
> To search out what might there be found;
> And what the sweet bird's trouble meant,
> That thus lay fluttering on the ground.
> I went and peered, and could descry
> No cause for her distressful cry;
> But yet for her dear lady's sake
> I stooped, methought, the dove to take,
> When lo! I saw a bright green snake
> Coiled around its wings and neck.
> Green as the herbs on which it couched,
> Close by the dove's its head it crouched;
> And with the dove it heaves and stirs,
> Swelling its neck as she swelled hers!'
>
> (531–54)

This "dream" interprets Geraldine's tale as a second remove, as a reading of Sir Leoline's (assenting) interpretation. First, the Bard adopts the terms or themes of his master. In his own comments on Geraldine's tale, Sir Leoline employs the terms of serpent and dove: he says that Geraldine's kidnappers have "reptile souls" (449), and is also quoted as calling Christabel a "dove" (532–33), a term that he later applies to Geraldine (569). Along with his master's terms, the Bard also adopts his instruments of reasoning, the tropes of metonymy and metaphor: he says that the serpent menaces the dove with its nearness or contiguity (metonymy of place), and with the powers of mimicry (metaphor) that make it almost invisible: "Green as the herbs on which it couched, / Close by the dove's its head it crouched" (551–52). But the Bard does not merely adopt the terms and reasoning, the concepts and values, of his master: he also subjects them to a systematic reversal.

Geraldine

Thus, the "dove" known as "Geraldine" is recast in the role of the "snake," and the verifying instruments of metonymy and metaphor are shown to be the vehicles of falsehood. Reversed and reinscribed in a new story, Geraldine's tale has been, in the strict sense of the word, "deconstructed."[2]

It goes without saying that the force of this deconstruction would be lost on Sir Leoline: a firm believer in the truth, he would not be tempted to connect the fiction of the dream to the real circumstances of the actual moment. And if he made the connection he could not accept the judgments implied in the dream, for it would annul the authority of his truth and so put an end to his standing as a master. And such an end would finish off the Bard as a servant; for the Bard depends on his master: he must hear what the master says before he can follow up with his own critical reply. Each supplies what the other lacks—a language on the one hand, and an insight on the other. Taken together, they round off the limits of a certain discourse, a discourse of assertions and counterassertions, of "truths" and "falsehoods," furnished in the first place by the text itself, by Geraldine, whose tale holds forth the invitation to make sense of her person, of arriving at her truth, be it a truth that lies in the veracity of her assertions or in their falsehood.

But does this understanding, Sir Leoline's or Bard Bracy's, come to any real and sufficient account of Geraldine? Certainly her story is open to interpretation, and indeed it inevitably sets that process in motion, with its drama of an innocent maiden in distress and its telling reference to Lord Roland de Vaux of Tryermaine. And the readings of master and Bard are not without a certain real interest: Christabel, for instance, pays careful attention to them both, and her responses inevitably influence our own reactions to them. On the one hand, she finds her father's reading almost effaced by the memory of the mark:

> And now the tears were on his face,
> And fondly in his arms he took
> Fair Geraldine, who met the embrace,
> Prolonging it with joyous look.
> Which when she viewed, a vision fell
> Upon the soul of Christabel,
> The vision of fear, the touch and pain!
> She shrunk and shuddered, and saw again.
> (447–54)

Bard Bracy's reading, on the other hand, has an actual impact or influence on the text it reads, on the image of Geraldine herself, which it transforms, briefly, into one of a snake:

> A snake's small eye blinks dull and shy;
> And the lady's eyes they shrunk in her head,

> Each shrunk up to a serpent's eye,
> And with somewhat of malice, and more of dread,
> At Christabel she looked askance!—
>
> (583–87)

This impact extends to Christabel, who, being gifted with a sympathetic imagination, mimes ("with a hissing sound," 591), the image of Geraldine thus transformed, an event that the poem goes on to relate in the following way:

> The maid, alas! her thoughts are gone,
> She nothing sees—no sight but one!
> The maid, devoid of guile and sin,
> I know not how, in fearful wise,
> So deeply had she drunken in
> That look, those shrunken serpent eyes,
> That all her features were resigned
> To this sole image in her mind:
> And passively did imitate
> That look of dull and treacherous hate!
> And thus she stood, in dizzy trance,
> Still picturing that look askance
> With forced unconscious sympathy.
>
> (597–609)

Certainly, then, the Bard's reading, unlike the master's, has a powerful impact on Geraldine and Christabel alike; and yet the image of the snake does not last: "the trance was o'er" (613), to be followed by the enduring and horrible memory of the mark, a memory to which the image of the snake does not finally adhere:

> And when the trance was o'er, the maid
> Paused awhile, and inly prayed:
> Then falling at the Baron's feet,
> 'By my mother's soul do I entreat
> That thou this woman send away!'
> She said: and more she could not say:
> For what she knew she could not tell,
> O'er-mastered by the mighty spell.
>
> (613–20)

The effacement of the vision of the snake by the memory of the mark is a signal moment in the poem: for, up to a point, Geraldine can be read as a being of truth or falsehood, as a "dove," or as a "snake" acting as a "dove." We could say, for example, that the tale she tells, like the dress she wears, is a veil of fiction that covers the truth of her mark. But what, in the end, is the *truth* of her mark? Does the mark give the lie to the tale? Yes, in the narrow sense that the tale does not include the mark, but differs from it; no, in the sense that the mark, being unintelligible, has nothing to add of significance to the tale. Which is to say that the tale, true or false, does not communicate with the mark but only coincides with it, and that the forms of reading that concentrate on the tale never attain the recognition of the mark. Christabel, who accepted the tale without challenge and saw the mark as a consequence, finds that the other readings do not engage her as the mark does. For the tale is joined to the mark not as a falsehood to the truth it conceals, but rather as the juxtaposition or superimposition of one text, containing truth and falsehood alike, and another text, or palimpsest, that says nothing, tells no truth or falsehood, and falls under no one's control. This palimpsest controls everyone instead, including the poet or poem called Geraldine, who, though she can use her body to certain effect and can make it tell a story, cannot make the body tell the only story that really matters, which is the story of the mark and how it got there.

Christabel is thus a poem that breaks off at the moment of least communication, with Christabel caught in her spell, Sir Leoline enraged at her strange behavior, and Bard Bracy sent off on an errand he wants to avoid. Clearly this scene of noncommunication, dramatically rendered as an interaction between various characters, also enacts the condition of Geraldine, who is made up of these different and incompatible strata, one level communicating with Sir Leoline and the Bard, and another level, that of the "mark," communicating with Christabel in her trance-like moments of recollection. Recalling that Geraldine is a kind of poem, we can see that the noncommunication of the end of *Christabel*, which enacts the condition of Geraldine, reflects the rhetorical condition of the text itself: the poem tells a story that does not communicate with its own mark or seal.[3]

Must we give up the quest for the seal?

Three issues remain unexplored. Taken together, they suggest a program. First is the matter of closeness: we have not drawn close enough to Coleridge for his mark to surprise us. In textual terms, we haven't sufficiently taken in the system of his tropes and their deconstruction.

Second, in reading the tropes we must bear in mind what they do *not* reveal, namely, the mark. They cover up the mark. But this covering up is not a resource of the tropes: if it were, they could also disclose the mark. Rather, the covering up belongs to the power of the mark itself, which can always efface itself by taking the form of something else, of something other than a mark, for example, of a story or a tropological system.

Third, this effacement and divulgence of the mark is a kind of alternation or winking movement: Christabel hears the story *and* recalls the mark, in alternation. The two movements never take place at the same time. In this respect, the relation of the mark to story is like the relation of a sign to its meaning. Mark and story are to be focused on in turn, but not together. Geraldine, that is, is structured in certain respects like a sign, and it is not an accident that Coleridge ends his poem with a meditation on the sign-structure:

> A little child, a limber elf,
> Singing, dancing to itself,
> A fairy thing with red round cheeks,
> That always finds, and never seeks,
> Makes such a vision to the sight
> As fills a father's eyes with light;
> And pleasures flow in so thick and fast
> Upon his heart, that he at last
> Must needs express his love's excess
> With words of unmeant bitterness.
>   (656–65)

This enigma stands in relation to the poem as a sign stands in relation to its meaning. It means the poem, but in a way that we cannot rationally analyze. And the meaning of this meaning is . . . a sign: a father who wishes to express a certain kind of thought ("love's excess"), does so by means of certain shocking words, words of "unmeant bitterness." It is the bitterness of the words that is "unmeant," their bitterness being used to signify "love" instead of "bitterness." If we take the bitter words to mean what they seem to mean, then we miss their intended meaning. If we read the words as a trope—as a metaphor, in which the bitterness of the words *resembles* the bitterness of the feeling—then we inevitably miss the import of the words, and we also miss, therefore, the bizarre coincidence of the words with their meaning, a coincidence which is not organized like a metaphor.

Trope, sign, and seal, then: a sequence of places to turn to. If not in the form of a progress, at least in the form of a juxtaposition.

II

Merely to find the tropology in the poems of Coleridge is not an easy thing to do. For the tropes pertain in some way to the hidden, elusive, or occulted dimensions of language that make up its rhetoric. It is not surprising that readers disagree on the definitions of the tropes—on the meaning, say, of the word "metaphor"; or, if faced with a figure in a given text, on the class of trope that it might be said to belong to. It is not unusual, in the literature surrounding a romantic text, for one reader to see nothing of the figural about it, while another sees the entire text as a figure that figures forth its own tropology. Moreover, the tropes "exist," if that is the word, not as facts of language but as arguments or positions taken by the text. They "exist" as arguments in support of their own existence, and, as arguments, they are open to dispute or rebuttal, counterarguments to be posed, indeed, by the very text that argues their existence in the first place. To "find" the tropes is thus to argue convincingly that the text in question poses an argument—and that there lies hidden, in the poetry of Coleridge, for example, an "art of rhetoric" that argues, in a certain way, that language works in a certain way, this argument having an impact on the organization of the poetry itself.

To argue the existence of such an argument—to lend our argument the force of an incontestible fact—we turn to a poem that is widely regarded as a founding text of British Romanticism:

FROST AT MIDNIGHT

The Frost performs its secret ministry
Unhelped by any wind. The owlet's cry
Came loud—and hark, again! loud as before.
The inmates of my cottage, all at rest,
Have left me to that solitude, which suits
Abstruser musings: save that at my side
My cradled infant slumbers peacefully.
'Tis calm indeed! so calm, that it disturbs
And vexes meditation with its strange
And extreme silentness. Sea, hill, and wood,
This populous village! Sea, and hill, and wood,
With all the numberless goings-on of life,
Inaudible as dreams! the thin blue flame
Lies on my low-burnt fire, and quivers not;
Only that film, which fluttered on the grate,
Still flutters there, the sole unquiet thing.
Methinks, its motion in this hush of nature
Gives it dim sympathies with me who live,
Making it a companionable form,
Whose puny flaps and freaks the idling Spirit
By its own moods interprets, every where
Echo or mirror seeking of itself,
And makes a toy of Thought.
                                    But O! how oft,
How oft, at school, with most believing mind,
Presageful, have I gazed upon the bars,
To watch that fluttering *stranger!* and as oft
With unclosed lids, already had I dreamt
Of my sweet birth-place, and the old church-tower,
Whose bells, the poor man's only music, rang
From morn to evening, all the hot Fair-day,
So sweetly, that they stirred and haunted me
With a wild pleasure, falling on mine ear
Most like articulate sounds of things to come!
So gazed I, till the soothing things, I dreamt,

> Lulled me to sleep, and sleep prolonged my dreams!
> And so I brooded all the following morn,
> Awed by the stern preceptor's face, mine eye
> Fixed with mock study on my swimming book:
> Save if the door half opened, and I snatched
> A hasty glance, and still my heart leaped up,
> For still I hoped to see the *stranger's* face,
> Townsman, or aunt, or sister more beloved,
> My play-mate when we both were clothed alike!
>
> Dear Babe, that sleepest cradled by my side,
> Whose gentle breathings, heard in this deep calm,
> Fill up the interspersed vacancies
> And momentary pauses of the thought!
> My babe so beautiful! it thrills my heart
> With tender gladness, thus to look at thee,
> And think that thou shalt learn far other lore,
> And in far other scenes! For I was reared
> In the great city, pent 'mid cloisters dim,
> And saw nought lovely but the sky and stars.
> But *thou*, my babe! shalt wander like a breeze
> By lakes and sandy shores, beneath the crags
> Of ancient mountain, and beneath the clouds,
> Which image in their bulk both lakes and shores
> And mountain crags: so shalt thou see and hear
> The lovely shapes and sounds intelligible
> Of that eternal language, which thy God
> Utters, who from eternity doth teach
> Himself in all, and all things in himself.
> Great universal Teacher! he shall mould
> Thy spirit, and by giving make it ask.
>
> Therefore all seasons shall be sweet to thee,
> Whether the summer clothe the general earth
> With greenness, or the redbreast sit and sing
> Betwixt the tufts of snow on the bare branch
> Of mossy apple-tree, while the nigh thatch
> Smokes in the sun-thaw; whether the eave-drops fall
> Heard only in the trances of the blast,
> Or if the secret ministry of frost
> Shall hang them up in silent icicles,
> Quietly shining to the quiet Moon.[4]

"Frost at Midnight" dramatizes the elements of Coleridge's tropology on the stage of the human subject, this drama turning, linguistically, on the different ways of readying the homonym at play in the word "stranger."[5] A footnote, appended to the text in two editions that were published during the poet's lifetime, and referring to a line in the first paragraph—"Only that film, which fluttered on the grate" (25)—reads as follows:

Only that film. In all parts of the kingdom these films are called "strangers" and supposed to portend the arrival of some absent friend.

Geraldine

The word "stranger," according to the note, not only means, in the etymological sense of the French *étranger*, a person in a distant place, but also "film on a grate." This homonym has been motivated by means of a tropological link with the secondary meaning made into the sign or "portent" of the primary meaning. The link between them is one of metonymy, of the connection of two independent entities by nearness in time, of antecedent and consequent.[6] The argument of the poem, developed in three separate moments—the nocturnal "musings" of the first paragraph, the recollections of the second paragraph, and the predictive assertions of the third and fourth paragraphs—builds on the semantic material set forth in the fugitive footnote. The second paragraph analyzes, generalizes, and dramatizes the metonymic motivation in terms of a state of mind:

> But O! how oft,
> How oft, at school, with most believing mind,
> Presageful, have I gazed upon the bars,
> To watch that fluttering *stranger*! and as oft
> With unclosed lids, already had I dreamt
> Of my sweet birth-place, and the old church-tower,
> Whose bells, the poor man's only music, rang
> From morn to evening, all the hot Fair-day,
> So sweetly, that they stirred and haunted me
> With a wild pleasure, falling on mine ear
> Most like articulate sounds of things to come!
> So gazed I, till the soothing things, I dreamt,
> Lulled me to sleep, and sleep prolonged my dreams!
> And so I brooded all the following morn,
> Awed by the stern preceptor's face, mine eye
> Fixed with mock study on my swimming book:
> Save if the door half opened, and I snatched
> A hasty glance, and still my heart leaped up,
> For still I hoped to see the *stranger's* face,
> Townsman, or aunt, or sister more beloved,
> My play-mate when we both were clothed alike!
> (23–43)

As a schoolboy with a "most believing mind" (24), Coleridge read all relations in terms of metonymy: he not only accepted the link between "strangers," he also awaited a stranger to whom he was connected by metonymy, either of place ("townsman," 42), of family ("Aunt," 42), or of place, family, and dress—the "sister more beloved, my playmate when we both were clothed alike!" (42–43)—the clothes of the children duplicating the very kind of coincidence to be found in a homonym. In keeping with this portrait, Coleridge also relates a dominant daydream of the time, the recollection of an earlier "portent," the sound of the bells on the "hot fair day" (30), that "stirred and haunted me / With a wild pleasure, falling on mine ear / Most like articulated sounds of things to come" (31–34). The bell-tones were not themselves the "things to come," but only associated with them metonymically.

As indicated by the phrase "most believing mind" (an earlier version reads "most believing superstitious wish"),[7] this mind is a deluded one, exposed repeatedly to error and disappointment. And to this portrait Coleridge opposes, in the first paragraph, the portrait of a mind which he calls "self-watching" and "subtilizing," awake when others sleep (4) and given to "abstruser musings" (5). This skeptical mind, like the "most believing mind," also construes such things as the homonym "stranger" in terms of a trope:

>   . . . the thin blue flame
> Lies on my low-burnt fire, and quivers not;
> Only that film, which fluttered on the grate,
> Still flutters there, the sole unquiet thing.
> Methinks, its motion in this hush of nature
> Gives it dim sympathies with me who live,
> Making it a companionable form,
> Whose puny flaps and freaks the idling Spirit
> By its own moods interprets, every where
> Echo or mirror seeking of itself,
> And makes a toy of Thought.
>   (13–23)

Here the "stranger" on the grate is taken not as a metonymy portending an arrival, but as an analogy duplicating a person: the "stranger" is now linked to a "stranger" as the vehicle to the tenor of a metaphor, and Coleridge calls the mind that can pose such a link "subtle" and "self-watching," error-free. In the third paragraph, the governing trope of this mind is generalized to the status of a language, the language of God himself, one that the infant son will learn to speak, as opposed to the language of metonymy:

> My babe so beautiful! it thrills my heart
> With tender gladness, thus to look at thee,
> And think that thou shalt learn far other lore,
> And in far other scenes! For I was reared
> In the great city, pent 'mid cloisters dim,
> And saw nought lovely but the sky and stars.
> But *thou*, my babe! shalt wander like a breeze
> By lakes and sandy shores, beneath the crags
> Of ancient mountain, and beneath the clouds,
> Which image in their bulk both lakes and shores
> And mountain crags: so shalt thou see and hear
> The lovely shapes and sounds intelligible
> Of that eternal language, which thy God
> Utters, who from eternity, doth teach
> Himself in all, and all things in himself.
>   (48–62)

Like the metaphor of the "stranger" in the first paragraph, the elements of God's "eternal language" are metaphors: the clouds "image in their bulk both lakes and shores / And mountain crags." And thus the superiority of metaphor to metonymy, argued in epistemological terms, harmonizes with the poem's related themes of psychology and theology, sharing a common metaphysical ground in the concept of a presence transcending language.

So runs, at least, the argument of the poem. But this argument only turns on the sign structure, favoring one version of the sign over others. And since the sign structure is itself just a fiction of the language as it ought to work, and not a description of the language as it is, should we not expect of a poem that celebrates the virtues of "'subtlety" and "self-watching" that it also acknowledge somewhere the realities to which the concept of the sign is opposed? May it not, for example, demote its claims for one trope by somehow reinstating the other as being just as "truthful" or valid? Or, since homonymy makes no sense, should we not expect of a rigorous poem that it will also recognize somehow that it makes no sense to make sense of a homonym by means of one trope rather than another? Our suspicions are encouraged in the first paragraph of the poem, where the metaphor of the stranger is called a "toy of Thought" (23): to coin a trope is a form of play, of make-believe, of "fantastic playfulness."[8] Its claims for truth are not scientific, but a playful mimesis of science.

How, then, does *Frost at Midnight* undo its own arguments for the trope of metaphor? Where does Bard Bracy challenge Sir Leoline in this text? Shall we find him lurking on the level of the argument, in the form of a logical contradiction? On what basis, for example, does Coleridge make the confident predictions of the last two paragraphs? Are they, like the predictions of the second paragraph, founded on a false portent? If so, the poem would certainly stand accused of posing an argument elsewhere shown to be false.

In fact, the poem is too well reasoned to be undone at the level of argument: the predictions of the last two paragraphs are not based on a "false" portent but, in the terms of this poem, on a "true" one, a portent grounded in metaphor. The passage from present to future—that is, from the poet's "present" to the babe's "future"—is effected on the basis of analogy: the metaphor of the stranger in the first paragraph is *like* the images that make up the "eternal" language in the third, the difference between them being that the first is a single particular, and the second a general law. Nor is the link between father and son merely contiguous or metonymic, as one might be led to expect by the line "Dear Babe, that sleepest cradled *by my side*" (44, emphasis added). By analogy with his father and with all other human beings, the babe will, indeed, *learn a language*. The argument of the poem is thus a syllogism, in which the movement from present to future, and from particular to general, is grounded in a universal experience: all people learn language, the Babe is a person, therefore the Babe will learn language. It is, logically speaking, an unshakably sound argument.

The deconstruction of the argument does not take the form of a logical contradiction, but the form, instead, of the supplemental *use* of the (supposedly) castigated metonymy in the organization of the text. In a surreptitious return, the trope of metonymy puts the trope of metaphor *in place*: thus, while metaphor is argued as error-free, metonymy is shown to be more powerful, because it distributes the metaphor according to the laws of contiguity and association. It is the son, for example, and not the father, who will acquire the language of God, the "eternal language which thy God / Utters" (not "our God," or "my God"); for the acquisition of language may be universal, and the language of God may be "eternal," but the "eternal language" is not a universal one. It is associated (by metonymy) with the countryside, as a rural dialect unknown in "the great city"; and if the father can speak it on this occasion, he does so in the context of a lifetime's association with another language.

Metonymy returns in a second way, one touching the language of God himself. If we examine the metaphor of the "stranger," we find that metonymy performs an invisible (or silent) but decisive role in its epistemological success. If the metaphor of the stranger does not delude us, then it differs from the "rose" in the *Christening* poem. How? Not only because the tenor of the metaphor "stranger" differs from the vehicle in every material respect, whereas the tenor and vehicle of the metaphor "rose" were both "roses"; but also because the tenor and vehicle of the metaphor "stranger" are associated with one another in space, like an object and its reflection in a "mirror" (22). And Coleridge repeats this gesture in the third paragraph, defining the figure as metaphor, but deploying it as a metonymy:

> But *thou*, my babe! shalt wander like a breeze
> By lakes and sandy shores, beneath the crags
> Of ancient mountain, and beneath the clouds,
> Which image in their bulk both lakes and shores
> And mountain crags: . . .
>
> (54–58)

Certainly the clouds "image" the forms of nature in their "bulk," but the two are also connected by virtue of their correspondent spacing: the forms are "beneath" the clouds just as the "stranger" on the grate is in the room with the "stranger" watching it. It is the "spacing," and not the duplication, that makes these shapes "intelligible" (59). More precisely, it is the spacing that makes the duplication possible in the first place: a metaphor is always and already metonymic, an affair of "duplicity" like the homonym from which it stems.

Thus the poem deconstructs the hierarchy of values that it claims to uphold: it aligns those values with one trope in the chain of its argument, but then it reverses that judgment and reinscribes it in a second chain, the chain of the poem's topography.

Bard Bracy, after all, does not *take issue* with his master.

III

The proteiform graph itself is a polyhedron of scripture.
Finnegan's Wake

Is it accidental that the tropes, and the readings that arise from them, should so thoroughly miss the mark? What would happen, for instance, if Geraldine disrobed before the court, before the judges or readers known as Baron and Bard? Could such a thing actually take place?

It seems unthinkable that Geraldine should disrobe if the court is to remain a court: the Baron is a Baron, and the Bard is his Bard, only if the rules that govern and bring the court into existence are strictly observed. The conventions of the court—as a place of judgment as well as of manners—requires that everyone wear clothes. Those conventions *are* the court, and this fact is the source of Christabel's distress at the close of Part II. She has seen something that interferes with the reality of courtly decorum, and her conduct suffers as a result. The logic of courtly behavior is no longer real, having been displaced by the shocking perception of the mark. Who doubts that the same would happen to Baron and Bard if they too were to see the seal? Geraldine's clothing belongs to the court, pertains to the scene of the tropes, to their construction and their deconstruction. Her garments *are* the tropes, and to take them off would be to finish off the scene, the court, the Baron, and the Bard.

The tropes, however, though a necessity of the court, are only Geraldine's cover-up, and it follows that their shape, their placement, their texture, and their appeal are all to be counted among the effects of the seal. The seal shapes the text—the text known as Geraldine, and also the text, the sequence of readings, known as *Christabel*. The force of the mark determines the text through a series of after-shocks, in the silence and dissembling of Geraldine, in the astonishment of Christabel, in the errancy of Baron and Bard, and in the ruminations of readers thereafter. And the common trait of all these after-shocks is their failure, their incapacity, to uncover the mark itself, to comprehend it, and so to arrest the unlimited repetition of its shock. The mark indeed *makes* sense, but it never makes *sense*—of itself.

Where do we turn?

Away from the tropes, from the logic and the premise of the sign, and from the hope that resides in those premises, of making the "seal" present, punctual, meaningful, sensible.

Let us pause at the turn-off, at the divergence of the road without a sign.

To turn away from the sign is to turn away from the usual mission of reading, which is to make sense, to locate the text's meaning, its truths, falsehoods, arguments, system of values, stance, and gestures. Essential for such is the force of the mark, Geraldine is personal to this mark, belongs to it as no other person does.

These three features—materiality, perdurability, and uniqueness—are the essence of any "seal" that is a signature, and they serve to explain why a signature is also the kind of seal that hides or encrypts.[9] For a signature encrypts or "seals" the story of its own formation, its uniqueness and pastness: no one can tell how or why a signature comes to be as it is, just as no one doubts, when seeing one, that it is invested with a history, the history of the person who carries it. Indeed, it furnishes that person with whatever history he has; and this, it seems, is where we find the chief interest of Geraldine's "horrible bosom and half her side"—in its condition as a signature. Our interest does not, for example, lie in its ugliness, because its ugliness is not essential to it. It would still be a signature, and a fascinating one, if it were beautiful, as Coleridge makes clear in his descriptions of another, lesser-known seal:

> As when a mother doth explore
> The rose-mark on her long-lost child,
> I met, I loved you, maiden mild!
> As whom I long had loved before.[10]

Since, then, a turn from the tropes is a turn from the claims of logic, of reason, and of truthfulness, the remarks that follow cannot claim to tell the truth, to break the riddle of the seal, to represent the seal. They can only speculate on certain possible apparitions of the seal, in hopes of breaking the silence that invests it. To break a silence is precisely not to solve a riddle: solving a riddle furnishes us with the last word; but breaking a silence, by process of speculation, is to merely open up, as riddles are known to do, a new and potentially limitless chain of discourse.

Here, then, are a few speculative comments on the mark, furnishing notes for other speculations yet to come.

We turn, as we must, to the person of Geraldine herself, to the body that stays when the clothes fall away. We observe three things: first, the mark belongs to the body, not as something applied, like a tattoo, but as a part of the body itself: "Behold! her bosom and half her side— / A sight to dream of, not to tell!" (252–53). Second, the seal of the body, or the body of the seal, *outlasts*, as the body does, the circumstances of its own formation, and furthermore outlasts, as the body does not, the material fact of its own bodily existence—in the infinite chain of repercussions that it sets up among its readers and the readers of its readers. Third, as Geraldine herself indicates when she calls the seal the "mark of my sorrow," this material mark that lasts is personal to her; or rather, as they are to the text, and therefore pertinent as they no doubt somehow are to the "seal," those topics and procedures do not prepare a passage to the "seal," do not disclose it, but hide it instead in a decent mass of fine folding cloth. This cloth is the fabric of rhetorical discourse, the fabric of the New Critics, with their infinitely patient attention to ambiguity, structure, and paradox; of the structuralists, with their refined applications of semiology and rhetoric; and the fabric, as well, of authors like Geoffrey Hartman and Harold Bloom, who aim to go beyond the formalism of their precursors. Great as the differences are between these critical tendencies, they all have it in common that they cover the seal with their meaningful folds, folds that go by the names of "metaphor," "metonymy," "synecdoche," "metalepsis," "allegory," "irony," "litotes," "hyperbole," "tessera," "clinamen," "kenosis," "daemonization," "askesis," "apophrades," "limitation," "substitution," "representation," "reaction-formation," "reversal," "undoing," "repression," "sublimation," "introjection," "pathos," "ethos," "misprision," "misreading," "poetic crossing," "aporia," "akedah," "after-image," "blending," and "omphalos." To recite this chain of coinings—and no reading seems possible that does not tarry in their conceptual space—is to indicate just how drastic a step the seal of Geraldine seems to pose, drastic, among other reasons, because Coleridge himself is a chief source of our habits of reading, of our logic, of our tropology.

Geraldine's scar is thus a signature. And what is the signature, the scar, of the poem known as "Christabel"? It is not the signature at the bottom of the page that we refer to, but the signature as it lies concealed in the body of the text, carried by the text as an invisible or unacknowledged but powerful force, material, individual, and persisting.

Because speculations must really take off at this point, we take a step backwards and sideways to another text called "A Tombless Epitaph," which itself traces a speculative movement backwards and sideways along a path:

> For not a hidden path, that to the shades
> Of the beloved Parnassian forest leads,
> Lurked undiscovered by him; not a rill

> There issues from the fount of Hippocrene,
> But he had traced it upward to its source,
> Through open glade, dark glen, and secret dell
> Knew the gay wild flowers on its banks and culled
> Its med'cinable herbs. Yea, oft alone,
> Piercing the long-neglected holy cave,
> The haunt obscure of old Philosophy,
> He bad with lifted torch its starry walls
> Sparkle, as erst they sparkled to the flame
> Of odorous lamps tended by Saint and Sage.[11]

This path leads beyond the "gay wild flowers," which we construe—and we hope that the reading is not an abusive one—as a figure for the figures themselves, the tropes, the "flowers" of rhetoric. The tropes are found in the Parnassian forest, by the light of day. The poet, turning away from the daylight of the tropes, enters a subterranean space, a "long-neglected holy cave," a place of darkness, where, by the light of his torch, he sees the "starry walls" of the cavern. Those stars are visible where the flowers are not, and vice versa; which is to say, in keeping with the trend of our own speculation, that the stars are situated like a signature. They are a metaphor for the signature.

Could they not also be a signature in their own right?

There are at least two poems by Coleridge that close with starlit settings, the "Dejection Ode" and "To William Wordsworth." The starlit settings act, in their respective contexts, as signatures in the sense of affirmations, endorsing a movement articulated by the poem. We quote the second of these passages, because there the poet seems to counter-sign, or endorse, the signature of the great poem that he was listening to:

> In silence listening, like a devout child,
> My soul lay passive, by thy various strain
> Driven as in surges now beneath the stars,
> With momentary stars of my own birth,
> Fair constelled foam, still darting off
> Into the darkness.[12]

Here the image of the constellation is certainly *situated* like a signature, but we are not yet prepared to insist that it literally is one, if only because it is an image, and because this image occurs so rarely in Coleridge's poetry, whereas a signature *should* occur repeatedly.

What we seek is something more frequent and more material, more literal, a literal sense of the figure "star," a sense that is lost, perhaps, in the word "star" itself.

Coleridge once again points the way in an epigram that was not published in his lifetime and which does not find a place in the anthologies:

> The stars that wont to start, as on a chace,
> Mid twinkling insult on Heaven's darken'd face,
> Like a conven'd conspiracy of spies
> Wink at each other with confiding eyes!
> Turn from the portent—all is blank on high,
> No constellations alphabet the sky:
> The heavens one large Black Letter only shew,
> And as a child beneath its master's blow
> Shrills out at once its task and its affright—
> The groaning world now learns to read aright,
> And with its Voice of Voices cries out, O![13]

This epigram condenses in epitome issues elaborated throughout this paper: it shows a night sky, sown with stars, in the process of being covered over with a storm cloud. The "groaning world" that "reads" this scene sees one text, the "constellations," that is cancelled out by a second "Black Letter" text, a text of academic ideology and coercion embodied in the letter "O"—the vocalic phoneme that *mimics* a cloud in its shape and the wind in its sound, and expresses as well a *meaning*, the terror imposed by the "master" and rendered back by a submissive readership. To this "right reading" of the sky—a reading, be it pointed out, that issues forth from the sky itself, as one of its levels or stratifications—the epigram opposes the text of the stars, which is nothing other than the alphabet itself: "no constellations *alphabet* the sky." It is the silent and graphic inscription itself that the storm-cloud hides, the multiform and meaningless winking of the stars. The letters of the alphabet—excepting the letter "O" (and perhaps the letter "I")—have nothing whatever to tell us: they do not say, and do not have, a meaning. They are not signifiers, and they certainly cannot be called "arbitrary"; as nonsignificant writing, the letters of the alphabet are readily confounded with stars, with natural forms. Lacking significance, they only play, "starting, as on a chace": they are the stuff of language before the drive for meaning sets in.

How, then, does an "alphabetical" constellation appear as a signature, in the literal sense of an arrangement of graphemes adhering to a single individual? When is a constellation not just a metaphor, but a real signature of Samuel Taylor Coleridge?

How does he sign his name?

As he does, for example, in the "Epitaph" that closes his works:

> Stop, Christian passer-by!—Stop, child of God,
> And read with gentle breast. Beneath this sod
> A poet lies, or that which once seem'd he.
> O, lift one thought in prayer for S. T. C.;
> That he who many a year with toil of breath
> Found death in life, may here find life in death!
> Mercy for praise—to be forgiven for fame

> He ask'd and hoped, through Christ. Do thou the
> same.[14]

Let us suppose, then, that "S. T. C." is one of the poet's signatures, the seal in its most graphic or alphabetical form. Where does he *fix* his seal? Where do we find it, and how do we know that it is his?

We take a step backward.

The issues opened up by the notion of the signature, of the presence or absence of the signature, seem to us enormously complex in that they ramify with the classical problems of literary criticism, the themes, for example, of intention (did the poet *mean* what he seems to say? Did he *mean* to sign this poem, and in this or that fashion?); of sincerity and authenticity, that is, of the presence or absence of the signature in the text (did he really express himself in this text? Is the signature really his own, or is it a forgery?); of context (does this text have a purpose or function that exceeds its explicit theme? Does this signature pertain to a contract, of whose terms and parties we are unaware?); and of the notion of text itself, of the *bord du texte*, as Derrida phrases it (what is the inside or the outside of the text? If the signature does not fall outside, but belongs to the body of the text, has the notion "inner/outer" been put into jeopardy?). But the most fundamental question posed by a signature is the question of its *eligibility*, which ramifies with the classical issues of *visibility* and *legibility*: a signature may be "visible" but not legible (because deformed), and therefore not eligible as a signature. There are different degrees of legibility, and, in the remaining paragraphs of this paper, we propose to touch upon a few of the differences in those degrees. It is a topic that defies rigor; nor have we reread the works of Coleridge in the vain hope of mastering the effects of the seal. It is enough to open up a thorough-way.

One clue lies in a footnote to the closing couplet of Coleridge's epitaph, "Mercy for praise, to be forgiven for fame / He ask'd, and hoped, through Christ. Do thou the same!" To clear up the syntax he appends a note in the manuscript and signs the note: "N. B. 'for' in the sense of 'instead of.' ἔστη κεῖται ἀναστήσει—stetit: restat: resurget. ΕΣΤΗΣΕ."[15] The signature passes through at least four transformations: first, "S. T. C." has been transliterated into the Greek letters sigma, tau, and sigma-eta; second, the Greek letters have been translated, by homophony, into the third person singular of the past tense, ἔστησε; this, in turn, into its Latin equivalent, "stetit"; the Latin form, in its turn, into a Christological chain describing the resurrection ("he hath stood; he rests; he arises"), which brings us back to the coincidence, in the name of Christ, of the letters S., T., and C., an association which is advanced, thematically, by the closing line of the epitaph—"he asked, and hoped, through Christ."

This irruption of the signature is not an isolated event: for example, the Greek word "ἔστησε" occurs as a signature repeatedly throughout the manuscripts of Coleridge's poetry, beginning at least in the year 1800.¹⁶ Coleridge includes it and insists on the value (as a signature) of its *meaning* in the autobiographical poem entitled "A Character":

> Thus, his own whim his only bribe,
> Our Bard pursued his old À. B. C.
> Contented if he could subscribe
> In fullest sense his name ἔδτηδε;
> ('Tis Punic Greek for 'he hath stood!')
> Whate'er the men, the cause was good;
> And therefore with a right good will,
> Poor fool, he fights their battles still.¹⁷

Where Coleridge *stands*, he may be said to sign:

> I sate, my being blended in one thought
> (Thought was it? or aspiration? or resolve?)
> Absorbed, yet hanging still upon the sound
> And when I rose, I found myself in prayer.¹⁸

But the chief feature of the seal, the one that the footnote to the "Epitaph" reveals, is its ability not only to overflow the boundaries of grapheme and lexeme, as it does in the figure "he hath stood"; but its ability to overflow any discursive boundary of any kind. It can be arranged and in any sequence and across any chain of signifiers, as, for example, in the word "Christ," or in the word "Christian," or, for that matter—a matter of some interest to this paper—in the word "Christabel." In the "Tombless Epitaph," Coleridge rearranges his initials and seals them up in the pseudonym "Idoloclastes Satyrane."¹⁹

The letters of the alphabet "start," as Coleridge says, "as on a chace." They occur, not as sequences but as groups, as constellations. As, for example, in the word "constellation," or in the word "inscription," instances in which the graphism of the word encrypts or seals the seal to which it refers. "Secret," another word connoting the seal, the sealing-up of the seal, encrypts the signature of the poet within. And since the letters really do play a game of hide and seek, what is to prevent us from noticing the seal in those thematically prominent words—prominent for Coleridge—that begin with "st?" For example, the word "star," or "stop," or "stood" (graphic as well as lexical), or "stranger."²⁰ Consider the effects of signature at play in the first line of "Frost at Midnight" ("The frost performs its secret ministry"), or the effects of signature in the closing lines of that poem, as they gravitate around the image of the "silent icicles." Consider, finally, the play of the signature in the "Inscription for a Fountain on a Heath," presenting a *locus amoenus* that may well be the scene of the signature itself, a "spring" in an hour of "Twilight" and "Coolness," where can be found, soundlessly and forever dancing, a "tiny cone of sand":

> This Sycamore, oft musical with bees,—
> Such tents the Patriarchs loved! O long unharmed
> May all its aged boughs o'er canopy
> The small round basin, which this jutting stone
> Keeps pure from falling leaves! Long may the Spring
> Quietly as a sleeping infant's breath,
> Send up cold waters to the traveller
> With soft and even pulse! Nor ever cease
> Yon tiny cone of sand its soundless dance . . .

NOTES

1. "Christabel," 1. 127, in *Coleridge: Poetical Works*, ed. E. H. Coleridge (New York: Oxford Univ. Press, 1967), p. 220. All quotations of the poetry of Coleridge are taken from this edition, and are cited by line in the text of the article.

2. As defined, for example, by Jacques Derrida in *Positions* (Paris: Editions de Minuit, 1972), pp. 56–58.

3. The "seal" functions in this poem like the "anacolouthon" described by Paul de Man in his essay on Rousseau entitled "The Purloined Ribbon" (*Glyph 1* [1977]: 28–49). The tropes of a text do not represent the anacolouthon (an effect of what de Man calls the nonreferential, performing grammar of the text), but instead are disrupted by it.

4. *PW*, pp. 240–42.

5. In a longer version of this essay, we argue that the logic of Romantic tropology begins with a meditation on the homonym and the synonym, *facts* of language that undermine the standing of the sign-structure as the definitive *model* of language, of language as seen as a transparent and univocal image of concepts. This (conservative) logic of the tropes, which was initiated perhaps by Du Marsais in his seminal study *On the Tropes, or On the Different Ways a Word Can Be Meant in a Given Language* ("Des Tropes, ou des diferens sens dans lesquels on peut prendre un meme mot dans une meme langue" [Paris, 1797]), proposes to dominate the homonym by posing one of its meanings as the proper one, and its other meanings as related, and tropical, deviations. We also argue that, though in England the concepts of sign and trope are mainly explicated in works on semantic theory, and by such authors as Hugh Blair and George Campbell, they also operate as guiding concepts in such different fields as theology, epistemology, and psychology, from which they are then woven back into the thematic fabric of Romantic poetry. It was a chief enterprise of Coleridge, Wordsworth, and their followers to extend the logic of the tropes to the dimension of greatest conceptual generality, while maintaining contact at all times with a specifically lexical (or homonymic) starting point.

6. Du Marsais, *Des Tropes*, pp. 84–90, calls this figure a "metalepsis," and classifies it as a subspecies of metonymy.

7. *PW*, p. 241.

8. Ibid., p. 240.

9. The pages that follow derive from the astonishing work of Jacques Derrida on the topic of the signature, notably in the essay "Signéponge" (*Digraphe* 8 [1976]: 17–39).

10. "Recollections of Love," 16–19, in *PW*, p. 410.

11. "A Tombless Epitaph," 21–22, in *PW*, pp. 413–14.

12. "To William Wordsworth," 95–100, in *PW*, pp. 403–8.

13. "Coeli Enarrant," in *PW*, p. 486.

14. "Epitaph," in *PW*, pp. 491–92.

15. Ibid.

16. *PW*, p. 345.

17. "A Character," 69–76, in *PW*, pp. 451–53.

18. "To William Wordsworth," 109–12.

19. "A Tombless Epitaph," 1.

20. Coleridge repeatedly refers to himself as a "stranger": thus, "I have roam'd through life / Still most a stranger, most with naked heart / At mine own home and birth-place" ("To the Rev. George Coleridge," 40–42, in *PW*, pp. 173–75); so, too, "Oft to my eager should I whisper blame / A Stranger bids it feel the Stranger's name" ("To Two Sisters," 30–31, in *PW*, pp. 410–12). See also the poem entitled "To Matilda Betham from a Stranger" (in *PW*, pp. 374–76). The force of this signature lies in its conjunction with the homonym "stranger," communicating with the theme of the double, and the emotion of "strangeness" which the double is said, by Freud in his essay on "The Uncanny," to inspire. That it arises, according to Freud, from a fear of castration; that the poem "Frost at Midnight" presents a scene between father and son, in which the father meditates on a future in which he imagines his son contemplating a "silent icicle," the paternal signature; that poem, icicle, and son are thus implicated in a limitless replication of the *detached* paternal phallus, where the effects of framing (*mis en abîme*) cannot be arrested, dominated, or put into place; all are issues whose interlacing we propose to untie elsewhere.

SIX
PRE-POSITIONAL BY-PLAY
Andrzej Warminski

> Men that, by custom, have got the use of a by-word, do almost in every sentence pronounce sounds which, though taken notice of by others, they themselves neither hear nor observe.
> John Locke, *An Essay Concerning Human Understanding*, book 2, chapter 9

THE QUESTION of the meaning of meaning provides an exemplary beginning, for, according to Hegel's *Philosophy of Religion*, it is a question of beginnings. To ask what this or that means—"was bedeutet dies oder jenes" (16, 32)[1]—is to ask for two different, indeed opposed, meanings: *which one* depends upon the question's point of departure. If "we" begin with the *Vorstellung* of an "expression, work of art etc.," we are asking for the inner, the universal, the thought (*Gedanke*). If we begin with the thought, then we are asking for the outer, the particular, the *Vorstellung*, an example of the thought's content (*ein Beispiel des Inhalts*). In each case, what we *want*—either *Gedanke* or *Vorstellung* depends upon what we *have*—either *Vorstellung* or *Gedanke*—and meaning would be the passage from one to the other. Yet the relation between these two passages is not (and in the System of Hegel *cannot* be) one of symmetrical side-by-side coexistence, for then the question of meaning would be divided irrevocably against itself:[2] the one *two-sided* question would disintegrate into two, mutually excluding, in Hegel's terms, abstract, *one-sided* questions. That such a reading would indeed be incomplete is already suggested by the strong wording at the end of the second passage: "through the example the difficulty is cleared up, the spirit is in this way at last present to itself in this content [*durch das Beispiel wird es [das Schwere] uns deutlich, der Geist ist sich so erst gegenwärtig in diesem Inhalte*]" (16, 33). The two passages can be read as *one* narrative movement of spirit (*Geist*) from (one-sided) *Vorstellung* through (one-sided) *Gedanke* to the recuperation of both *Vorstellung* and *Gedanke* in the spirit's presence to itself. Such a movement would be nothing less than the task of philosophy itself, as it is formulated succinctly in the *Encyclopaedia of the Philosophical Sciences*: "The difference between representation and thought [*Der Unterschied von Vorstellung und von Gedanken*] has further importance because in general it can be said that philosophy does nothing else but transform [*verwandeln*] representations into thoughts,—but of course from there the mere thought into the concept [*Begriff*]" (8, 73–74). But if *Begriff* can be identified with the presence of spirit to itself, "das Absolute," then the passage of *Gedanke* to *Begriff* is already "present" in the first passage: "Consequently it means that the concept [*Begriff*] should be given, and hence the *concept* is the meaning; it is the absolute, the nature of God grasped in thought, the logical knowledge of the absolute, that we want to have" (16,32). In other words, by ending with the concept, the absolute, the presence of *Geist* to itself, each of the two passages—*Vorstellung* to *Gedanke* and *Gedanke* to *Vorstellung*—contains the entire narrative of the movement from the first to the second passage: from *Vorstellung* through *Gedanke* to their dialectical mediation in *Begriff*. Each movement—each meaning of meaning as point of departure—presupposes and posits the other: the entire narrative is always already and never yet present in each of its moments.

This double movement of position and presupposition is made possible by the work of two compound words—*Vorstellung* and *Beispiel*—and the play of their prepositions. That is, each of these words can play the rigorously dialectical roles of point-of-departure and end-point on account of its peculiar status. Rather than being a merely outside—particular and sensuous—*representation* opposed to an inner—universal and spiritual—*thought*, *Vorstellung* is neither outside nor inside, neither particular nor universal, neither sensuous nor spiritual: although no longer mere representation, it is not yet real thought. Later in the *Philosophy of Religion* Hegel carefully distinguishes *Vorstellung* from both *Bild* ("image") and *Gedanke*. Unlike *Bild*, which "takes its content from the sphere of the sensuous and depicts it in the immediate mode of its existence, in the particularity and arbitrariness of its sensuous appearance" (16,139), *Vorstellung* is *Bild* elevated to the form of universality: "the content is not grasped immediately in sensuous perception, not in the figural mode [*auf bildliche Weise*], but rather *mediated* through *abstraction*, and the sensuous figural [*Bildliche*] is elevated to universality" (16,140). This elevation necessarily entails a negative relation to the figural: "mit dieser Erhebung ist dann notwendig das negative Verhalten zum Bildlichen verknüpft" (16,140). But precisely on account of this (one-sidedly) negative relation to the sensuous and figural— *Erhebung* is not (yet) *Aufhebung*—*Vorstellung* is still essentially implicated (*wesentlich verwickelt*) with the sensuous: that is, *Vorstellung* needs the sensuous and this battle against it in order to be itself (*sie bedarf desselben und dieses Kampfes gegen das Sinnliche, um selbst zu sein*) (16,141). The sensuous belongs essentially to *Vorstellung* (*es gehört also wesentlich zu ihr*); only real thought can free itself absolutely from the sensuous and elevate the sensuous determinations of a content—and not merely negate them immediately—to the universal determinations of thought, to the certainty (*Bestimmtheit*) of the Idea. So that the position of *Vorstellung* is, in a sense, to have no position; its status is constant unrest: "Daher steht nun die Vorstellung in beständiger Unruhe zwischen der unmittelbaren sinnlichen Anschauung und dem eigentlichen Gedanken" (16,141). This (non)status of being in-between, constantly on the way, is well conveyed by the word's meaning as a (spatial or temporal) "placing *before*": *Vorstellung* is a (posited) outside on its way to becoming a (presupposed) inside, or, more precisely, it is a movement *away* from exteriority and *towards* interiority. But it should not be forgotten that this movement *away* and *towards* would at the same time be a movement in the other direction: that is, in order to become *Begriff*, *Idee*, the presence of *Geist* to itself, etc., thought also has to *come out* to *Vorstellung*. This is formulated in the first passage of the meaning of meaning: although we have the *Vorstellung* (*die Vorstellung haben wir wohl*) and are asking for the inner (*nach dem Inneren fragen wir*), what we must do is bring this inner to *Vorstellung* (*dies ist es, was wir zur Vorstellung bringen wollen*). In short, the movement towards the "inner" meaning would also always already be the movement towards the "outer" meaning. *Vorstellung* would be the name of this movement because it contains both (spatial) position and (temporal) presupposition: the question of—i.e., the movement towards—meaning would be the dialectical mediation of the two meanings of *Vorstellung*.[3]

Although *Beispiel* would seem to function in much the same way as *Vorstellung*, its status in the text of Hegel is even more problematic. Like *Vorstellung*, *Beispiel* has a peculiar non-status, but the nature of this non-status is considerably different. Whereas the mediating function of *Vorstellung* is essential to the working of the System—it is hardly necessary to recall the crucial role played by *Vorstellung* in distinguishing the "places" of religion and philosophy (in the *Phenomenology*, the *History of Philosophy*, or the *Philosophy of Religion*, for example), or the role *Vorstellung* (subdivided into two layers of triads, one of which includes *zeichenmachende Phantasie* and the creation of linguistic signs) plays as a mediator between *Anschauung* and *Denken* in the *Encyclopaedia*—*Beispiel* has no official place to fill or role to play: rather than in-between, *Beispiel* is to the side. But if its existence is marginal in relation to Hegel's System, *Beispiel* is nevertheless ubiquitous in Hegel's text:[4] not only every time that "Hegel"—the text—says "zum Beispiel" but in other, ostensibly more serious, contexts as well. The question of the meaning of meaning would certainly be one of these, for according to this text the spirit (*Geist*) can be present to itself—by implication "satisfied" (*befriedigt*) and "at home" (*zu Hause*) as it could *not* be in a pure (i.e., one-sided) determination of thought—only through an example of the thought-determination's content:[5] *Geist* would be truly "by itself" (*bei sich*) only by being "beside itself" (in a *Beispiel*). As in the case of *Vorstellung*, the text makes use of prepositions indicating spatial direction to convey the double role of *Beispiel*: although it is an exterior example, it is the example of an interior content (*In-halt*); although by positing an example the spirit would seem to be going outside, it is only in this way that it can be inside (*in diesem Inhalte*). Once again this speculative word-play on *Beispiel* accounts for itself by the word's *meaning*, for *Beispiel* means both "model" (*Vorbild, Muster*) and "example" or "illustration" (*veranschaulichendes Gleichnis*).[6] In other words, it both precedes and follows, it is both inside and outside, exemplary and derived: *Beispiel* would be "its own" *Beispiel*. Like the para- of parable, the *bei-* of *Beispiel* would mean both "at, towards, straight to" and "beside, to the side of."[7] The narrative of the meaning of meaning could be read as an interpretation of the "one" word *Beispiel*—a word that, like the question of meaning, is *one* only to the extent that it is different from, indeed opposed to, itself.

But all the questions have not been answered. If *Beispiel* can in fact play the role of *Vorstellung*, if it can be *in apposition to*, a stand-in (stand-by?) for *Vorstellung*, then what would its status of systematic invisibility *mean*? Indeed, it would be something of a surprise if *Beispiel* turned out to be another "speculative word," for "Hegel"—the System—can admit any kind of presence "to the side" only by dismissing it as *one-sided*.

A good example—aside from the frequent complaints about the understanding (*Verstand*) which leaves its determinations "side by side" (*nebeneinander*) because it can link them only by the mere "also" (*Auch*)⁸— would be the list of pejoratives Hegel uses in the *Aesthetics* to put in its place "the conscious symbolism of the comparing form of art [*Die bewußte Symbolik der vergleichenden Kunstform*]": *Beiwerk, Schmuck, Zierat, Zutat, bloßes Beiwesen, Nebendinge, Nebenarten, zwitterhafte Gebilde, das nur Danebenstehende, Nebensächliche, das Beiherspielende*, etc. 13, (486–491, 507). All of these (and others) proliferate within the space of a few pages, one next to the other, without apparent need to bring their disseminating meanings back to the one meaning: as though their metonymical disorder and lack of *system* were proof of their marginal status as excessive decorations—an *Unsinn* so insignificant as to need no sublation to *Sinn*. But it is not insignificant that this exorcising rhetoric of the speculative philosophy is applied to a "conscious symbolism" that, to a great extent, means *figures of speech:* including *Fabel, Parabel . . . Rätsel, Allegorie, Metapher, Bild, Gleichnis*.⁹

A better way to ask the question of *Beispiel* may be to ask the question of the meaning of meaning again, *a second time*: if a question of meaning is two-fold, then what would be the other, the *second*, meaning of meaning? The *Philosophy of Religion* provides two meanings of meaning, but they turn out to be *one* double (two-sided) movement of position and presupposition.¹⁰ In other words, the text answers the question of the meaning of meaning *in the first sense only*: it tells what the inner, the universal, the thought, of the meaning of meaning is, but it does not give the example (*Beispiel*) to "house" that thought. What is the *Beispiel* of the meaning of meaning? What is the *Beispiel* of *Beispiel*? But the question cannot be asked so simply, for the System has a ready answer: *Beispiel* is its own *Beispiel*, and since the question of this context is the meaning of God, *Christ*—God's positing himself in his other— would be the *Beispiel* of *Beispiel*, as is suggested in the very next paragraph: "But this is God: not only in itself [*an sich*] but also essentially for itself [*für sich*], the absolute spirit that is not only the being that maintains itself in thought, but also one that *appears*, gives itself *objectivity* [*der nicht nur das im Gedanken sich haltende Wesen ist, sondern auch das* erscheinende, *sich* Gegenständlichkeit *gebende*]" (16,33). In *Reason in History* the nature of God—as the spirit able to produce himself by positing *his own* object—is in fact called "the most sublime example [*das erhabenste Beispiel*]." The same text, however, also provides a way to redefine the *second* question, for the following sentence reads: "Properly [*eigentlich*] speaking, it is not an example, but the universal, the true itself, of which all the rest is an example."[11] What "we" want—and who would this (other) "we" be, if it cannot be a "we" included in the systematic play of the meaning of meaning?—would be precisely the *Beispiel* of the meaning of meaning, the *Beispiel* of *Beispiel*, that is *still* an example.[12] As the above sentence suggests, "properly speaking" such a *Beispiel* would not, could not, belong to the economy, the propriety, of the "proper" (in *all* senses) sense, the two mutually positing and presupposing meanings of meaning. But, again, the question of the other meaning, the setting of the other scene (*ein anderer Schauplatz?*) for the play of *Beispiel*, is not an easy matter, for do "we," can "we," even know *what* "we" are asking? Or, for that matter, *when?* It is clear that asking the question of the meaning of meaning a second *time* cannot belong to the self-redeeming temporality of the movement *Vorstellung/Gedanke/Begriff*. What would it be like, such an other *Beispiel* and its other temporality? No doubt it would be like—yet it could not be "like" anything since it would be the condition of (im)possibility of *all* "like"—Hölderlin's parable of the sower,[13] but such thematic prejudicing of the question does not lead very far because "Parabel" is one of the figures assigned a not too prominent place in the equally peripheral conscious symbolism of the comparing form of art.

As in the case of the "two" meanings of meaning, the status of a comparison (*Vergleichung*) within the system of this symbolism depends upon the point of departure (*Ausgangspunkt*): the artist—but he is not (yet) really an artist because this form of art is not (yet), properly speaking, *art*: it is a "pre-art" (*Vorkunst*)—begins either with the outer representation or with the inner thought, the meaning (*Bedeutung*), to be represented. *Parabel* belongs to one of the former, less explicitly subjective, forms of comparison, and although Hegel mentions the parable of the sower as an example of Gospel parable—"die Parabel vom Sämann z.B."—it is only in order to dismiss the story *itself* as of insignificant import (*eine Erzählung, für sich von geringfügigem Gehalt*). If the parables of the Gospel are "of the deepest interest," it is on account of their "meanings": the parable of the sower, for example, is "important only because of its comparison with the doctrine of the kingdom of heaven [*wichtig nur durch die Vergleichung mit der Lehre vom Himmelreich*]." In fact, the relation between the religious teachings and the human incidents which represent them in *Parabel* is somewhat like the relation between the human (meaning) and the animal (representation) in Aesop's fables.

But another use of parable, which Hegel mentions only "by the way," may be its jesting tone through which Goethe, for example, was able to write off from his soul that which is unpleasant in life (*durch welchen er sich das im Leben Verdrießliche von der Seele losschrieb*) (13,503). It would seem that Goethe, at least according to Hegel, made a practice of disburdening himself on the reader. The *Encyclopaedia* tells of the beneficial effects of being able to exteriorize "overpowering feelings" and how Goethe, "especially through his *Werther*, was able to relieve himself, while subjecting the readers of this novel to the power of feeling [*Empfindung*]" (10,251).

A more promising way to formulate the question would be to concentrate on what was called the "textual"—as opposed to "systematic"—status of *Beispiel*: its systematically unrecognized presence in, or rather to the side of, the System. But the label "text" is no answer, for it presupposes that which is being sought: it assumes that the text has been *read* when it is precisely a question of *reading the text*. And how would *such* a text—a *Beispiel* of *Beispiel* in the other sense, the improper sense, the sense that is, properly speaking, unreadable—be read?

In the first place, it would probably be, would have to be, *mis*read. Two pages after the meaning of meaning, the *Philosophy of Religion* discusses the dangers, indeed necessity, of misreading a text in general and an "unsystematic" text in particular.[14] The words of the Bible, namely, are "a discourse that is not systematic [*ein Vortrag, der nicht systematisch ist*]," and a positive religion that takes the Bible for the essential foundation of doctrine is exposed to grave abuses. The danger lies not so much in the text or in the interpreter as in the nature of interpretation itself, or rather in what the nature of interpretation *brings along with it* (*mit sich*): i.e., that the thought speaks along with it or by it (*daß der Gedanke dabei mitspricht*). While seeming to stay "with the sense [*bei dem Sinn*]," one "in fact develops further thoughts [*entwickelt in der Tat aber weitere Gedanken*]." In other words, as soon as the interpreter goes beyond "mere word-interpretation [*bloße Wortinterpretation*]"—which, strictly speaking, is not interpretation because it entails the substitution of one word by another of the same "compass" ("*Umfang*")—he must misread the text because he always brings along thoughts conditioned by his own time. And yet it is neither the accompanying thoughts nor the necessity of bringing the sense of the Scriptures out "into consciousness, into representation [*Vorstellung*]" that is responsible for the misreading, but rather the "presentation of what the sense is supposed to be [*Darstellung dessen, was der Sinn sein soll*]" (16,36): it is *then* that the differently determined *Vorstellung* makes itself count, and this is why the commentaries on the Bible do not make us acquainted with its content but rather contain the attitudes (*Vorstellungsweise*) of *their own time*. This description of the necessity of misreading simultaneously completes and complicates the description of the movement through (from and to) *Vorstellung* described in the narrative of the meaning of meaning. That is, on the one hand, it states explicitly the nature and the necessity of the difference between the two meanings of meaning (the difference *within* meaning): i.e., it is a temporal difference which can be compared to, which is, the temporal difference separating the (*Vorstellung* of the) text and the (*Vorstellung* of the) interpreter. On the other hand—and this is the complication—it is not so much the interpreter or his *Vorstellung* that creates the difference of meaning, the difference of misreading, but rather the attempt to present the meaning of the text: in short, the temporal difference between text and interpreter can be called more precisely a difference between text *read* and text *written*. What kind of relation such a difference describes is difficult to say, for the relation between *Vorstellung* and *Darstellung* in this passage is very much "like" the relation between *Vorstellung* and *Beispiel* in the meaning of meaning: a problematic *a*pposition which can turn into unsublatable *o*pposition if the "right" ("wrong," properly speaking) question is asked. Whatever the relation may be, the "writing" of *Beispiel* and *Darstellung* would make possible the reading of meaning and its (speculative mis-)interpretation. Yet the same—and can it ever be the same?—writing of *Beispiel* and *Darstellung* also makes reading imposssible, for this writing cannot itself be read except when translated into the mediating language of *Vorstellung*; and such a translation always brings along with it the necessity of *Darstel-*

lung and its writing: *Darstellung* would be its own condition of (im)possibility. Although the other question "What is the *Darstellung* of *Darstellung*?" leads to the "same" aporia as the other question "What is the *Beispiel* of *Beispiel*?," some progress towards the "right" question has been made. Hegel's presentation, example, of the difference between *Vorstellung* and *Beispiel, Vorstellung* and *Darstellung*, as the difference between text *read* and text *written* throws into better relief the precisely *textual* dimension of the problem: that is, the peculiar status of *Beispiel* cannot be thought as a merely spatial, appositional, (non)presence to the side of the System—such a *Beispiel*, if not sublatable, is nevertheless too easily deposited in the shadow realm of *Nebending, Schmuck*, etc.— if the relation (between text read and text written) is intrinsically temporal. But since the peculiarly "textual" temporality of *Beispiel* and *Darstellung*—like the textual space they occupy—would not be that of the System, it cannot be thought *in terms of* either space *or* time: in order to become "itself" (undialectically) the text has to clear an "other space" in which it may develop in an "other time" (and this somehow outside of, different from, other than, the oppositions inside/outside, identity/difference, self/other). The necessity of misreading neither clears up nor develops how such clearing and development are possible, but it does indicate a direction: it is the interpretation of *Scripture* that leads to the most contradictory opinions; it is *Scripture* that all heresies as well as the Church invoke. And "Scripture" means not only the unsystematic discourse of the Bible: on the contrary, misreading is a necessity that holds sway even in the presentation of an in itself already developed philosophical *system*, that of Plato or Aristotle for example (*"bei der Darstellung eines in sich schon entwickelten philosophischen Systems, z.B. des Platon oder Aristoteles*). Thanks to the (re)writing of *Darstellung*, even the text of a System, for example, may suffer the fate of so-called Holy Scripture (*sogenannte Heilige Schrift*) and be made into a waxen nose (*zu einer wächsernen Nase*).

Hegel's presentation of Aristotle's system in the *History of Philosophy* may serve as a rereading of the question of *Beispiel*, for this presentation is, to a large extent, a question of (re)reading Aristotle's examples. If Aristotle has not been understood, it is because previous interpreters did not know how to read him, and for this reason to reread the text means also to tell *how* it should be read. For Hegel, nowhere is this more necessary than in the case of *De anima* and its examples. To illustrate the workings of sensation (*Empfindung*) Aristotle uses "that famous *comparison* which has so often been the occasion of misunderstanding, which has been so wrongly construed [*jene berühmte Vergleichung, die so oft Mißverständnis veranlaßt hat, so schief auf-*

gefaßt worden ist]" (19,207). It is not immediately apparent *why* this should be so, for Hegel has no problem stating directly what Aristotle says: "He says namely that sensation is the taking up of the perceived forms [*die Aufnahme der empfundenen Formen*], without the matter; in sensation only the form comes to us, without the matter." Such behavior is to be distinguished, according to Hegel, from practical behavior like eating or drinking, when we act as particular individuals who, as materially existent, relate to the material in a material way. For Hegel, there is no need to dwell on *such* activity, and he dismisses what Aristotle has to say about the vegetative soul (*die ernährende Seele*) as insignificant: "What Aristotle says about feeding [*Ernährung*], 'whether like on like or on the opposed [*ob Gleiches vom Gleichen oder vom Entgegengesetzten*],' is insignificant [*unbedeutend*]" (19,205). Sensation is "more interesting" since in its taking up of the form (*Formaufnahme*) the material is "consumed" or (more "correctly," especially in regard to etymology) "effaced" (*vertilgt*). Obviously, such a consumption would be more of an "effacement" and is not to be confused with the consumption that occurs in nourishment, for "form is the object as universal [*die Form ist der Gegenstand als Allgemeines*]" (19,208); in sensation we relate only to the form and take it up without the matter. To tell *how* this occurs is the task of the misread example: " 'as the wax takes in only the sign of the golden signet ring, not the gold itself, rather purely its form [*wie das Wachs nur das Zeichen des goldenen Siegelringes an sich nimmt, ohne das Gold selbst, sondern rein seine Form*]' " (19,208). But if it is possible to repeat the meaning of the example[15] without difficulty—and Hegel does so several times (even before citing it)—then what has gone wrong in its interpretation? Hegel is expansive on this matter, and it is worthwhile to follow him: the unnamed misinterpreters—"man," "jeder"—have stopped in a crude way with the coarseness of the comparison (*Man bleibt roherweise beim Groben des Vergleichs stehen*). When one holds on to the example (*bloß an dies Beispiel hält*) and goes over (*übergeht*) to the soul, then one says that the soul behaves (*verhalte sich*) like the wax, that representations (*Vorstellungen*), sensations, everything is only impressed into the soul; the soul is a *tabula rasa*, empty, and exterior things only make an impression, as the material of the signet ring works on the material of the wax. This is the misreading, and it is the lot of most philosophers when they "adduce a sensuous example [*ein sinnliches Beispiel anführen*]" because "everyone understands this and takes the content of the comparison in its entire compass [*Umfange*],—as though everything that is contained in this sensuous relationship were also valid for the spiritual" (19,208). In the case of the wax/ring example, the comparison applies only (*nur*) to the determination that in sensation only (*nur*) the form is taken up, only (*nur*) the form is for the perceiving subject, only (*nur*) the form comes to the subject; only in regard to this side is a comparison being made (*nur nach dieser Seite ist verglichen*). Hegel's repeated "only" stresses the distinction to be made, the overlooked difference (*Unterschied*) between the image (*Bild*) and the behavior of the soul. In short, Hegel's ability to tell the difference between the two "sides" of the example—the side meant to be compared and the side meant not to be compared, the side of similarity and the side of difference—is what makes it possible for him to read it: he can tell the difference between the material and the form because he can tell the difference between the sensuous and the spiritual sides of the example. In order to read the example Hegel uses the difference that the example is meant to read: as though he were able to read a difference between matter and form, sensuous and spiritual—the difference between the interpreters who see only the similarity and overlook the difference and Hegel who sees both—inscribed in the *Beispiel* of that difference. But if in order to be read the *Beispiel* has always already *to have been read*—if reading is a rereading—then how is it possible to read *in the first place*? In other words—and the problem is precisely the impossibility of finding *other words* to read the words of the *Beispiel* of *Beispiel*—how can Hegel claim to read a text that his own reading has rendered, properly speaking, unreadable? Indeed, it would not be improper to ask "Who is reading whom?" in the case of a text that has its (mis)readers (including Hegel) inscribed within "itself": perhaps Aristotle has as much of a claim to reading Hegel as Hegel has to reading Aristotle.[16]

But Hegel's rereading of the *Beispiel* does not stop with a reading of the difference inscribed in the example: if he has a claim to rereading the text, it is because he *rewrites* it. What previous interpreters overlooked in the example is that the wax in fact does *not* take up the form: that is, "the impression remains an exterior figure, a design on it, but not a form of its essence [*dieser Eindruck bleibt eine äußerliche Figur, Gestaltung an ihm, aber keine Form seines Wesens*]"; "if this form became the form of its essence, it would cease to be wax" (19,209). The soul, on the other hand, takes up the form into its own substance, *assimilates* it, and in such a way that the soul is in itself, to a certain extent (*gewissermaßen*), everything that is perceived (*alles Empfundene*). The example means to say that *only* the form comes to the soul, but *not* that the form is and remains exterior to the wax and that the soul, like wax, has no form in itself. In short, the soul neither is nor behaves like wax, and Hegel repeats the denial several times: "In no way is the soul supposed to be passive wax and to receive determinations from the outside." He goes so far as to say that the taking up of the form (as the universal) is *not* like that of the wax: "Die Seele ist die

Form, die Form ist das Allgemeine; und das Aufnehmen desselben ist nicht wie das des Wachses." Since the wax/ring example too easily suggests the passivity of the soul in sensation, Hegel proposes his own version: although it cannot be denied that passivity is a moment in sensation, this passivity is *sublated*, the soul *holds away (hält . . . ab)* the material, *repels (repelliert)* it, *relates (verhält sich)* only to the form, and *transforms (verwandelt)* the form of the exterior body into its own. Just as Hegel's rereading of Aristotle's example was a repetition of the soul's behavior in sensation, so is his new version of the soul's behavior in sensation a repetition of his rewriting of Aristotle's example: that is, the soul is supposed to hold away, repel, the material just as Hegel holds away the material of Aristotle's example by denying that the soul behaves like wax. Unlike the misreader who stays with the coarsely material of the comparison and *holds on* to the *Beispiel (an dies Beispiel hält)*, Hegel relates *(verhält sich)* only to the form and transforms, appropriates, Aristotle's example by rewriting it. Such a rewriting is active in its relation to the material whereas the taking up performed by the misreader is merely passive. By holding on to the material, the wax, of Aristotle's example, the misreader becomes like wax himself: he who attempts to read the writing of *Beispiel* without *re*writing it risks being turned into a waxen nose. In being able to write off the unpleasantness of the material, Hegel would be like Goethe: just as Goethe was able to disburden himself of excess *Empfindung* by writing *Werther* and subjecting the *readers* of this novel to the power of feeling, so Hegel disburdens himself of the material excess of Aristotle's example by rewriting it and subjecting the *readers*—the waxen *mis*readers inscribed in his text. But if such a rewriting can take place only at the expense of the (mis)reader, does it not also occur at the expense of Aristotle's text? In short, is not Hegel doing precisely what he blames other readers for doing: i.e., turning the text into a waxen nose? Is Hegel's new example—a process of *aufheben/abhalten/sich verhalten/ assimilieren/verwandeln*—simply to the side of Aristotle's wax/ring example, a case of mere metonymical substitution? Whence comes the authority of rewriting and its new—its other—*Beispiel*?

Since to a certain extent—and the question is precisely to *what* extent—Hegel's new example substitutes a *digestive* model for Aristotle's *mimetic* model, another way to formulate the question would be to ask: "how can the *form* be eaten?" If the soul "assimilates" and "transforms" the *form* of the exterior body into its own, the question of feeding, " 'whether like on like or on the opposed,' " would apparently not be as insignificant as Hegel would have it. But Aristotle's explanation of the body's digestion in *De anima* is indeed not of too much help because it is very much like Hegel's version of the soul's digestion: i.e., as long as the food remains undigested, the body feeds on that which is opposed to it; as soon as the food is digested, it feeds on something like itself.[17] The two moments would correspond to the succeeding moments of passivity and activity in Hegel's version of sensation. But since in sensation the soul digests not the material but only the form of its object, the digestive analogy cannot explain *how* that process takes place: indeed, as Hegel emphasized at the beginning of this passage, sensation is to be understood precisely in its *difference* from nourishment. To stay with the analogy of nourishment would be once again to stay with the *wax* of the comparison. Aristotle compares the relation between body and soul to that between wax and its form, and Hegel quotes his example earlier in his presentation: " 'One should therefore not ask whether soul and body are one,' "—and Hegel paraphrases (i.e., rewrites) this to mean "one ought not to say this, that they are one"—" 'just as one does not ask whether the wax and its form are one' " (19,201). But if the digestive model cannot satisfy the appetite of Hegel's new *Beispiel*—"L'Homme ne vit pas seulement de pain," says Georges Bataille in the course of rewriting another (or the same?) Hegel text, "mais des comédies par lesquelles il se trompe volontairement"[18]—all that remains is the model of rewriting—to "eat" the form would be to rewrite it—and why should this model have any more authority than digestion? In fact, rewriting would seem to be even more questionable as an analogy than nourishment, for it puts in question *all* models, analogies, comparisons, by substituting (active) *production* (in particular *textual* production) for all (passive) mimetic models. The authority of the new example produced by Hegel's text would be the authority of its own production: rewriting (as the activity that denies authority) would be its own authority. But the authority of Aristotle—or that of Hegel—is not written off so easily. In order to explain the difference between potentiality and reality, passive and active knowledge, Aristotle introduces the example —one not cited (explicitly[19]) by Hegel—of three men: the first can be said to be "knowing" because man as such is a knowing creature; another can also be said to be knowing because he understands the art of "(reading and) writing" (*grammatikēn*); but only he who really thinks, who actively practices his knowledge, can be properly said to be knowing.[20] If Hegel can rewrite Aristotle's example—or should it be: "If Aristotle can rewrite Hegel's example . . ."?—it is because he has read Aristotle's text—or should it be: "it is because he has read Hegel's text"? Hegel's distinction between passive "taking up" and active, appropriating rewriting is always already inscribed in Aristotle's distinction between passive and active knowledge. So that the authority for rewriting Aristotle's *Beispiel* comes from Aristotle himself—but if the *Beispiel* can be only *re*written, if it can *be* only *as* rewritten, who writes the *Beispiel*? Who is "Aristotle" that he may write the *Beispiel*? For that matter, who is "Hegel"?—or, more precisely, it is the authority of *thought* itself. Although Hegel does not cite the example of the "three" men, his other example, which takes the place of Aristotle's "famous" example, nevertheless comes from "an other, infamous example [*ein anderes berüchtigtes Beispiel*]" (19,214): the *Beispiel* of thought.

Aristotle's treatment of thought in *De anima* is "essentially speculative" (*wesentlich spekulativ*), and it marks the place where his language most coincides with Hegel's: "In our language the absolute, the true, is only that whose subjectivity and objectivity are one and the same, are identical; this is precisely contained in Aristotle as well [*In unserer Sprache ist das Absolute, Wahrhafte nur das, dessen Subjektivität und Objektivität ein und dasselbe, identisch ist; dies ist ebenso auch im Aristoteles enthalten*]" (19,218). Aristotle's *nous* thinks the identity of identity and difference, "it is the thought of thought, the thinking of thought [*Er ist der Gedanke des Gedankens, er ist das Denken des Gedankens*]" (19,219). As such, it can be summarized only in superlatives: "This is the highest peak of Aristotelian metaphysics, the most speculative that can exist [*Dies ist so die höchste Spitze der Aristotelischen Metaphysik, das Spekulativste, was es geben kann*]" (19, 219). As the very peak, what Aristotle says about thought is to be elevated above its context. That Aristotle simply "goes over [*geht . . . über*]" (19,212) from sensation to thought—as Hegel states at the beginning of his presentation (of Aristotle on thought)—is mere appearance, for thought is not "beside" and does not come after anything: "It only appears as though thinking is discussed beside other things; this form of succession of course appears in Aristotle. But what he says about thinking is for itself the absolutely speculative and does not stand beside something else, sensation, for example, which is only *dynamis* for thinking [*Es hat nur den Schein, als ob von dem Denken gesprochen würde neben anderem; diese Form des Nacheinander erscheint allerdings bei Aristoteles. Aber was er über das Denken sagt, ist für sich das absolut Spekulative und steht nicht neben anderen, z.B. der Empfindung, die nur dynamis ist für das Denken*]" (19, 219). If Aristotle's presentation of thought is so close to the truth of the speculative philosophy, then a great deal would be at stake for Hegel in the proper understanding of the infamous *Beispiel* of thought: " 'The *nous* is like a book, on the pages of which nothing is really written [*Der nous ist wie ein Buch, auf dessen Blätter nichts wirklich geschrieben ist*]' " (19,214). This is the well-known example of the *tabula rasa*, and Hegel had signalled its misreading at the very beginning of his presentation of Aristotle's philosophy: common opinion believes that "according to Aristotle the soul is a *tabula rasa*, that it receives its determinations passively from the exterior world [*Außenwelt*], that his philosophy is empiricism, the worst Lockeanism etc." (19,133). This misreading of the *tabula rasa* was also denounced proleptically in Hegel's reading of the wax/ring example. So that the scene for the drama of *Beispiel*, misreading, and Hegel's rereading is set in advance, and there are no surprises in the manifest plot: exteriority and passivity are once again the principal villains. As the misreaders of the wax/ring example held on to the coarsely material of the comparison and overlooked the *difference*, so here "one overlooks all thoughts [*übersieht alle Gedanken*] of Aristotle and grasps only such an exterior comparison [*und faßt nur solche äußerliche Vergleichung auf*]" (19,214–15): according to the misreading "Aristotle says that the spirit [*Geist*] is a *tabula rasa* on which exterior objects [*äußere Gegenstände*] are first supposed to write." "Such accidental comparisons are grasped [*aufgefaßt*] particularly by representation [*Vorstellen*], instead of holding on to the concept [*statt sich an den Begriff zu halten*], as though they expressed the fact [*als ob sie die Sache ausdrückten*]." The key to a proper reading is once again the recognition of a difference, a limit to the breadth of the comparison: "Aristotle does not at all mean [*ist gar nicht gemeint*] the comparison to be taken in its entire extent [*in ihrer ganzen Ausdehnung*]; understanding is not a thing, does not have the passivity of a writing-tablet [*Schreibtafel*] for then we forget all concept). " Thought is active, and hence "the comparison limits itself [*beschränkt sich*] only to this, that the soul has a content only insofar as one really thinks"; just as a book in potentiality contains everything but in reality nothing before one writes in it (*ehe darauf geschrieben ist*).

Like the example of sensation, the example of thought is bound (even more?) inextricably to its reading: that is, if to think means to write in the blank book of thought, then to *think* the *Beispiel* means to write in the blank book *of* the *Beispiel*. Like the thinking soul, the *Beispiel* of thought contains everything in potentiality but nothing in reality until it is written. And "everything" includes the misreaders who fail to write in, to think, the blank book of the *Beispiel*: *everyone* can understand a book on which nothing is written (*Ein Buch, auf das nichts geschrieben ist, kann jeder verstehen*). As long as one does not write in the book of *Beispiel*—as long as one does not put the "book on which nothing is written" *within quotation marks* and understand it *as* a *Beispiel*—one remains an anonymous (every)one—"man," "jeder"— inscribed in the book that in reality contains nothing: the misreader would be a passive writing-tablet waiting for exterior things to write on it. The "book on which nothing is written" and which *everyone* can understand because *no one* has read it——i.e., because no one has rewritten the "nothing" of the book of *Beispiel* (on which "nothing" *is written*) so that it would mean something—would be like *Also sprach Zarathustra*: "Ein Buch Für Alle und Keinen." Hegel, on the other hand, precisely because he is able to distinguish between the thought, the concept, the *Sache*, of the example and its "nothing"—i.e., the exterior, accidental comparison, the extent to which the example is *not* to be taken—Hegel can write in the blank book of the *Beispiel*: that is, he writes in the book in which "nothing" is written by rewriting it, i.e., by reinscribing the "nothing" within his own text so that it may mean something—by negating the negation. Unlike the misreader—everybody —who passively accepts the book on which nothing is written and thereby becomes a blank book himself—nobody—Hegel actively rewrites the book on which nothing is written and thereby becomes a real book himself—somebody—(and simultaneously allows Aristotle to become a real book—himself). By rewriting and rereading Hegel turns the one—unwritten, unread—book of Aristotle into *two* books: the one unwritten and unread; the other rewritten and reread. But the relation between these two books remains problematic. It is not just that Hegel once again presupposes the reading of the example in order to read it—i.e., he can understand the example of *thought* because he can distinguish between the *thought* and the excess passivity and exteriority of the example—even if the assumption may seem less immediately justifiable than his rewriting of the example of sensation on the authority of thought. Presupposing what it posits is, after all, the very truth of a dialectical scheme, and where could it be more true than in the movement of thought thinking itself? If in rewriting the "nothing" of Aristotle's example Hegel renders it unreadable, it is a *determinate* unreadability. Nevertheless, another unreadability may accompany the other *Beispiel*, and a way to begin its reading may be to ask another question: how is it possible to think, to *(re)write*, nothing? But if this question is not to be taken as an invitation to the (re)writing of the big *Logic*,[21] then it needs to be reposed (deposed?), and repositioning the apposition may help: how is it possible to think nothing *as* (re)written? Or, again, what is the "nothing" *of thought*, that it may be (re)written?

The other *Beispiel*—Aristotle's *or* Hegel's?—replies of itself: the "nothing" of thought is the *Beispiel* of thought, and it cannot be thought *except* as (re)written. That is, the *Beispiel*—the excess exteriority and passivity of the comparison, its *non-thought*—is that which thought needs to posit in order that it may presuppose itself. But if *Beispiel* is the "nothing" of thought, or, to put it in more Hegelian terms: if *Beispiel* is the "negation" of thought, the negation *within* thought without which thought cannot negate the negation, then a reinscription of its two excesses—passivity and exteriority—is necessary. Hegel's difference between an exterior and passive *Beispiel* and an interior and active thought is more problematic than mere (sublatable) opposition, for the two sides contaminate one another by means of an (chiasmic) exchange of properties. In order to become the interior activity that it is, thought has first of all to be an interior *passivity* in that a passive taking up, *reading*, is necessary for a (re)writing of *Beispiel*: in this case a reading of the *difference* between *Beispiel* and thought. But if this "interior passivity" alone can be relegated to the status of a moment in the dialectical movement, together with its complement (its crossing) it presents more of a problem: namely, the writing read by the interior passivity, the difference between the interior thought and the exterior comparison, between the extents to which the comparison is and is not to be taken, is inscribed *in* the *Beispiel by* the *Beispiel*. Rather than merely passive exteriority, the *Beispiel* is an *active* exteriority: the *Beispiel* "itself" inscribes the difference between the "extents" of the comparison, between thought and nonthought. That "the comparison limits itself only to this ... [*die Vergleichung beschränkt sich aber nur darauf* ...]" means that the comparison *limits itself*. The *Beispiel* produces the excess (passivity and exteriority) of *Beispiel*: the simile *dis*sembles, *dis*simulates (die Vergleichung vergleicht?[22]). If *Beispiel* is the "nothing," the *nonthought*, of thought, it is nevertheless—also always already—a nonthought that *thinks*: a thinking nonthought that cannot itself *be thought*—"la non-pensée pensante, cette réserve de la pensée qui ne se laisse pas penser."[23] To say that "it makes no difference," that then *Beispiel* may as well be called thought, is no answer because this is precisely the problem: in order that the difference between thought and *Beispiel* may make sense, what is called thought and what is called *Beispiel has* to make a difference. The real problem is not that thought needs to presuppose itself as different from *Beispiel* in order that it may be thought, etc., but that it cannot do so without rendering itself *indistinguishable* from *Beispiel*: in*different* to *Beispiel in terms of* identity and difference. If there is a difference between thought and *Beispiel*, it is an undecidable and therefore excessive difference. In the same movement that produces sublatable passivity and exteriority, the excess of *Beispiel* produces an unsublatable interiority and activity. And this excess, rather than coming from anywhere outside thought, is inscribed within thought itself: *not* as the "nothing," the "other," the "excess" *of* thought, but as the unthinkable nonthought whose thinking makes thought (im)possible. Thought would be the dissimulation of *Beispiel*. To rewrite and reread the blank book of *such* a *Beispiel* would be to become *nobody* in a different way from those—"man," "jeder"—who became nobody by leaving the blank book unread and unwritten. The reader who (re)writes the "nothing" of *Beispiel* only allows the blank book to write itself, to write itself as always already written. Unlike the *History of Philosophy*, the excess of *Beispiel* needs neither (the thought of) "Aristotle" nor (the thought of) "Hegel" to be written: indeed, it would be more correct to say that the excesses of *Beispiel*, just as it dissimulates (as) thought, just as it writes the fiction of the authority of thought, writes the fictions of "Aristotle" and "Hegel," the dissimulations of authority and authorship. The book of *Beispiel*—as the book in which nothing *is* written—is a book for all and for none: a book that is unreadable and unwriteable because it can be read and written (only) by nobody.

But if[24]

NOTES

1. All page references within the body of the text are to the twenty volume *Theorie Werkausgabe* of G. W. F. Hegel published by Suhrkamp and are given by volume and page number. Translations are my own.

2. Cf. Jacques Derrida, *Glas* (Paris: Editions Galilée, 1974), p. 256 (left-hand column).

3. A helpful introduction to the problem of *Vorstellung* in Hegel—especially in its relation to *Reflexion* and the logic of essence (in the big *Logic*)—is: Malcolm Clark, *Logic and System* (The Hague: Nijhoff, 1971).

4. In terms of *context*, the distinction—between "System" (and the role of *Vorstellung* in it) and "text" (and the role of *Beispiel* in it)—is not an idle one, for the motive of Hegel's asking the question of the meaning of meaning is to describe the relation of the philosophy of religion to the *system* of philosophy (*Verhältnis der Religionsphilosophie zum System der Philosophie*).

5. Cf. the following page: "der Geist, der nicht erscheint, *ist* nicht" (16,34).

6. Gerhard Wahrig, *Deutsches Wörterbuch* (Gütersloh: Bertelsmann Lexikon-Verlag, 1975).

7. See Erich Przywara, "Bild, Gleichnis, Symbol, Mythos, Misterium, Logos," *Archivio di Filosofia, Filosofia e Simbolisme* ed. Enrico Castelli, (Roma: Fratelli Bocca Editori, 1956), 7–38.

8. See, for example, the *Encyclopaedia* (§20): "Die Vorstellung trifft hier mit dem *Verstande* zusammen, der sich von jener nur dadurch unterscheidet, daß er Verhältnisse von Allgemeinem und Besonderem oder von Ursache und Wirkung usf. und dadurch Beziehungen der Notwendigkeit unter den isolierten Bestimmungen der Vorstellung setzt, da diese sie in ihrem unbestimmten Raume durch das bloße *Auch* verbunden *nebeneinander* beläßt" (8,73). See also "das Erklären" in the *Phänomenologie des Geistes* (Hamburg: Meiner, 1952), pp. 118–21. What is called the mere "also" is called the mere "and" in the *Jenenser Logik* (Hamburg: Meiner, 1967), pp. 47ff.

9. The reason these "deficient forms" (*mangelhafte Formen*) (13,491) belong "almost exclusively" to linguistic art is this art's *additional* capacity: "Die Scheidung nun der beiden Momente des Kunstwerks führt es mit sich, daß die verschiedenen Formen, welche in diesem ganzen Kreise ihre Stellung finden, fast durchgängig nur der Kunst der Rede angehören, indem die Poesie allein solche Verselbständigung von Bedeutung und Gestalt aussprechen kann, während es die Aufgabe der bildenden Künste ist, in der äußeren Gestalt als solcher deren Inneres kundzugeben." (13,490).

10. In the introduction to the *History of Philosophy* the discussion of "was Verstehen heißt" entails a similar two-sided movement (18,91–92).

11. G. W. F. Hegel, *Die Vernunft in der Geschichte*, ed. Johannes Hoffmeister (Hamburg: Meiner, 1955), p. 58. See Jacques Derrida, *Glas*, p. 38 (lefthand column): "Seule la figure du Christ peut donc régler l'échange producteur—amortissement et bénéfice—entre la rhétorique et l'onto-logique."

12. In relation to Hegel's logic of the Holy Family such a *Beispiel* would be an illegitimate child, a bastard. Cf. the *OED*: "Byspel, bispel. *Obs.* ?*dial.* ... (ME. *bispell*, OE. *bi-spell*, *biz-spell*, f. bi, By+Spell tale, story, narration; cogn. w MHG. *bîspel*, *bîspil*, 'instance,' 'example,' ... 1. A parable.... 2. A proverb.... 3. *dial.* One whose worthlessness is proverbial, who becomes a byword.... 4. An illegitimate child, a bastard. Cf. By-blow."

13. A preliminary attempt to read the unreadability of Hölderlin's parable is: Andrzej Warminski, " 'Patmos': The Senses of Interpretation," *MLN* 91 (1976): 478–500.

14. The context is a discussion of the relation of the philosophy of religion—*this* text—to positive religion—i.e., a religion based on interpretation of a text, the Bible (*Verhältnis der Religionsphilosophie zur positiven Religion*). Cf. note 4.

15. Although Hegel calls the example *Beispiel* most often, he also calls it *Gleichnis*. He uses *Vergleichung* for the comparison itself (i.e., the relation between the soul and wax) and *Bild* for the side of the comparison that is the image (i.e., the wax stamped by the ring).

16. And perhaps Plato has a better claim to reading both, for, after all—or is it "first of all"?—the wax/impression example as a model for perception occurs in the *Theatetus*—and is abandoned for reasons that would not be without interest for another reading.

17. Aristoteles, *Über die Seele*, trans. Paul Gohlke (Paderborn: Ferdinand Schöningh, 1961), p. 68: "Ist nun Nahrung das, was der Körper schließlich aufnimmt, oder das, was man zunächst ißt? Das ist ein Unterschied. Wenn beides Nahrung ist, die eine in unverdautem, die andere in verdautem Zustande, dann könnte man in beiderlei Sinn von Nahrung sprechen: solange sie noch nicht verdaut ist, wird etwas durch seinen Gegensatz genährt, sobald sie verdaut ist, durch etwas Gleichartiges. Offenbar also haben beide Richtungen recht und unrecht."

18. Georges Bataille, "Hegel, la mort et le sacrifice," *Deucalion* 40 (October 1955): 34.

19. The introduction to the *History of Philosophy* contains an "implicit" citation as it distinguishes between *potentia* and *actus* in order to describe the movement of *Entwicklung*: "Wir sagen, der Mensch ist vernünftig, hat Vernunft von Natur; so hat er sie nur in der Anlage, im Keime...." (18,39–40).

20. Aristoteles, *Über die Seele*, p. 71: "Etwas kann nämlich entweder wissend sein, wie wir von einem Menschen sagen, er sei wissend, weil der Mensch überhaupt zu den wissenden Wesen gehört. Bisweilen nennen wir aber auch erst den wissend, der schon die Kunst des Schreibens versteht. Jeder von diesen hat die Anlage, jedoch nicht auf die gleiche Weise, der eine, weil seine Gattung und sein Körper entsprechend veranlagt ist, der andere, weil er, wenn er nur wollte und von außen ihn nichts hindert, sein Denken betätigen könnte. Erst wer wirklich denkt, ist im eigentlichen Sinne wissend und kennt dieses bestimmte Alpha, die beiden ersten sind nur in der Anlage wissend, und zwar der eine, weil er sonst schon viel gelernt hat und schon oft aus dem Zustand der Unwissenheit herausgetreten ist, der andere, weil er

die Arithmetik oder Schreibkunst schon besitzt, sie nur nicht betätigt, da er etwas anderes zu tun hat." Cf. Aristote, *De l'Ame*, trans. E. Barbotin (Paris: Société d'Editions Les Belles Lettres, 1966), p. 44: "En un premier sens, un être est savant à la manière dont nous dirions l'homme savant, parce que l'homme compte parmi les êtres capables de savoir et de posséder la science. En un second sens, nous appelons savant celui qui possède actuellement la science de la grammaire...."

21. It would be a literalization of Hegel's statement (in the preface to the second edition) that the big *Logic* should be reworked not just seven but seventy-seven times.

22. See *vergleichen* in Jacob Grimm und Wilhelm Grimm, *Deutsches Wörterbuch* (Leipzig, 1956), 12:1, p. 456: "in neuerer zeit hat *vergleichen* vielfach eine etwas andere färbung in der bedeutung angenommen. während früher die nebeneinanderstellung und gleichstellung das zumeist betonte war, nimmt das wort später den sinn des kritischen betrachtens, abschätzens an; früher ist es mehr die gleichheit, welche bei *vergleichen* hervorgehoben wird, heute mehr das unterscheidende neben dem gleichen."

23. Maurice Blanchot, "Discours sur la patience," *Le Nouveau Commerce* 30–31 (1975): 42. Cf. p. 24: "S'il y a rapport entre écriture et passivité, c'est que l'une et l'autre supposent l'effacement, l'exténuation du sujet: supposent un changement de temps: supposent qu'entre être et ne pas être quelque chose qui ne s'accomplit pas arrive cependant comme étant depuis toujours déjà survenu—le désoeuvrement du neutre, la rupture silencieuse du fragmentaire."

24. This text is part of a longer reading of Hegel in progress (which in turn is part of a series of readings of Hölderlin, Hegel, and Nietzsche).

SEVEN
REALIGNMENT: ALOIS RIEGL'S IMAGE OF LATE ROMAN ART INDUSTRY
Barbara Harlow

... there is a picture in the foreground [*Vordergrund*], but the sense lies far in the background [*Hintergrund*]; that is, the application is not easy to survey.
                        Wittgenstein, *Philosophical Investigations*

ALOIS RIEGL, looking on the late Roman age and its art as a *bahnbrechende*, a "ground-breaking," epoch, took a critical stand against the art historians and history writers of his own day and outside the traditional purview of antiquity. Riegl's *Spätrömische Kunstindustrie*[1] was first published in Vienna in 1901. At that time the late Roman Empire was generally viewed as a period of decline and decay, the dissolution of the once flourishing ancient world. Its art was seen as even more catastrophic, ugly and lifeless (*unschön und leblos*) when compared with the classical forms. Thus dismissed as useless and unworthy of tradition by the nineteenth-century critics, the Late Roman Empire itself had fallen into neglect.[2] Riegl's approach to the age was less straightforward. An epoch can be *bahnbrechend*, ground-breaking, in two ways: it can, in the usual sense of the word, establish a new pattern from which a tradition is said to develop, or it might, more literally, indicate the radical interruption of such a tradition. The ambivalence inscribed in the word *bahnbrechend* used by Riegl to describe the Late Roman period and its art likewise critically marks Riegl's representation of that art in his *Spätrömische Kunstindustrie*.

According to the theory of decline and decay (the *Verfallstheorie*) that dominated the ancient scholarship and art history of Riegl's time, the Late Roman period was a regrettable interruption of the once ascendant progress of the art of antiquity. Riegl represents the defenders of this argument as claiming that "never, by way of a natural development [*natürlicher Entwicklung*], could a Late Roman art have grown out of the classical." (SK, 6). Not, at least, those products of the art and crafts of the third, fourth, and fifth centuries known to the modern art historian. The *Verfallstheorie*, however, is necessarily connected with a particular theory of evolution and development (the *Entwicklungstheorie*). Late Roman art, viewed as an interruption in the development of antiquity, threatened to undermine the very foundations and structure of the evolution theory itself. The upholders of progress thus saw themselves obliged, for the sake of their theory, to appeal to the barbarians. The barbarians, outsiders, provided a most convenient excuse for the historians and theoreticians, whose constructs were on the verge of foundering in the abysmal rubble of Late Roman art. Riegl caught their ploy: "And so one helped oneself out," he writes, "by imagining [*mit der Vorstellung*] a forceful interruption [*Unterbrechung*] of development [*Entwicklung*] by the barbarians" (SK, 6). The barbarians, held responsible for classical art's deterioration into offensive ugliness and lifelessness, were made the scapegoats for the threatened decline of the theory. And the modern historians of decline and decay left Late Roman art to the decay which comes to neglect.[3]

Riegl, however, likewise a believer in progress, is bent on rescuing not only the theory of historical development, but Late Roman art as well. And with the rescue of Late Roman art from the decline to which it had been consigned by Riegl's coevals, the *Entwicklungstheorie* will also be recuperated—without enlisting the aid of the barbarians. Like his contemporaries, Riegl saw Late Roman art as a crucial interruption between the art of antiquity and modern art. But from Riegl's viewpoint, it is also a necessary, unavoidable—even via the barbarians—link in the chain that reaches from classical forms and normative ideals of beauty to modern, more subjectivist, works of art. Nor are the barbarians to be deemed responsible for the ugly and lifeless turn that art might appear to have taken in the last centuries of the Roman Empire. Rather it is the modern eyes, the eyes of the timebound art historians of Riegl's day, that present it in such a light. The problem, contends Riegl, is this, that the "art historian is incapable of overcoming the aesthetic demands of his contemporaries" (SK, 3). The art historian sought recourse to the barbarians in order to save his theory. Riegl in turn makes barbarians of his critics in order to save Late Roman art from any further decline and decay.

The nineteenth-century art historian, looking at Late Roman art, saw nothing, or something still worse: the rubble of a tradition in decay. From these remains, however, the art-historical refuse that is Late Roman art, Riegl fashions a sort of viaduct, one which would realign Late Roman works of art as an integral part of the mainstream of Western artistic development. Riegl criticizes the unseeing upholders of the *Verfallstheorie*: "One imagines for oneself an unbridgeable cleft ripped out [*aufgerissen*] from between Late Roman art and preceding classical antiquity" (SK, 6–7; my italics). The cleavage between Late Roman art and its precedents, a cleavage that is Late Roman art, is the work of the art historians themselves. With the force of their theory, they have ripped (*aufgerissen*) Late Roman art from out of the Western artistic tradition, and sundered thereby the very tradition itself. Riegl reworks the gaping fault they have rent. His representation of Late Roman art, the *Spätrömische Kunstindustrie*, rejoins, rearticulates a hitherto faulty tradition.

Riegl, however, in no wise admits that "Late Roman art simply succumbed to the negative task of *tearing down* [*Niederreissen*] for the sake of making room for new constructions" (SK, 12–3; my italics). It is neither a question of "ripping out [*aufreissen*]" Late Roman art from a classical tradition, nor a matter of "tearing down [*niedereissen*]" the works and norms of classical art. The *Riss*, the fault or fissure, must be otherwise transcribed. Its outlines describe a figure of a different sort. From the "aufgerissenen Kluft," from the "Niederreissen der klassischen Kunst," Riegl translates a revolutionary image of antiquity, realigned, for the modern beholder. His image, the work of disruption, is itself a work of art, what he himself has defined as "*outline* and color on surfaces or in space [*Umriss und Farbe in Ebene oder Raum*]" (SK, 6; my italics).

What has made Riegl's project necessary in turn renders it treacherously difficult. According to the *Verfallstheorie*, there are no grounds for a Late Roman art. It is nothing but a fault, a flaw, maintain the critics, a break in tradition, with tradition. The art of the Late Roman Empire can in no developmental way be said to be rooted in the classical. But if not as an outgrowth of the preceding classical culture, whence then spring the productions of the third and fourth centuries? Is there even such a thing as a Late Roman art, one anyway worthy of the appellation "art?" Late Roman art is, after all, neither beautiful, in the classical sense, nor alive. In other words, if there is indeed no late Roman art, is there then any ground for a further elaboration of it? It is just such a ground that Riegl is working out in his *Spätrömische Kunstindustrie*, the groundwork on which he might construct his own theory, the background against which to display his accomplished work of art, the grounds from which both, theory and work of art, might be developed. "Der Grund," according to Riegl, "ist der Scheidewand" (SK, 96). The ground is the interface. The ground, the background that is. In its special and unique regard toward background Late Roman art delineates itself most markedly from the art which preceded it. That this should be so is not altogether self-evident. The supporters of decline and decay in the art of the Late Empire claim that, insofar as there can be said to be a Late Roman art at all, which is already dubious, it could not have developed out of an earlier tradition. At best one can attribute it to the barbarians. Not only are there no grounds for a Late Roman art, Late Roman art has no background. From the point of view of the *Verfallstheorie* there is nothing there, not even a nothing, at most an abyss, an *Abgrund*.

Riegl, more perspicacious perhaps, more farsighted, at any rate, than his contemporaries, elaborates his representation of an art-historical development, at least from the Egyptian period through the Late Roman, as the progressive emergence of the background in the work of art. Ultimately, in Riegl's work, this background will take on foreground proportions. It is first brought out, however, in the art of ancient Egypt, which is described in the *Spätrömische Kunstindustrie* as essentially tactile (*haptisch*) and accordingly apperceptible through the sense of touch. Greek art, contrariwise, is said to be optical (*optisch*), thus requiring of its beholder his sense of sight, rather than of touch. Albeit Late Roman art, like the Greek, is also primarily optical, neither the observer's sense of touch nor that of sight are adequate or appropriate for its apperception. Late Roman art requires in addition the help of what Riegl terms an *ergänzende Erfahrung*, an "expanding consciousness or enlarging experience," on the part of its observer. Seen through this schema, once it has been focused on the works of art themselves, the background looms more perceptible in its process of emerging, its progressive importance becomes more self-evident, even decisive. Riegl turns first to look, with his mind's eye, at the pyramids of ancient Egypt, and describes the vision, partial, granted their beholder. "Before whichever of the four sides the observer stations himself, his eye encounters but the unified surface of the equally proportioned triangle whose sharply defined sides in no way remind one of the depth connection [*Tiefenanschluss*] behind it" (SK, 36). In looking at the pyramids, the observer's close-up vision (*Nahsicht*) is quite sufficient, indeed most apt. Those imposing edifices having been considered to the fullest extent possible, Riegl shifts his gaze somewhat forward in time and several geographical degrees north. He is looking at the Greek portico and pillared temple, and what he sees looks somewhat different from the pyramids he has just quit. Here, "each of the sides may still, on the whole, be surface, but, individually, they are no longer undifferentiated tactile flatness. Rather they dissolve into formal rows of pillars and porticoes." Riegl appends his description, perhaps in order that his follower might better focus his own mind's eye: ". . . should the eye wish to appreciate them [the pillars and porticoes] in their desired relation as parts of an harmonious whole, a certain retreating distantiation from the partial surfaces is requisite. It follows then that the Greek temples can be taken in only at an appropriate distance corresponding to normal vision" (SK, 38). If the esthete found his close-up vision most suitable at the foot of the pyramids, he discovers here, before the pillars of the Greek temple, that he requires instead his normal vision (*Normalsicht*). This observer, however, if he is to view, at Riegl's side, the Pantheon in Rome, must distance himself, both temporally and spatially, still further again. "Whereas the pyramid depended on a close-sighted [*nahsichtigen*] impression [*Aufnahme*], and the pillared temple on a normal-sighted [*normalsichtigen*], farsightedness [*Fernsicht*] must come in with the Pantheon, where no two points of a single zone lie on the same surface, and which thus demands a unified perspicuous view [*Übersicht*] over them all if the desired unity (symmetry in height and breadth) is to be perceived' (SK, 42). But a perspicuous view (*Übersicht*), from any standpoint, is beyond the ordinary observer's ken. And here, in face of the Pantheon, even a farsighted vision (*Fernsicht*), visionary as it may be, is found to be lacking in perspective. "This constant variation in depth furthermore draws the observer's glance [*Blick*] irresistibly towards the depth; but because this depth is in part incompletely (on the flanks), in part not at all (on the rear side) visible, the Pantheon . . . appeals to the enlarging assistance of the subjective consciousness [*die ergänzende Hilfeleistung des subjektiven Bewusstseins*]" (SK, 42–44).

"The depth [*Tiefe*]," Riegl has recalled to the observer's attention, "is not only perceptible to no sense whatever . . . but is to be understood as surface dimension solely on a further complicated route of thought process [*auf einem weit verwickelterem Wege des Denkprozesses*]" (SK, 29). This *Tiefe*, the depth that emerges into Late Roman art, which the art critics and history writers of Riegl's day mistook for nothing, which their point of view wholly obfuscated, is brought out again in the *Spätromsche Kunstindustrie*. Riegl, with the critical assistance of his "ergänzende Erfahrung," his "subjektiven Bewusstseins,"[4] re-presents it once more before the mind's eye. The circuitous way taken by his thought process (*der Weg seines Denkprozesses*) leads him to probe into the depths of this background whence he emerges once again on the track of Late Roman art. The background itself turns into a critical leitmotif in Riegl's *Spätromische Kunstindustrie*, and this into a translation of sorts of his *Denkprozesses*.

Riegl fabricates the background to his own work by way of an elaboration of the background as represented in the development of Late Roman art. In the gradual but decided evolution of the acanthus leaf, for example, Riegl recognizes the phenomenon of a progressive emergence of the background into the foreground.[5] Once, the acanthus leaves appeared as a carefully delineated design traced against an otherwise undifferentiated background. Then, in the leaves on the marble capital in Salona (situated approximately between the end of the fourth and the beginning of the sixth centuries) Riegl sees the background itself become design. The acanthus leaves are no longer isolated individual forms applied to an unassuming surface, but are rather arranged in such a fashion that the space between them, around them, appears also as a designed pattern. Riegl describes the configuration. "The leaves, first of all, are so closely packed together that but little of the background surface [*Grundebene*] is visible. Secondly, they are interconnected by their pointed tendrils in such a way as to splinter the still remaining background [*stehengebliebene Grund*] into myriad symmetrical and isolated compartments" (SK, 72). The background no longer holds itself back, but instead renders itself remarkable as immanent pattern and design.

This outstanding phenomenon, the radically crucial emergence of the background into unmistakable prominence, is visible throughout Late Roman art: on its reliefs, its freestanding sculpture, in the paintings and mosaics, as well as in the products of its art industry.[6] It reaches a critical and pivotal point at the end of Riegl's work with the garnet inlays in gold (*Granateneinlage in Gold*). On a particular gold buckle from Apahida the design is no longer to be distinguished from the background—or the other way around. The background has moved forward to the point where it now competes with design for a position of eminence in the foreground. The undecidable interplay between pattern (*Muster*) and background (*Grund*) is transfixing to its beholder. "Welche Rolle spielt hiebei das Gold und welche der rote Granat?" Which role does the gold play and which the garnet? Is it the gold outlines in which the garnets have been set that represent a pattern, or are these simply a surface against which the crimson stones figure in a design of their own? From a given perspective the dilemma might appear to have been answered, the arrangement fixed upon. This Riegl admits: "Academically the question can be answered: for the gold constructs not only the enclosing margin, but the sole connected surface, whereas the garnet fields stand isolated against each other" (SK, 326). Riegl, however, is not one to be satisfied with academic answers. His point of view is other, and what he sees looks different altogether. He turns the academic solution round on itself: "on the other hand, it must be admitted that everything has been done here so as to allow the relationship to appear as just the opposite—the gold as pattern [*Muster*] and the garnet as background [*Grund*]" (SK, 327). What Riegl refers to as the "dissimulation [*Verschleierung*] of the relationship between background and design" (SK, 327)[7] is complete. In a moment of illusion the one might just as well be mistaken for the other. This *Verschleierung*, the devious concealment, lies, in the last analysis, in the ever-shifting interplay between *Muster* and *Grund*, background and pattern. They masquerade as each other, the background standing out as pattern, the pattern retreating into the background, and vice versa. Analysis itself is distorted. The most perspicacious and penetrating of hermeneuts is at a loss to figure out once and for all the multifarious designs concealed and revealed in this confusing process of veiling/unveiling. No wonder then that the more superficial art critics should have failed to catch, even fleetingly, the background in Late Roman art, of Late Roman art. Nor does the accomplishment of this *Verschleierung* yield in any way a total picture. Background and pattern are not to be told apart from each other. The incessant transforming and deforming of the image demand that a new form be ever and again given to it. The perspective that translates the image in one way or another is in turn transposed with the shifting of the image.

What Riegl, with the German word *Grund*, designates as ground and further elaborates as background, *Hintergrund*, is not, however, to be mistaken for that other ground, referred to in German as *Boden*, the ground one treads on, stands on. It is a feature, Riegl points out, of Late Roman art that, despite its unique and singular regard (*Rücksicht*) towards the *Grund*, it does not recognize the ground in the sense of a *Boden*. Rather than establishing its figures firmly, feet down, on the ground, it portrays them instead as if dancing quite freely in the air. Witness, for example, the Felix Diptych from 428: "Late Roman painting, indeed Late Roman relief work, leaves its figures to hover with downward turned feet over the ground [*Boden*], and declines to establish them in a hard and fast relation to it" (SK, 213). Perhaps the art critics, with an eye to the ground, were, in a sense, on the right track after all. Late Roman art, were it not already in an abysmal state of decline, might seem to be threatening to founder in a gulf of its own making. The history writers too seem to have seen this freeswinging, oscillating, indeed groundless (*bodenlos*), appearance of the art of the Late Empire as typifying a general lack of principles, dependability, resoluteness, constancy, in short an overall unruliness, in the period. Such a nugatory judgement notwithstanding, this very ground(*Boden*)-lessness lies in the historical role of the Late Empire as a *bahnbrechende*, a "ground-breaking," epoch. The age itself was rent with political strife and cultural confusion, torn and splintered by inner factions and numerous wars. The Christians, now legitimized, were gradually assuming power. With Constantine's conversion the state religion has changed. Apart from conflicts between pagans and Christians, heresies split the Christian community as well. Even the Empire itself has been divided in two, the East and the West, and is usually ruled by two, although often still more, emperors at any given time. This inner confusion is further increased with the onslaught of barbarian invasions from without, barbarians who fought as often for as against the Romans, on Roman frontiers, and remained for all that outsiders still.[8] If its background (*Hintergrund*) is spurious, the very grounds (*Boden*), political, cultural, territorial, on which the Late Empire stands are fissured with the seeds of conflict and turmoil that it has sown.

The argument that there are no stopping points in historical progress and evolutionary development holds especially in application to the late Roman period. This is Riegl's contention as well: "not only is there no regress [*Rückschritt*] in development [*Entwicklung*], but there is furthermore no stopping point [*Haltpunkt*], everything instead flowing continuously forward" (SK, 18). At most there are pointers which, followed up, lead to particular, often arbitrary, images and representations of a given, momentary, epochal configuration. Accordingly, the freeswinging aerial figures of Late Roman art are to be seen less as an anachronistic regression to a more primitive form of artistic expression, and more as a stationary, instantaneous representation of an irremediably continuous temporal process.

By way of its position vis-à-vis space, whether it be *Hintergrund*, *Grund*, or *Boden*, its disposition in space, its self-exposition in space, Late Roman art elaborated the parameters of its own unique place in the history of art. This production of space took over and transformed the preceding spatial configurations, thereby making way for a further artistic manipulation of space. Thus Riegl contends that

Constantinian art (and the Late Roman especially), with its coloristic conception [apparent, for example, in the shiftily changing motives, *Muster/Grund*, light/shade, etc.] of the individual forms taken in absolute unity of depth, was the necessarily final transition [*Durchgangsphase*] of ancient art, which had to open the way [*die Bahn . . . freizumachen hatte*] for a new artistic concept bringing objects into a more equal relation with the space between them. Through its regard [*Berücksichtigung*], albeit at first forced, for space as such, Late Roman art did indeed open the way [*die Bahn . . . freigemacht hat*]. (SK, 93)

The space worked out in and by the art of the Late Roman Empire, like the time in which its works were produced, is crisscrossed by manifold faults and fissures. A representation of that art, such as Riegl seeks to execute in the composition of his *Spätrömische Kunstindustrie*,[9] must thereby be sketched out with similarly fluid, self-transposing outlines (*Umrisse*). Like the groundplans for the architecture of the period, which Riegl has described as oscillating between a "production of (closed) space as such [*Schaffung des (geschlossenen) Raumes als solchen*]" and the "production of the spatial boundaries [*Schaffung der Raumgrenzen*]" (SK, 26), Late Roman art vacillates undecidedly to and fro, its works as much epoch-making as destructive of art and tradition. Whether, extending the constructive analogy, that art is to be seen as the creation of a new order of space (*Schaffung des Raumes*) or as the final limit to a hitherto progressive development of artistic space (*Schaffung der Raumgrenzen*) is not to be decided from any one given perspective. Where the art began, the point to which it will ultimately lead, the extent of its sway, are not to be established on any prefabricated theoretical grounds. The Late Empire's function as *Durchgangsphase*, as "transitional phase," interval, is eminently displayed in its works of art. Its boundary lines and markers are themselves made up of intervals, ceaselessly shifting, the evanescent manifestation of its *bahnbrechende* role in progress. Riegl's description of Late Roman art, that

> now the uninterrupted tangible connection of all parts of the surface was no longer upheld as an absolute and principal artistic requirement, and an interruption of the same through optical pauses whose connecting bridges [*verbindende Brücke*] were fashioned by a mental experience assumed validity. (SK, 390)

likewise describes the period itself.

The late Roman images, outlines designed in and by the intervals that riddle and disarticulate a concept of the epoch's art, are in a state of constant transposition. These intervals, that once resided inconspicuously between, almost behind, the elements and pieces of the pattern, have themselves become pattern. The designing of the pattern and the elaboration of the background work reciprocally on each other: "the complete isolation of the individual form resulted thereby in an [emancipation of the interval], the elevation of the hitherto neutral and formless background to an artistic, that is, closed individual unity, potential of form" (SK, 390). The representational image is in turn transformed in this continuous process into an optical illusion. What was once a picture has turned out a picture puzzle, one that knows no definite solution, whose incongruity admits of no resolution. What is *Muster*? What is *Grund*? The academic answers succeed neither in dismissing, nor in explaining away, the question. It is bound to resurface in another form. *Muster* and *Grund*, pattern and background, dissolve disconcertingly into one another and reappear. Riegl repeatedly discovers this phenomenon in the products of the chisellers (*Keilschnittarbeit*) of Late Roman art industry. In the work of this particular craft the ornamentation is fashioned in such a way that, once again, *Muster* and *Grund* appear in a reciprocally untenable relation to each other. The artfulness of this handiwork is especially remarkable in the decoration on a buckle found in Pannonia (modern Hungary). "This technique can be taken with the same correctness or incorrectness either positively (as relief) or negatively (as engraving). We find ourselves subject to the same doubt when we endeavor to perceive the motif as pattern [*Muster*], foundering here on the preliminary question, what must be pattern [*Muster*] and what background [*Grund*]." Recourse to other examples in art, other modes of formation, in order to decide the dilemma, is in vain: the riddles only proliferate. "Were it a relief that we had before us, then clearly the ridges must represent the pattern; an engraving, then the recesses would have above all to be caught by the eye." A single point of view, however, is, from another angle, just as discomfitting. "Because, as already remarked, uncertainty governs this relation, there is nothing left for us but to attempt to dig out [*eruieren*] the meaning [*Bedeutung*] from the ornament's configuration" (SK, 293–94). The ornament itself yields no final definition.

The question meanwhile arises for Riegl's observer of whether Riegl is describing a confusion in the art object or his own disoriented state and disordered frame of reference. Where does the complication lie: with the observer or the observed? Is it the observation which is awry? The perceptual picture puzzle encountered by Riegl time and again in the course of his observations on and of Late Roman art is as much a fabrication of his day, its mind's eye, as it is the result of the Late Roman Empire's peculiar *Weltanschauung* and the temporal distance across which Riegl is studying it. An analogical example of Riegl's perplexity, excerpted from Wittgenstein's *Philosophical Investigations*, comes to mind: the duck/rabbit, which Wittgenstein has taken from Jastrow's *Fact and Fable in Psychology*. According to Wittgenstein's explanation, which turns out to be no explanation at all, "the figure can be seen as a rabbit's head or as a duck's."[10] Similarly, the Late Roman Empire can be seen as an interruption, a rupture, in a continuous history of art and culture, or as an epoch-making breakthrough, the establishment of a tradition. Glancing back at the buckle, the picture becomes still more complicated again. Meanwhile, writes Riegl, "the relationship on the bronze [buckle] alters with  each movement of its wearer; what was just now the light-side can become at the next moment shadow-side . . ." (SK, 295). The solution to the picture puzzle, transitory, fugitive as it may be, depends on the point of view taken vis-à-vis such a picture. The outlines remain, so much is ascertainable, but they shift with the viewpoint. And the picture comes out different each time.

If Wittgenstein's duck/rabbit illustrates a general perceptual

problematic, a second sketch from the *Investigations* demonstrates the more particular problem posed by the reciprocally changing relationship between *Muster* and *Grund*: what Wittgenstein calls the "double cross,"
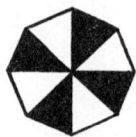
the *Doppelkreuz*. In his elucidation of this example, Wittgenstein makes no decision as to whether the figure represents a white or a black cross, and describes it simply "as a white cross on a black background [*Grund*] and as a black cross on a white background [*Grund*]" (PI, 207). Nor does he make an either/or dilemma out of the puzzle. Both possible configurations are immanent in the figure and included, though no longer simultaneous, in Wittgenstein's scriptural representation of it. Perhaps still more remarkable is the metaphorical turn given to the description: "as," writes Wittgenstein in both cases. For Wittgenstein, the problem exemplified by the "duck/rabbit" as well as by the "double cross" is a philosophical problem, namely the problem raised by "descriptions of the alternating aspects" (PI, 207).

This "description of alternating aspects" is the problem that Riegl faces as well. How, in other words, is he to describe the Late Roman Empire and its art? As pattern against a mistaken background, or as the groundwork from out of which modern art grew? As interval between classical and modern art, or as inevitable limit to a classical tradition, its last frontier? The image of Late Roman art is composed rather of its revolutionary ambiguity: a pivotal point, a turning point. From its outlines, definitive and well-defined as they might seem, there is always still another image to be developed. Just as the matter stood with architecture, at once a "Schaffung des (geschlossenen) Raumes" and the "Schaffung der Raumgrenzen." However the picture may be described, it remains, in Riegl's words, "to carry out the one part of the task at the expense of the other" (SK, 26).

Intricated in Riegl's representation of Late Roman art there is the outline for a project to transform the formation, aesthetic, historical, scientific, of his day, to reform the background of his contemporaries.[11] Riegl finds their centricity and conformity to a classical ideal of art and beauty itself barbaric. He takes these critics to task for the partiality of their standpoint: "If the works of Late Roman art upset our modern conception, it is just that, by representing [*vorstellen*] the individual form tactilely to ourselves in close-up vision [*Nahsicht*] with little regard [*Rücksicht*] to space, we are thus unable to represent it in optical farsightedness [*Fernsicht*]." It is regrettable "the extent to which we are rooted in [our] fundamental [*grundsätzlichen*] point of view" (SK, 254).

Whereas the modern observer of ordinary repute recoiled at the sight of the stiffly contorted Late Roman figures, seeing in them but a poorly executed regression to the art forms of ancient Egypt, Riegl looked these figures in the eyes and noticed there the very subtlest of movements. "In the sidelong glance [*Seitenverdrehung*] of the eyes," Riegl discovered "a positive artistic means . . . whereby the figures in all their cubic spatiality are loosed from the visual surface and set into a relation to each other . . ." (SK, 249). For all their assumed lifelessness, the animation in their eyes betrays these petrified emperors, senators, and imperial notables. The figures relate not only to one another but with their beholder as well.[12] Their eyes meet momentarily. A hitherto unsuspected dimension is opened. Not only a background has been unveiled, but a visionary foreground is revealed. It turns somehow on the eyes: how they look, what they look like, how they are looked at. It happened, for example, in the instance of Wittgenstein's duck/rabbit: when the eye was seen in such a way that it appeared to be looking left, the image looked like a duck, looking right, like a rabbit. The more perspicacious observer will recall the statues of the good shepherd, more or less abundant in Late Roman art, whose "yearning and soulful upward glance . . . manifestly translates inner spiritual movement into outer, momentaneously fleeting, material appearance" (SK, 205).

The eyes then, under close scrutiny, are seen in turn to work like windows in that they establish an "immediate communication between the inner and the outer" (SK, 38). Now it so happened, however, according to Riegl's version, that these windows were held to be inadmissible in architecture by the Egyptians, who disdainfully dismissed them as nothing more than "disturbing breaches [*störende Löcher*]" in an otherwise perfect whole. Windows were furthermore rejected by the Greeks when building their temples as an "unpleasing interruption [*Unterbrechung*]" of the tactile-material through a purely optical-colored inessential Nothing" (SK, 49). The Roman artists and artisans of the Late Empire, however, the same artists who turned their eyes towards the still undefined distance, saw more in windows than their predecessors. They accordingly built them into their architectural edifices. And Riegl saw more through these windows than did his near-sighted contemporaries. "With the windows, which opened vision from restricted narrowness into freeness, an art of the future became for the first time manifest" (SK, 50–51). Through the windows of Late Roman art is revealed not only a preceding background but a still to be elaborated foreground. Like the eyes.[13]

In this fugitive meeting of the eyes Riegl fashions a trajectory which is to cross, however fleetingly, centuries of misprision, and in the course of which a new, if not revolutionary, aesthetic configuration is to be established. If Late Roman art is *bahnbrechend*, so likewise is Riegl's representation of it. Riegl's project, however, should not be mistaken as the attempt to raze and lay waste to the current theories of art.[14] No, these rather are recognized as a certain, necessary background to his own work, a background that must be transposed if Riegl is to prepare the ground for an edifice of his own design and making. Thus Riegl's work elaborates the parameters for a new and progressive apprehension of the place of Late Roman art in art history. Riegl will, as he claims, "break [*brechen*]" the prevailing prejudice that "Late Roman art means not an advancement but only a decline" (SK, 7). In the face of the bias-obscured eyes of his contemporaries Riegl proposes a new art of seeing, a new art of perceptive description.

The *Spätrömische Kunstindustrie* oscillates, in Riegl's own words, between a "tactile clarity of details [*taktische Klarheit der Details*]" and an "optical perspicuous view over the whole [*optische Übersicht über das Ganze*]" (SK, 38). A vademecum of sorts, it recounts the "voyage of discovery" into the "dark part of the world on the map of art-historical research," into the "latest phase of ancient art" (SK, 2). Riegl was a museum curator. If from his standpoint at the turn of the century he is gainsaid the perspective of a certain distantiation vis-à-vis the Late Roman period, a farsighted, indeed visionary, perspicuous view of its art, he also finds himself in the singular historical position of being able to view its works at close hand. These works have left their native ground to find shelter within museum walls.[15] The experiential dimensions of time and space vacillate between irreconcilable discrepancy and inarticulable continuity. The dimensions of Riegl's book, his theoretical constructions, vacillate with them.

The same ambivalence that has been ascribed to the Late Roman age and its art is in turn inscribed in the composition of Riegl's text. Each of the exemplary figures that it designs and produces, of art and works of art, can likewise be seen as a model, a stencil, for Riegl's own art-critical task. It might happen, in other words, that Riegl should find himself subject to derisive critiques not unlike those practiced against Late Roman art. It could be objected, for example, that Riegl, like the skilful Late Roman artisans who worked out their perforated designs in laying them over a second surface (*durchbrochene Arbeit*), is himself simply placing preconceived, prefabricated patterns, like *Muster/Grund*, to name one example, against a given background. Upon closer examination, however, this work reveals an optical illusion similar to that rendered manifest by the Late Roman art objects under Riegl's scrutiny. The ambivalence, everywhere prevalent, discovers the objection itself as but a misdirected point of view. What is, after all, the *Muster*, and what the *Grund*, in the *Spätrömische Kunstindustrie*?

From Riegl's standpoint, art history represents a development. This development may not always proceed directly, straightforwardly; more often than not it is complicated and contorted. Nonetheless, it reveals a necessary evolution. In the development of the line in surface decoration, for example, Riegl detects the line of development of surface decoration. Its traces are found in the art of ancient Egypt. "The line was for the Egyptians essentially mere outline [*Umrisslinie*], tactile, tangible that is in things of nature, but not visible." The line leads further to the Greeks, their ideals of form and beauty. "At the hands of the classical Greeks, the line long received the same use as outline [*Umrisslinie*], although it was employed on the side as well for modelling effects. . . . Through broadening and lack of definition . . . [the lines] betrayed themselves as shadows" (SK, 120–121). Thus historical epochs too cast shadows.

Meanwhile, however, the line does not simply disappear with the shades, dissolve into these shadows. It develops further, rendering still other forms of ornamentation, outlines, sketches: acanthus leaves, tendrils, and vines, palmettes, arabesques, and the like. Riegl apprehends in the display of these motifs a compositional law, the law of the so-called "contrasting curves," the *kontrastierenden Kurven*. The line has been bent, crooked, and this has happened in such a way that "the individual curves do not develop, as they did in the waved runners, out of each other, in uninterrupted connection [*ununterbrochene Verbindung*], but break instead their flow in order that the succeeding curve should, where possible, spring immediately forth in the opposite direction" (SK, 267). The compositional law of "kontrastierenden Kurven" that has been designed in the lines of ornamental motifs is again to be traced, in translation, in the outlines of Riegl's representation of Late Roman art. Like the decorative curve that departs, gracefully yet abruptly, from the established line, that "springs forth in the opposite direction [*nach der entgegengesetzten Richtung ausspringt*]," so too Riegl's depiction of Late Roman art and art industry can be seen as interrupting a long-standing tradition of art criticism. It takes a turn which contradicts in a sense the foregoing and hitherto prevailing "ununterbrochene Verbindung" of that tradition. Riegl's representation of the art of the Late Roman Empire finds a model of its own in that art. The line develops. It becomes figure.[16]

The representation of Late Roman art which Riegl has sketched out in the *Spätrömische Kunstindustrie* is made up of myriad fragments, the bits and pieces of a larger work still in progress. The very text of the book is perforated, riddled, with pictures, illustrations, selective and partial, of his own configured image of what was Late Roman art. At the same time each of these fragments contains the elements of its further elaboration. They are all figures designed according to the ornamental construct that Riegl terms *unendlichen Rapport* ("infinite relationship, endless connection"). Begun no matter where, the image can be continued indeterminably in any direction. Like the acanthus leaves that

spiral round pillars and capitals, across ages, entwining thereby the development of art-historical epochs into a necessary evolutionary process. In this then, the law of "unendlichen Rapport," Riegl's representations resemble too the enamelled bronze plate, found in the Themse and now displayed in the British Museum. It is reproduced in Riegl's text.

And what an ornament! We ask: what is *Muster* and what *Grund*? We think to recognize shields, scrolls, but the shifting enamel coloring drives us to bewilderment. We see light-colored and dark-colored scrolls thrust into each other, but no background [*Grund*] between. Yet we remain at first at the midpoint: the four-leaf rosette in the center. The entire pattern [*Muster*] seems to conflue in it. But what of the oval leaves pushing in from the four corners? The key to the understanding of the whole pattern lies in these leaves, for each of them is nothing but a quarter of the middle rosette. Were we to extend [*ergänzen*] each of these corner leaves to a complete rosette and everywhere imagine the continuation as indicated by the middle rosette, we would recognize that on all four sides of the oblong the same pattern repeats itself. (SK, 361)

The trajectory pursues its course.[17]

By means of his close-sightedness, his normal vision, his visionary point of view (*Nahsicht, Normalsicht, Fernsicht*), and with the direction of his subjective consciousness, his *ergänzende Erfahrung*, Riegl has translated the art works and crafts of the Late Roman Empire into the words of his book. In the preface to the *Spätrömische Kunstindustrie*, which represents the work as an architectural accomplishment, Riegl describes with hindsight his prospective undertaking: "What I am hereby proposing is a display of the essence of Late Roman style and its historical development [*Werdens*]; I believe thereby to have largely closed the last great and already-too-long-left-open [*die letzte grosse und bereits allzulange offengebliebene Lücke*] gap in our knowledge of the general art history of mankind" (SK, 22). In the concluding afterword, "Die Grundzüge des spätrömische Kunstwollens [the fundamental characteristics of the Late Roman *Kunstwollens*]," Riegl appealed to the literary works of Late Roman writers, notably Saint Augustine and Plotinus, to provide the *Prufstein*, the touchstone, to the foundations of his edifice. Riegl sees it as incumbent on him to discover "whether what at that time was in fact desired of the fine arts is that which we, as ground for the investigation of the monuments, imagine to ourselves as the desired." It is in this hypothetical agreement [*Übereinstimmung*] that, for Riegl, "the true and only admissible touchstone [*Prufstein*] for the whetting of our research results will first be laid" (SK, 393). Finally, however, the stopping of this gap, the "allzulange offengebliebene Lücke," which lay open at the beginning of Riegl's work, does not bring the edifying construction of art history to the fullness of completion. If the *Spätrömische Kunstindustrie* is indeed a *bahnbrechendes* book, then it too has excavated a breach, constructed an interruption, and thereby established a site for still further developments. The scriptural, figural representations in Riegl's work are yet again to be analyzed, disassembled, and reconstructed. The perfection lies in their imperfection: they must be repeatedly elaborated, their contrivances puzzled out. New configurations emerge. An *unendliche Rapport*. "Gaps [*Lücken*]," Lou von Salomé once wrote, "work best as holes [*Löcher*] through which one looks into endlessness [*Unendlichkeit*]." "Gaps [*Lücken*]," she continues, "are positive building blocks [*Bausteine*]." The important thing is, ultimately, the "endlessness [*Unendlichkeit*] shining everywhere through, *which first makes a world of it all.*"[18] The image thus produced oscillates with the standpoint of its observer, his designs, his background, his *ergänzende Erfahrung*.

NOTES

1. Reference, however, will be made to Alois Riegl, *Spätrömische Kunstindustrie*, 3d ed. (Darmstadt: Wissenschaftliche Buchgesellschaft, 1964). Hereafter cited as SK. Translations are my own.

2. Why the Late Roman Empire should have suffered such neglect is

not immediately obvious. It can certainly not be for lack of source material, which is more than abundant. Perhaps it was the baroque turn the Latin language had taken that offended scholars reared on Ciceronian periods. This linguistic and literary evolution is examined by Erich Auerbach in his study of the Latin historian, Ammianus Marcellinus. Cf. Erich Auerbach, *Mimesis* (Bern: Francke, 1964).

3. Riegl claims that Jakob Burckhardt alone was not prone to such interpretations, attributing this to his interdisciplinary approach. Burckhardt, he says, was an "art historian of the old school to whom any division of labor was foreign and who, for just that reason, became one of the greatest and most perspicacious" (SK, 4). A reading, however, of Burckhardt's study *Die Zeit Konstantins des Grossen* reveals that he too held the barbarians responsible for the level reached by Late Roman art, although he does not find this to be a deplorable state of affairs.

4. The importance of the *ergänzende Erfahrung* in aesthetics is reemphasized in Riegl's later work, *Das holländische Gruppenporträt*, a study of the development of the group portrait in the Dutch art of the 16th and 17th centuries. Riegl refers to it here as "that authentic Dutch one-sided communication in the old group portraits which stops halfway and requires extension [*Ergänzung*] through the observer's experiential conscoiusness [*Erfahrungsbewusstsein*]." Alois Riegl, *Das holländische Gruppenporträt*, 2 vols., 2d. ed. (Vienna: Oesterreichischen Staatsdruckerei, 1931), I: 197. Hereafter cited as HGP. Translations are my own.

5. Riegl's first book, *Stilfragen*, subtitled "Grundlegungen zu einer Geschichte der Ornamentik," and published in 1893, was a study of the development of the acanthus leaf in design. Contrary to the prevailing opinion that the acanthus leaf as ornament arose as a direct copy of the leaf as it existed in nature (*acanthus spinosa*), Riegl takes it back to the Egyptians and follows the leaf's evolution up to and through the 5th century, when "the individual multi-sectioned tips are loosed from the former whole or half acanthus leaves and construct their own configurations with independent meaning [*Bedeutung*]." Alois Riegl, *Stilfragen*, 2nd ed. (Berlin: Richard Carl Schmidt, 1923), pp. 277–78. Translations are my own. The acanthus leaf in the *Spätrömische Kunstindustrie* is as if but a single sprig excerpted from the series. It begins again a new sequence: the acanthus leaf in the works of Alois Riegl.

6. Its title, *Spätrömische Kunstindustrie*, notwithstanding, only one chapter, the last, is concerned specifically with art industry. The earlier sections treat of what are usually classified, as long as the distinction holds, as "fine arts": painting, sculpture, architecture, etc. Riegl, who did not hold with this distinction, projected a second volume of this work, but died before finishing the task.

7. Riegl discovers this relation between *Muster* and *Grund*, already critical in *Stilfragen*, again in the "Dutch group portrait": "the group of figures sharply demarcates itself, as *Muster* from *Grund*, against the room's space... (HGP, 191). Has the relation *Muster/Grund* itself become *Muster* to Riegl's art-critical eye?

8. For a perhaps all-too-detailed account of the history of the period, see A. H. M. Jones, *The Later Roman Empire*, 2 vols. (Norman, Oklahoma: Oklahoma Univ. Press, 1964).

9. Riegl continues the story of space in Late Roman art, already begun in *Stilfragen*, in *Das holländische Gruppenporträt*. "An art which, like ancient

art, viewed formed individual things as objective givens, could never have succeeded in representing free space. Emergent Christianity in the Roman Empire first emancipated free space, albeit only in a very narrow depth still close to the nearlying surface" (HGP, 22).

10. Ludwig Wittgenstein, *Philosophical Investigations*, 3d ed., trans. G. E. M. Anscombe (New York: Macmillan, 1968), p. 194. Of Riegl's contemporaries, Ernst Mach most notably represents the psychological and philosophical dilemmas confronting the turn-of-the-century scientists and scholars. Cf. in particular *Die Analyse der Empfindungen* and *Erkenntnis und Irrtum*.

11. Nor is the project limited to the *Spätromische Kunstindustrie*. As he once began his *Stilfragen*, Riegl opens *Das holländische Gruppenporträt* with an attack directed at contemporary art history and criticism. In each of these instances, Riegl has selected an area of study, formal, in the case of ornament, or historical, as with Late Roman art industry and the Dutch group portrait, which has been singularly, if not studiously, neglected by the critics. He then levels his charge of centrism and selective blindness, followed by a presentation of his own theory. The procedure becomes at once subject and object of his works. The fate to which Late Roman art fell victim will also be the fate of Riegl's compositions and theories, which, despite a certain immediate interest and controversy aroused by their appearance, have since been relegated to general neglect. Such neglect, however, arouses sporadic interest. There is a modern bibliography, scant though it be, attached to Riegl's name. The most recent of these articles, "Alois Riegl: Art, Value and Historicism," by Henri Zerner, which first appeared in *Critique*, Aug.–Sept. 1975, and was reprinted with modifications in *Daedalus*, Winter, 1976, presents a summary of the latest interest inspired by Riegl.

12. In his study of the Dutch group portrait, Riegl appeals to the eyes of Late Roman art to bring out the characteristics of a later age. "It was the Roman Empire that granted the eye, that most eminent of means of expressing attention, a hitherto unheard-of formation [*Ausbildung*], one that, for the future and not least for Christian art, was ground-breaking [*bahnbrechende*]. During the Roman Empire art dared for the first time to permit a deviation of the eye's direction from the head's direction . . . " (HGP, 15n). The eyes of the members of the Dutch companies in portrait then establish a "relationship with a third party (more precisely numberless third parties), which, missing in the picture, must be thought into it" (HGP, 43). Riegl fancies himself a member of this third party. His own mind's eye appeals, like the sculpted Roman emperor's once did, like the painted Dutchman's did, to still another third person.

13. Heinrich Wöllflin, who could not have been uninfluenced by Riegl, perceives the windows in a building as the eyes of the work of architecture. "In windows we discover organs that resemble our eyes. One might say that they 'spiritualize' the building." Heinrich Wöllflin, "Prolegomena zu einer Psychologie der Architektur" in *Kleine Schriften*, ed. J. Gantner (Basel: Benno Echwabe, 1946), p. 38. My translation.

14. In particular the iconographical and the material-technical theories of art interpretation, which Riegl considers as necessary but nonetheless insufficient preliminaries to the task of the art historian and critic. These are represented, in the *Spätromische Kunstindustrie* and *Stilfragen*, by G. Semper, *Der Stil in den technischen und tektonischen Künsten oder praktische Asthetik* and W. G. Goodyear, *Grammar of the Lotus*, respectively. A key concept

in Riegl's theoretical structure is that of *Kunstwollen*, which has not been discussed here. It has been variously interpreted, most notably by Erwin Panofsky ("Der Begriff des Kunstwollens" in *Zeitschrift für Asthetik und allgemeine Kunstwissenschaft*, 14, 1920).

15. Riegl finds fault with the modern criticism of Late Roman art that berates the entrepreneurs of the time, Constantine's "Antiquitätensammler," as having to import art from the lands which they conquered in order to compensate for a lack of artistry of their own. He turns the charge against the critics, pointing to the modern imperialism which has looted and pillaged its victims, an act as barbarian as that laid to the account of the Romans (SK, 174).

16. Riegl has figured out the linear process in *Stilfragen*. The line, which he describes there as the "silhouette, the outline [*Umrisslinie*], which in reality do not exist and were first invented by men" (SF, 2), he reinscribes in his image, his representation of *Spätrömische Kunstindustrie*. The artist has, as Riegl puts it, "to form a work of art from out of the line" (SF, 3). Riegl does.

17. Riegl, "although it means a deviation from the straight line [*gerade Linie*] of representation of our object" (SF, 308), continues to pursue his investigation of the origins and development of this compositional law of *unendlichen Rapport*. His works themselves become part of the *unendlichen Rapport*.

18. Lou Andreas-Salomé, *In der Schule bei Freud* (Zurich: Max Niehans, 1958), p. 118–9. My translation.

EIGHT
ABSENCE, AUTHORITY, AND THE TEXT
Richard Jacobson

I PRESENCE AND THE LAW

WHAT FOLLOWS is the examination of the effects of a certain defect, of a de-function in the realm of the imaginary. The resonances of that defect in the literary remains of a civilization have been profound and continuous, since the lack which gave rise to all that followed was no less than the silence of God. The primary monument to that silence is an amplitude of words, in particular that law and that writing which we customarily privilege by the dignifying deixis of capitalization: The Law, and The Scriptures, as if to say at once both *"our* law, *our* scriptures" and also "law and writing *par excellence."*

Law, in the sense of law codes and statute books, is in essence the expropriation of a real or imagined former social presence.[1] At one time, so we like to assume, the king dispensed justice beneath a tree to all who came before him. When faced with contradictory claims, or when codes which stood outside the law were at issue, the king or the judge allowed an ordeal: the joust, the bitter waters, the duel. Decisions of a nonjuridical nature might be taken by a structurally similar practice: the lot-oracle or some similarly technical mantic device. At what point the decision of such an ordeal was referred to the manipulation of God is uncertain, but presumably it is a rather late and relatively sophisticated projection of the king onto the cosmic stage in the form of divinity.

Insofar as resort to written codes expropriates these essentially *present* modes of Authority, the existence of the code itself points to an *absence*—an authoritative absence, no doubt, an absence paradoxically filled with a host of real or imagined sanctions, an absence in the cultural regime whose internal counterpart is to be found in the range of socially determined superegos (the "shame" sanction, the "guilt" sanction, the multifaceted objectifications of "conscience").

The Old Testament, read in an appropriately deconstructive mode, offers a specially privileged field for examination, since it offers the prospect of locating the precise moment(s) in its mythified history when the plenitude of Absence replaced the (imaginary?) memory of a divine Presence, when God was replaced by Text. One such moment can be dated more or less precisely to the beginning of the fourth century B.C. At the same time, the dichotomy between Priest and Prophet, never as clearly defined in fact as in convention before this date, came into effect. And at this same time, prophecy came to an end.

Properly speaking, prophecy died *twice* in ancient Israel, each time directly following upon the promulgation of a book of the Law.

Since it is the regular practice of the final Priestly redactors of the Pentateuch to attempt (and fail) to conceal the construction of their text, it will be necessary for our purposes to make a careful methodological distinction, one well known to Biblical scholars, but even more crucial to the present project: we must distinguish carefully between the fictive date of any fragment of text and the era of its production. Apart from usual reasons of historical scruple, this distinction will have the heuristic value of demonstrating the unexpected fact that the *later* portions of our text are the most highly mystical and "mystified," while the earlier ones are in a certain sense, *mutatis mutandis*, far more "rational" and "natural." It is only quite late in the game that one must not pronounce the name of one's God. When he was a friend, chief, battle companion, warlord—one saw his mighty deeds and acclaimed him. Only much later does he recede from this intercourse—which the mythic history allows only to Moses—into the vague and magnetic invisibility of an imageless existence, of a voice, if that, from the still silence, of a euphemism.

The nature of the priesthood of Yahweh (it is only appropriate in speaking of the era of Presence to speak of the Israelite God by his proper name) in the pre-exile period (before 587 B.C.) was apparently not, as later, limited to or even primarily centered around the sacrificial cult. We read of numerous early Kings and leaders of the Israelites carrying out sacrifices, quite apart from the priesthood. The aphorism, quoted in Jeremiah (18:18) and Ezekiel (7:26) to the effect that "Instruction (*torah*) shall not perish from the priest, nor counsel from the wise, nor the word from the prophet" speaks of a priestly role inscribed in the folklore as primarily that of *"torah."* This word only came to mean "law" (*nomos*) centuries later. In the preexilic period, the word is closer in meaning to its original derivation from a root meaning "to cast" or "to point," related to cognate words for "teacher" and "parent." The "casting" in question must originally have been divination by use of the Urim and Thummin, a binary lot-oracle restricted to and eventually, after the loss of its function, emblematic of the priesthood.[2] From this consultation of the divine comes the secondary association of priests with *torah*, that of instruction in the *noninstitutionalized, customary* law. Long before it became a law-code, *torah* meant, in effect, priestly practice, neither set rule nor abstract teaching. To a certain extent this original meaning is preserved as a trace in the distinction in later Jewish liturgical language between *torah*, the body of both written and traditional ("oral") law, and *sepher torah*, the physical scroll on which the Pentateuch is written. Perhaps the clearest example of the locus of authority in this early period, and its marked *presence* in the retrospective view, is the catch-phrase of the D document (ca. 621–550 B.C.). When speaking of the anarchy of the early years: "there was then no king in Israel" (e.g., Judg. 19:1, et al.)—not "there was then no *law*."

II THE LAW FROM SINAI

The Ten Commandments appear three times in the Pentateuch, the Five Books of Moses which later Judaism ascribed as a matter of dogma to God's direct dictation to Moses. The first version (following the syntagmatic line of the text in its final form) appears as an interpolation in Exodus 20:1–17. Its interpolated character is clear in the continuity in narrative between the end of ch. 19 and 20:18, as well as in the apparent non sequitur at the beginning ("So Moses . . . spake to the people. And God spoke these words, saying . . ."). This version of the decalogue is part of the Priestly Document, the final addition to the Pentateuch which was the work of scribes in the exilic and immediate postexilic period (i.e. from ca. 587 through ca. 450 B.C.). An earlier "ritual decalogue," in contrast to the "ethical" mode of Exodus 20, appears in Exodus 34. An intermediate, "Deuteronomistic" form of the text appears in Deuteronomy 5:6–21; it differs from the Priestly form only in detail.

Prophecy died for the first time following the discovery of the early form of the book of Deuteronomy. When Josiah, King of Judah (ca. 639–609 B.C.) initiated a refurbishing of the Temple, the priest Hilkiah announced that he had found "the Book of the Law" (Heb. *sepher haTorah*) in the Temple. It takes no great insight to conclude that the book Hilkiah found was one he intended to find. In fact, the narrative (2 Kings 22:8) does not report that Hilkiah actually *found* the book, merely that he reported finding it. The subsequent reading of the book and the religious reform which followed make it clear that the book was some form of the present Deuteronomy.

Julius Wellhausen, in whose works the nineteenth-century deconstruction termed "Higher Criticism" or the "Documentary Hypothesis" reaches its definitive articulation, compares the account in 2 Kings with the much later parallel in Chronicles, completed ca. 300 B.C. In Kings, Hilkiah's book can be read in one sitting to Shaphan, the Royal Scribe, and similarly repeated to the king. In 2 Chron. 34:18 Shaphan reads merely a *portion* of the book to the king.[3]

Two preliminary observations are to the point: (1) Hilkiah and/or his circle almost certainly wrote the book they delivered to the king. (2) Sometime between the completion of the Books of Kings (ca. 560 B.C.) and Chronicles (ca. 300 B.C.), the conception of what was found changed: formerly it had been understood to be a single book, the Urdeuteronomium. Some centuries later, the "book" was regarded as too long to be read in its entirety in one sitting; it had become the complete Pentateuch. Between 560 and 300 B.C., the Pentateuch had been completed, all of its constituent parts arranged into an apparently coherent chronological sequence, and its origin was retrojected into a by-then remote past. But it is merely the discovery of the Pentateuch that was placed in the seventh century B.C.; its composition had by this time been cast even further back, to the covenant ceremony at Sinai that both constituted the Israelites as a people and determined (in the view of a later age) its alliance with God.

The first death of prophecy followed directly upon the promulgation of Deuteronomy as *the* book of the Law (or Instruction, *torah*) of Moses. Jeremiah, who was perhaps eighteen when the book was found, apparently saw him*self* inscribed in it as the prophetic successor to Moses:

A prophet will the Lord thy God raise up unto thee, from the midst of thee, of thy brethren, like unto me [sc. Moses]; unto him ye shall hearken. (Deut. 18:15)[4]

It is apparently in response to the "discovery" of this book that Jeremiah, referring to a happier past, says

> Thy words were found, and I did eat them;
> And Thy words were unto me a joy and the rejoicing of my heart;
> Because Thy name was called on me, O Lord God of hosts. (Jer. 15:16)

Yet the book's acceptance must have meant that prophetic oracles, no less than the priestly practice of customary instruction, were *no longer necessary*. The medium of prophecy was now expendable: in contrast to its intermittency and uncertainty was the fixed and certain written word.

Absence, Authority, and the Text

Jeremiah stands in the Temple court and denounces worshippers' reliance on the Deuteronomistic religious ideology:

Trust ye not in lying words, saying, "The Temple of the Lord, the Temple of the Lord, the Temple of the Lord, are these" (7:4)

—i.e., do not rely on the special character of the Temple in Jerusalem as proclaimed by Deuteronomy, but rather "thoroughly amend your ways and your doings." Not only is Jeremiah nearly lynched by the crowd (26:8–15), but we are told that a contemporary prophet with a similar message, Uriah, was in fact assassinated (26:20–23). And Jeremiah's biographer and amanuensis, Baruch b. Neriah, includes in his text the ultimate disqualification of prophecy: he quotes a letter from one of the leaders of the first Exiles in Babylon to the Judean authorities, ordering the appointment of "officers in the house of the Lord for [the restraint of] every man that is mad, and maketh himself a prophet, that thou shouldest put him in the stocks and in the collar. Now therefore, why hast thou not rebuked Jeremiah of Anathoth, who maketh himself a prophet unto you?" (Jer. 29:26f.).

The second and decisive deathblow to prophecy came some centuries later, with the arrival in Jerusalem of Ezra the Scribe, a priest from Babylonia armed with a commission from the Persian King.[5] The commission, quoted in the Book of Ezra, refers to his having "the law (Aram. *dath*) of thy God which is in thy hand" (7:14), and "the wisdom of God, that is in thy hand" (7:25). Wellhausen, along with most Biblical scholars, believes that Ezra brought at least the Priestly code, and most likely the final redaction of the Pentateuch from Babylon to Palestine. The text says that "on the first day of the seventh month" he formally read "the book of the Law of Moses, which the Lord had commanded to Israel" (Neh. 8)—a reading which continued onto the following day.

By what means could the dogma have so thoroughly taken hold that this text, the result of centuries of editorial effort, was given by God to Moses on Mt. Sinai at the very beginning of Israelite national history—a dogma taken for granted by the writer of Chronicles, probably living less than a century after Ezra himself promulgated the text? Also, how could the term *torah*, which earlier meant a priestly *practice*, come to be limited and specified to the extent that not long after Ezra's time it meant that very text?

The answers are certainly connected. It is no surprise that any group claiming authority will mystify the origins of its authority. But how can both Ezra's contemporaries and the succeeding generations that so closely scrutinized the words of the Pentateuch to the extent of finding significance even in its calligraphic ornamentation, fail to see in the text the very signs of its own constructedness? I think that the cognitive dissonance, by which contradictory items of knowledge or perception are perceived and sometimes forcibly harmonized, may be explored through the legends which survive in the Talmud (completed in two stages, about A.D. 200 and A.D. 500). Such an exploration will show, among other things, that in the midst of asserting the divine origin of the Pentateuch, that very dogma is in fact questioned. But at the same time, an increasing mystification of the material signifiers of the text deflected awareness from the painful contradiction, so that the *torah* as law and as ritual came to signify—in its totality—the divinity whose discourse was at best an historical, or otherwise, an imagined memory.

According to the (Babylonian) Talmud, Ezra was responsible for ten ordnances, two of which require that the Pentateuch be read publicly in the afternoon service of Sabbaths, and on Mondays and Thursdays as well (*Baba Qamma* 82a).[6] Yet Josephus (ca. A.D. 100) says that Moses ordained the reading on the Sabbath (*Contra Apionem* 2, 175). Furthermore, Deuteronomy, which of course antedates Ezra by some centuries, calls for the reading of "this book" once every *seven years*. The significance of institutionalizing this much more frequent reading is the fact and emblem of the replacement of God by text. By ritualizing the reading of a discourse *about* God by reading three times a week what Ricoeur calls "l'annonce de grande geste de Jahvé,"[7] the substitution of the discourse in the present for an impossible discourse in the past is effected. That discourse is now the subject of a communication *within the community* of Israelites, or more properly, Jews. But the ritual carries with it the imaginary element that the discourse about God as the "absent person," the subject of the message, is in fact an exchange *with* him. The Torah is now the grand and complex *sign* of the Divine, and something akin to worship is accorded the physical book, which by virtue of its dogmatically asserted *contiguity* with God replaces the contiguity lost when the second person of the discourse became, by virtue of his silence, the third, when the addresser became the message.

It is this contiguity which is of course reflected in the etymology and use of the word tradition (*traditio*, "handing over"). Thus, in the Mishnah: "Moses received the Torah at Sinai and transmitted it to Joshua, Joshua to the Elders, and the Elders to the Prophets, and the Prophets to [Ezra's] Great Assembly" (*Aboth*, ch. 1). Thus too the Talmudic dictum, "In ancient times when the Torah was forgotten from Israel, Ezra came up from Babylon and established it" (*Sukkah* 20a).

The means Ezra used to promulgate the "Law of God" which was "in his hand" and to manage its effective supersession of the previous documents on which it was based involved an ingenious and quite literal *re*writing. Until the Babylonian Exile (587 B.C.), Hebrew had been written in a Semitic script substantially identical to the Phoenician. In Babylonian Exile, if not before, the Israelites became acquainted with the Aramaic branch of this script (the "Assyrian script," or "square letters"). The older script was sometimes put to use during the following centuries, in the Samaritan Pentateuch and in the coins of the Bar Kokba era (A.D. 132–135).

Mar Zutra, or as some say, Mar ᶜUqba said, Originally the Torah was given to Israel in Hebrew characters and in the sacred [Hebrew] language; later in the times of Ezra the Torah was given in Assyrian script and the Aramaic language. [Finally] they selected for Israel the Assyrian script and Hebrew language, leaving the Hebrew characters and Aramaic language for the *hedyoṭoth* (Gr. *idiotes*). Who are the *"hedyoṭoth?"* R. Hisda said, the Samaritans. (*Sanhedrin* 21b)

And even though the Torah was not given through him [Ezra], its writing was changed through him. (ibid.)

Furthermore, the Mishnah, in tractate *Yadayim*, notes "The Aramaic sections in Ezra and Daniel render unclean the hands [i.e., are holy]. If an Aramaic section is translated into Hebrew, or a Hebrew section into Aramaic or [Old] Hebrew script, it does not render unclean the hands. It never renders unclean the hands unless it is written in the Assyrian script, on hide, and in ink."

Hence, for a text to be holy, it must be written in the square script, a script manifestly unknown to Moses, even though a form of the script which had survived from ancient times, the Old Hebrew, was still known and in occasinal use.

What else came from Sinai? An assertion, which, if offered in full awareness of its plain meaning must be ironic, is offered as follows:

R. Isaac said: the textual reading, as transmitted by the Scribes [Ezra was admitted to be the first such Scribe], their stylistic embellishments read [in the text] but not written, and words written but omitted in the reading are all from Moses at Sinai. (*Nedarim* 37b)

That is to say that the various *qre* and *ktib* annotations, words which appear in the text but are not to be read, or words which do not appear but are traditionally added, were all given by God to Moses at Sinai— instead of a clear text which, of course, had it been so transmitted, would have included the words originally intended. Furthermore, anonymous legal decisions, *for which no authority can be named*, are identified numerous times in the Talmud as "a legal decision from Moses at Sinai."

Two further traditions about Ezra may reflect a special kind of unknowing knowledge about his historical role. As noted above, Jeremiah's secretary was Baruch b. Neriah (Jer. 36:4: 45:1). Baruch must have been long dead by the time of Ezra's return, whether it occurred ca. 458

or 397 B.C. Yet in reply to the question why Ezra was not among the first to return from Babylon, the Talmud states "for as long as Baruch b. Neirah was alive, Ezra would not leave him to go up to the land of Israel" (*Megillah* 16b). Elsewhere in the same tractate, "R. Joshua b. Korha said Malachi is the same as Ezra, and the sages say that Malachi was his proper name" (15a).

That the sages of seven centuries later than Ezra lacked a clear chronology of the past may be assumed, and that they were often playful with history for homiletic purposes is no doubt true. But traditions which connect Ezra in the one case with the man who *wrote down* the final pre-exilic prophecies, and in the other identify him with the post-exilic prophecy which is both *anonymous* (Malachi is not properly a name: it means merely "my messenger") and is also traditionally the last legitimate prophecy ever to have been delivered, only point to an awareness, denied at the instant it is implied, that Ezra's work involved both the writing of a text and the conclusion of the prophetic era. The identification of Ezra with Malachi, while absolutely uncertain in historical terms, takes added significance from the reference in that prophecy to a divine Book whose author is made anonymous by a grammatical device:

Then they that feared the Lord spoke with one another,
And the Lord hearkened and heard,
And a book of remembrance was written before him
For them that feared the Lord and thought upon his name. (Mal. 3:16)

An anonymous addition to the book of Zechariah (ch. 9–14), dated to the generations immediately following Ezra, bears witness to the unmistakeable and utterly final demise of prophecy:

And also I will cause the prophets
And the unclean spirit to pass out of the land.
And it shall come to pass that, when any shall yet prophesy,
Then his father and his mother that begot him shall say unto him
Thou shalt not live, for thou speakest lies in the name of the Lord,
And his father and his mother that begot him shall thrust him through
When he prophesieth. (Zech. 13:2f.)

One final anecdote from the Talmud will demonstrate how thoroughly the intercourse with the divine was now rationalized. R. Eli^cezer b. Hyrkanos is convinced of his judgment in a minor legal detail. Failing to convince his colleagues, he cries out, "If the *halakah* (legal doctrine) agrees with me, let it be proved from Heaven." Whereupon a heavenly voice cries out, "Why do you dispute with R. Eli^cezer, seeing that in all matters *halakah* agrees with him? But R. Joshua arises and exclaims, "It [the law] is not in heaven!" (Deut. 30:12). "What did he mean by this?" R. Jeremiah says that he meant that since the Torah had already been given at Mt. Sinai, we pay no attention to a heavenly voice. "Because Thou hast long since written in the Torah at Mt. Sinai, 'After the majority one must incline'" (Exod. 23:2). Elijah the Prophet (ninth century B.C.), who according to legend frequently revisited the world of the living, asked what the heavenly response to this colloquy was, replied that God laughed with joy, exclaiming, "My sons have outsmarted Me, My sons have outsmarted Me" (*Baba Mesia* 59b).

III THE HOLY OF HOLIES

No reliable account exists of the design and furnishing of Solomon's Temple. The fictional accounts that are included in the Old Testament presumably reflect in large part the Second Temple, built by the returned exiles and their compatriots ca. 520–515 B.C. This forcing of the image of the successor onto the original is part and parcel of the practice of the final, Priestly redaction of the text, which suppresses whatever the earlier documents reflected of the diachronic, replacing the historicity of the text as far as possible with the synchrony of present discourse. As intercourse with the divine recedes from present to past imagination, the *told thing* loses its quality of process and all perspective is reduced to the narrow lines of the present, spoken language. Still, a certain limited historical memory may have been allowed.

Within the structure of the Temple itself, one third of the area was reserved as the "Holy of Holies," or *debir* ("oracle"?). Into this most holy place, separated from the rest of the interior by a curtain, the presiding Priest entered only on the Day of Atonement (Lev. 16). Our text, a portion of the Priestly Document, identifies "the holy place within the veil" as the very locus of divine presence: "For I appear in the cloud upon the mercy seat" (16:2).[8] The furnishings of this room are described (in a heavily reedited text) in 1 Kings 6:23–28. At some point, either in Solomon's Temple or early in the history of the Second Temple, two cherubim (not the figures of Italian painting, but very likely winged serpents) whose wings outstretched touched both walls and met in the middle of the room, stood over the "ark of the covenant" (1 Kings 8:6). "There was nothing in the ark save the two tablets of stone which Moses put there at Horeb" (8:9). Yet in Deuteronomy, Moses commands the Levites to put the "book of this Torah" next to or in the ark (31:26). It is not hard to conclude with Wellhausen (pp. 392 ff.) that what is significant in the original story is not the words of the "Torah" or the decalogue inscribed on the stone, but at least in the earliest period the ark itself. Only later, as presence yielded to ritual, and discourse to Law, did the secondary, metonymic addition to the stones become the locus of the sacred. "If there were stones in it at all, they probably served some other purpose than that of writing materials." If there was any message on the stones, they would have been exposed to public view, like the Twelve Tables or other such engraved laws or treaties. The stones, if they existed at all, were almost certainly blank. Or else they were lost in the Babylonian destruction of Jerusalem, and the reservation of the Holy of Holies to the annual visit of the High Priest amounted to the mystification of their absence. In either case, they testify to an Absence nearly as profound as that enforced by later doctrine in an imageless God whose very name could not be pronounced.

In fact, the history of the Holy of Holies is a history of an accretion of absence. If there was an ark, it must have been removed before the Temple was rebuilt. If there were cherubim at all in the Second Temple, they must at some other, undertermined moment in history have been removed as well. Only the astonishment at finding an utterly vacant room at the very center of awe could have given rise to the slanders current in the Hellenistic world about the mysterious contents of the sanctuary. Josephus denounces two such blasphemies:

Apion dared to claim that in this sanctuary the Jews had placed the head of an ass, which they worshipped with all piety. (*Cont. Ap.* 2, 80)

[Apion] claims that Antiochus [Epiphanes, who broke into the Temple ca. 169 B.C.] found a couch in the Temple with a man reclining before a bedecked table. (ibid. 2, 91)

Elsewhere, Josephus states simply that "in this room there was nothing at all" (*Bell.* 5,5,5).

The Gospels appear to use the Old Testament as recurrent, if intermittent, intertext. A kind of semioclastic intertextuality occurs in the narrative of the two women who come to dress the body of the crucified Jesus (Luke 24:1 ff.). For what they find, instead of the body, is a significant and profound emptiness. They find in fact, no *thing* at all, but instead of the object, a message. The tradition which was to base itself on the Gospels appropriated, if that is the word, the eloquent, atoning, emptiness.[9]

It seems inevitable that the systematic alteration we have reviewed involves a set of complex coordinations, all of which are mutually dependent. God is replaced by Text, which then becomes the signifier both of God and the index of his silence. The impossibility of speaking *with* God is replaced by speaking *of* God. Practice becomes Law, engendering a skewed infinitude of legal discourse in the legal compendia of the Talmud and its progeny. Perhaps most interesting is what happens to the name of God. It is written into the Hebrew text as YHWH, a word which became utterly forbidden to pronounce. Seeing the now ineffable Name, the Jew pronounced (and pronounces) a euphemism, *Adonai* ("My Lord"). In thus encountering God through the deixis of a refusal to pronounce, he practices *différance*, or indeed, *déference*. The *différance* between the letters read and phonemes pronounced diagrams the very space between the Name and Whom it denominates, a speaking space, a gap filled by a mystery.

NOTES

1. This observation is further elaborated in my "Law, Ritual, Absence," *Hartford Studies in Literature* 9 (1977): 164–74.
2. Julius Welhausen, *Prolegomena to the History of Ancient Israel* (Cleveland: World Publishing Co., 1957), p. 394. (First German ed., 1878.)
3. Robert Pfeiffer, *Introduction to the Old Testament* (New York: Harper, 1948), p. 791, claims that "the Chronicler is the first writer to attribute the entire Pentateuch to the inspired pen of Moses."
4. This observation is due to William L. Holladay, "Jeremiah and Moses," *Journal of Biblical Literature* 85 (1966): 17–27.
5. The text says that Ezra was commissioned in the seventh year of Artaxerxes. It is uncertain whether the First or Second Artaxerxes is intended. The dates would be either 458 B.C. or 397 B.C. Due to a variety of chronological problems within the narrative, other dates in between these two have been suggested. Even Shakespeare confused the Edwards in his history plays.
6. The pagination of the Talmud cited in each case is the traditional form used in all editions. A convenient English translation (adopted here, with corrections) is published by the Soncino Press (London, 1952).
7. In "Structure et herméneutique," *Esprit* (Nov. 1963), pp. 596–628.
8. The word *kapporeth* may mean "ark-cover," or else should be amended to *paroketh*, by a simple metathesis, in which case the phrase should read "I appear in the cloud opposite the veil."
9. This moment in the text has been treated at length by Louis Marin in "Les femmes au tombeau," *Langages* 22:39–50.

NINE
ON THE MESSIANIC STRUCTURE OF WALTER BENJAMIN'S LAST REFLECTIONS
Irving Wohlfarth

> The smallest guarantee, the straw at which
> the drowning man clutches . . .
> Benjamin

IN THE BEGINNING was the world of the Greek epic; in the end its equivalent is to be re-established; the present is the fallen interim, alienation. Such is the three-part story, beginning, middle, and end, thesis, antithesis, and synthesis, told by Georg Lukács in *Die Theorie des Romans*. The major work of his pre-Marxist phase, it was, on his own later account, heavily indebted to German Idealist sources.[1] Triadic patterns did not, furthermore, cease to structure his thinking even after his self-proclaimed break with his idealist past. Nor is such idealist materialism an isolated case. *Die Theorie des Romans* was to become an influential source book for an esthetics that generally provides ample material for the positivist critique of Marxism as a disguised form of Messianism. In the celebrated parable of the dwarf and the automat that inaugurates his last reflections on the philosophy of history, "Über den Begriff der Geschichte,"[2] Walter Benjamin interpreted his own Marxism as just that. Now that its accompanying notes and fragments have also been published, it is possible, thanks largely to their cross-references to his earlier writings, to piece together Benjamin's version of the messianic triad. To reassemble its elements into such a structure is no doubt to risk oversystematizing Benjamin's fragmentary and disparate corpus. On the other hand, fragmentariness and reunification belong precisely to the periodicity of the triadic scheme.

I

The history of esthetic forms sketched in Benjamin's essay on the storyteller, "Der Erzähler," acknowledges its indebtedness to Lukács's theory of the novel. It refers back to its epic point of departure:

> Mnemosyne, the rememberer, was the Muse of the epic art among the Greeks. This name takes the observer back to a world-historical parting of the ways. For if the record kept by memory—historiography—constitutes the creative indifference [*schöpferische Indifferenz*] of the various epic forms (as great prose is the creative indifference of the various metrical forms), its oldest form, the epic, encompasses in undifferentiated form [*kraft einer Art von Indifferenz*] the story and the novel. (S, 2, p. 245)

The epic is "the oldest form" of historiography. It is a kind of *a priori* synthesis, an originary, undivided unity that contains within itself the latent potentialities of the two forms that will be heir to the dissociation of epic sensibility. That division marks a "world-historical parting of the ways." This does not, however, signify their parallel, if opposite, evolution in time. If both are originally given as simultaneous possibilities within the epic, their later actualization is not synchronic. On the contrary, the rise of the novel, which, as Ian Watt has also shown, coincides with the rise of the bourgeoisie, marks the beginning of the end of the story.

> The earliest sign of a process which ends with the decline of storytelling is the rise of the novel at the beginning of the modern period. . . . It took the novel, whose beginnings go back to antiquity, hundreds of years before it encountered in the developing middle class the elements which brought it to fruition. With the emergence of these elements storytelling began quite slowly to recede into the archaic. . . . (ibid., pp. 233, 235)

(Marx argues likewise that many of the features of capitalism can be traced back to antiquity but crystallize *into* capitalism only in the modern period.) Esthetic forms evolve according to millennial rhythms. The decline and fall of storytelling is a very gradual process, which approaches its final end only with the First World War (ibid., p. 230). Thus the historical relation between novel and story is one neither of simultaneity nor of succession. They overlap. Even where they coexist in time, they have "wholly different historical coordinates" (ibid., p. 247). The storyteller *in* modern times is *of* a different time and place. Nikolai Leskov, Benjamin's chosen example, adheres to the world of the Greek Orthodox Church. Notwithstanding the "world-historical parting of the ways," the story is earlier, closer to the epic than the novel. Among the "variations of the epic" it takes "first place" (ibid., p. 245). Even though it cannot be located at the point of "creative indifference" already occupied by the epic proper, it implicitly assumes its function. Indeed, Benjamin proceeds to contrast the novel and the *story* to exactly the same effect that Lukács counterposes to the novel and the *epic*: "immanence of meaning" and a transcendental "home" versus the quest for meaning and "transcendental homelessness" (ibid., p. 246) in Lukács's scheme, wisdom ("the epic side of truth" [p. 233]) and counsel versus "profound perplexity" in Benjamin's. The story here takes over something of the role there performed by the epic.³ But as only one of two derivative forms it must also be more partial than the epic, which encompasses them both. Mnemosyne is the Muse of the epic, and it is in terms of two subtypes of memory that the story and the novel are contrasted:

Memory establishes the chain of tradition that hands events down from generation to generation. . . . It encompasses the . . . varieties of the epic. First among these is the one embodied by the storyteller. It ultimately establishes a whole network of interrelated stories. The next one starts where the last left off, as the great storytellers, especially the Oriental ones, always liked to show. In each of them there lives a Scheherezade to whom at every point a fresh story occurs. Such is epic *memory [Gedächtnis]* and the storyteller's Muse. Against it is to be set another principle, the Muse of the novel, which initially—that is to say, in the epic—lies concealed, not yet differentiated from that of the story. In epics it can at most be occasionally divined, particularly at such solemn Homeric moments as the initial invocations of the Muse. What these passages prefigure is the perpetuating [*verewigend*] memory of the novelist as opposed to the short-lived [*kurzweilig*] reminiscences of the storyteller. The former is dedicated to the *one* hero, the *one* odyssey or the *one* struggle; the latter, to the *many* scattered [*zerstreut*] occurrences. It is, in other words, *remembrance [Eingedenken]* that, as the novelist's Muse, joins memory [*Gedächtnis*], the storyteller's, their original unity having come apart with the disintegration of the epic. (Ibid., pp. 245–46)

Since the "fall" of the epic, Mnemosyne has been separated into *Gedächtnis* and *Eingedenken*,⁴ the memory of the many and the remembrance of the one.

Historiography represents, according to our original quotation, the "creative indifference" of all the epic forms. The relation is likened to that of white light to the colors of the spectrum (ibid., p. 243). The epic, another instance of creative indifference, is the oldest form of both. And the epic genre that, like the story in relation to the epic, has *historiographic* pride of place (and functions in turn as the common denominator for the other narrative forms) is the chronicle, which is indeed defined as "history-telling." Like all stories, chronicles are essentially oral even where they appear in print. And between the oral chronicle and written history there is, after all, a decisive difference. Unlike the chronicle—and like the novel, which is also predicated on the printing press—historiography proper, which aims to "explain" chains of events, cannot "rest content" to embed them in a divine scheme of things (ibid.). Telling stories and writing history remain quite different activities even when the framework of the story is no longer unambiguously religious:

> Is its perspective that of religious or natural history [*heilsgeschichtlich oder naturgeschichtlich*]? All that is certain is that . . . it stands outside all properly historical categories. Leskov tells us that the age when man could believe himself to be in harmony with nature has run its course. Schiller called this era the age of naive poetry. The storyteller keeps faith with it. . . . (Ibid., p. 244)

The storyteller keeps faith with a pre-historical paradise lost, and Benjamin's own historical narrative, itself a sustained act of memory, keeps faith in turn with the irrevocably disappearing figure of the storyteller. In *Die Theorie des Romans* such *dédoublement* took the form of a thoroughgoing identification with the novel. Protagonist, novelist, and philosopher-critic respectively mourned the memory of the epic. Nor did the constitutive irony in which Lukács grounded the novel form do anything to mitigate this collective triadic nostalgia. The recurrence of such triadic patterns in analyses that reproduce them in the very act of situating them is eloquent testimony to their power. They then function as both part and whole, structure analysis and analysed alike.

Like "Der Erzähler," "Über den Begriff der Geschichte" is devoted to the "problem of remembrance (and forgetting)" (*GS*, 1, 3, p. 1226)—namely, to the pressing issue, here and now in 1940, of writing and, almost synonymously, making history "against the grain" (*GS*, 1, 2, p. 697) of prevailing history and historiography. Whereas the latter (which Benjamin summarily equates with historicism) "feels its way into the victor" (ibid., p. 696), a messianic materialism must swim against the stream (ibid., p. 698) and help break open the historical continuum. Historical materialism is to "take theology into its service" (ibid., p. 693) and to "save" past and present together. To do so is, among other things, to remember memory itself, to rescue from oblivion the two forms of memory that have, according to "Der Erzähler," been distributed among various more or less literary forms of narration. If historiography proper was there distinguished from them, the forms of memory they embody are here invoked in its name. Memory, regressive by definition, has been superseded—that is, forgotten—in and by the headlong "progress" of modern history; and by "remaining content to establish a causal nexus of various moments of history" (ibid., p. 704) modern historiography—which came into being with the distinction between "resting content" to "exhibit" the way of the world and "explaining" it as a "precise chain [*Verkettung*] of particular events" (*S*, 2, p. 243)—now merely serves to ratify this oblivion. It is Benjamin's central thesis that genuine historical memory takes the form of messianic contacts between the present and specific moments of the past. This may also be said to apply to the relation between memory itself and its two increasingly archaic constituents, *Gedächtnis* and *Eingedenken*. In each Benjamin discovers a messianic potential at the very moment when they are threatened with final extinction—namely, at the beginning of the Second World War.

Leskov was, we read in "Der Erzähler," decisively influenced by the Greek Orthodox doctrine that *all* souls enter paradise, and "interpreted the Resurrection less as transfiguration than as the breaking of a spell [*Entzauberung*], in a sense akin to the fairy tale"—namely, as "magical escape" (ibid., p. 251). The third section of "Über den Begriff der Geschichte" returns to the figure of the chronicler, the history-teller, and interprets his epic enumeration of "the many, scattered events" in similarly redemptive terms:

The chronicler who recounts [*hererzählt*] events without distinguishing the large from the small thereby takes into acocunt the following truth: nothing that has ever taken place is to be given up as lost for history. To be sure, only a redeemed humanity is granted [*fällt zu*] the fullness of its past. (GS, 1, 2, p. 694)

The history-*teller* (re)counts [(*herer*)*zählt*] all souls. He tells time, all of it, and his chronicle is utopian because it is unselective. If it anticipates the Last Judgment, this is because it makes no discrimination. It does not focus exclusively on the great events of history; it does not, that is, feel its way into the victors. By contrast, the storyteller's mystical materialism enables him to feel his way into matter itself. The hierarchy of his world, far from coinciding with that of the social order, is that of "all created creatures" (S. 2, p. 253), including the very lowest, which are not simply the underlings of the highest: "The mineral is the lowest stratum of created things. For the storyteller, however, it is directly joined to the highest" (ibid., p. 256). The chronicler who does not distinguish between large and small events in his historiographic counterpart. He helps history magically escape from itself. But his resurrection of the past is messianic in a further sense. It is possible only under utopian conditions.

Eingedenken shares similarly messianic potentialities, but it is not only in a redeemed world that they are activated. "Über den Begriff der Geschichte" twice cities it by name:

The sense that they are exploding the continuum of history is peculiar to revolutionary classes at the moment they enter into action. The great revolution introduced a new calendar. The inaugural day of a calendar functions as a historical time-lapse camera. And it is essentially the same day that keeps recurring in the form of holy days, which are days of remembrance [*Tage des Eingedenkens*]. Thus calendars do not count [*zählen*] time like clocks. (GS, 1,2, pp. 701-2)

The soothsayers who elicited what time had in store certainly did not experience time as either homogeneous or empty. Anyone who bears this in mind will perhaps get an idea of how past time was experienced in remembrance [*Eingedenken*]—namely, in just the same way. The Jews are known for having been forbidden to investigate the future. The Torah and prayer, on the other hand, instruct them in remembrance. This stripped the future of its magic [*entzauberte*] to which all those succumb who fetch enlightenment from soothsayers. (ibid., p. 704)

Jewish prayer and revolutionary action are hardly identical. Common to both, however, is the interruption of the ongoing time of hours and weeks, "progress" forever on the way to a future which is both more of the same and never-never land in one. The calendar, be it religious or revolutionary, arrests the progress of the clock; or rather it combines quantity with quality:

The temporal order that places its homogeneity above [Bergson's] *durée* cannot but allow for the continued persistence of heterogeneous, outstanding fragments of time. To have combined the recognition of quality with the measurement of quantity was the work of the calendars, which leave spaces for remembrance [*Stellen des Eingedenkens*] blank, as it were, in the form of holy days. (Ibid., pp. 642–43)

Such forms of memory mark an emphatic experience of time and the temporality of experience. Their disappearance means the end of experience and the mere marking of time; the transformation of holy days into holidays and weekends deprives the week of its end. If historiography originates as the casual explanation of punctual events in linear sequence, pure homogeneous successivity punctuates historical consciousness out of existence. Where time is equivalent to perpetual motion, the revolutionary possibility of historical standstill is precluded.

Thus calendars do not tell time like clocks. They are monuments of a historical consciousness of which not the slightest traces have been apparent in Europe for a hundred years.

. . . calendars leave spaces for remembrance blank, as it were, in the form of holy days. The man who is bereft of experience feels as if he had been dropped from the calendar. The city dweller knows this feeling on Sundays: Baudelaire has it *avant la lettre* in one of the *Spleen* poems.

Like the *Gedächtnis* of the chronicler, *Eingedenken* rescues the past, but rescues it, if not from the chronicler, then at least from the chronological time marked by his historicist descendants. It is in this context that the partial nature of such *Gedächtnis* and the antithesis between the two forms of memory comes most clearly into focus. The chronicle, too, tells time by the calendar, not the clock. It is, however, hardly equipped to arrest the flow of time, but only to attend to the broad diversity of its rhythms. Epic *Gedächtnis* "assimilates the course of events" (*S*, 2, p. 245). How, then, could it "interrupt the course of the world"? (*GS*, 1, 2, p. 667). It is *kurzweilig*, diverting, but also easily diverted; it does not hold firm to any particular event, but goes on to the next.

The "angel of history," in stark contrast, backs into the future, stares in fascinated horror at the wreckage of the past, and would "dwell" (*verweilen*) on it—a melancholy version of the Faustian *Verweile doch*. He could not tear himself away from it; he is torn away only by the force of destruction itself:

There is a picture by Klee called "Angelus Novus." It shows an angel who looks as if he were about to move away from something he is staring at. . . . His face is turned toward the past. Where a chain of events appears before *us*, he sees a single catastrophe that ceaselessly piles wreckage on wreckage and hurls it in front of his feet. He would doubtless want to stay [*verweilen*], to awake the dead and join together what has been smashed. But a storm is blowing from Paradise. It has got caught in his wings, and is so strong that the angel can no longer close them. This storm propels him inexorably into the future, to which his back is turned; meanwhile the pile of debris before him grows to the heavens. What we call progress is *this* storm. (*GS*, 1, 2, pp. 697–98)

Today's historian cannot see the wood for the trees. Not to perceive in the disaster called history anything but a harmless, orderly "chain of events" is to succumb to the short-sightedness of latter-day *Gedächtnis*. Never was *Eingedenken*, the persistence of memory, more needed. It is best translated as "recollection" or "remembrance": the angel's *Eingedenken* is motivated by the urge to re-collect the broken past, to re-member the dismembered. The novelist's "perpetuating" remembrance is devoted to the *one* hero, the *one* odyssey, the *one* struggle. Similarly, the angel's wide-open eyes perceive the whole of history as a "single catastrophe"; therein they outdo the calendrical "time-lapse camera." If *Gedächtnis* is synonymous with expansiveness, "epic breadth," diversity and diversion, *Eingedenken* connotes concentration on the particular moment and the "enormous abridgment" (ibid., p. 703) that telescopes mankind's history into a moment. The angel of history, the allegorical embodiment of *Eingedenken*, reenacts the allegory of melancholy, and the melancholy of allegory, anatomized in *Ursprung des deutschen Trauerspiels*. Differing forms of memory embodied in divergent genres, each nevertheless animated by the same impulse to break the mythical spell cast over the past, *Gedächtnis* and *Eingedenken* perhaps also function as the antidote to the other's potential relapse into myth—*Gedächtnis*, to the paralyzing spell of melancholy; *Eingedenken*, to complicity with Chronos.

Eingedenken is associated in "Der Erzähler" with the novel and in "Über den Begriff der Geschichte" with Juadism.[5] Could it be that these heterogeneous identifications come together in the figure of one of Benjamin's favorite novelists, Marcel Proust? Proustian memory, at all events, embodies an authentically modern form of *Eingedenken* and combines novelistic *Eingedenken* with epic *Gedächtnis*. "Der Erzähler" showed how the historical dynamic that underlay the rise of the novel gradually undermined the story and, with the spread of the press, finally imperilled both (S, 2, p. 235). To undertake in modern times to tell the story of one's life would, in this perspective, be to swim against the world-historical tide. Such, according to "Über einige Motive bei Baudelaire," is Proust's strenuous wager:

> The insulation of information against experience further derives from the fact that the former does not enter "tradition." Newspapers appeared in mass circulation. No reader so readily has at his disposal the stories someone else might want to hear him tell [*was sich der andere von ihm erzählen liesse*].— Historically, the various forms of communication competed with one another. The replacement of older narratives by information, and information by sensation, reflects the increasing atrophy of experience. All these forms in turn emerge against the background of the story, which is one of the oldest forms of communication. . . . Proust's eight-volume work conveys an idea of what was involved in restoring the figure of the storyteller to the present. (*GS*, 1, 2, p. 611)

Proust reconstructs his life's experience in an age that Benjamin variously describes in terms of the "impoverishment of experience." He is the storyteller out of his natural element. It is, under the *right* conditions, granted to the storyteller "to reach back over a whole lifetime. . . . His gift is his life, and his dignity the ability to tell it in its entirety" (S, 2, p. 258). Proust's venture is correspondingly problematic:

> From the outset he was confronted with the basic task of giving an account of his childhood. In claiming that it was a matter of chance whether it could be done at all, he gave the full measure of its difficulty. In this context he coined the notion of *mémoire involontaire*. It bears the traces of the situation that gave rise to it. It belongs to the inventory of the variously isolated individual. Where experience [*Erfahrung*] in the strict sense obtains, certain elements of an individual's past combine in memory [*Gedächtnis*] with those of the collective past. Rituals, with their ceremonies and feasts (which Proust, it seems, nowhere recalls [*gedacht*]) kept intermingling these two components of memory [*Gedächtnis*] afresh. They would prompt remembrance [*Eingedenken*] at particular times and remained its handles for life. Voluntary and involuntary memory thus lose their mutual exclusiveness. (*GS*, 1, 2, p. 611)

Storytelling and, correlatively, "experience in the strict sense" are possible, according to "Der Erzähler," only under certain socio-historical conditions. Collective artisanal production constitutes their economic substructure; spinning yarns has to do with spinning yarn. Storytelling is itself a kind of "handicraft"; and calendrical feast days (*Feiertage*), the "days of remembrance," represent in turn "handles" of memory. The calendar, the temporal precondition of experience, intermingles its private and public dimensions, measurable time and its "heterogeneous, outstanding fragments." Just as the decline of the epic entails the dissociation of epic memory, so the bourgeois secularization of the calendar results in a (Bergsonian) dichotomy between subjective and objective time. The novel is written and read in isolation (*S*, 2, p. 234); therewith the social conditions of epic totality have disappeared. Deprived of the mnemonic institutions whereby a society renews its traditions and prompts the individual to recall his past, the isolated subject, unlike the storyteller, no longer has his biography at his disposal. All that he is "granted" are haphazard epiphanies, heterogeneous fragments, intermittent, entirely private memories. If *Eingedenken* was from the outset synonymous with the difficulty of recapturing past time—it first appears in the solemn (*feierlich*) epic invocation of the Muse—it is now to an unprecedented degree beyond individual control: "It is, according to Proust, a matter of chance whether the individual gets a picture of himself, whether he can take hold of his experience" (*GS*, 1, 2, p. 610). Memory—or at least the memory that counts—is fragmented into "involuntary" shocks and flashes that arrest the temporal continuum and enact "dialectics at a standstill" (*S*, 1, p. 418). Benjamin translates *mémoire involontaire* as *unwillkürliches Eingedenken*. Though lacking in either the element of conscious concentration elsewhere associated with *Eingedenken* or the easy, relaxed continuity with which stories "occur" (*einfallen*) to their teller, it proves, contrary to appearances, the most promising form of remembrance available to the present. With this latest dissociation of memory the hardening alternative lies between good fragments and bad wholes, between voluntary memory, which, as in the case of historicism, makes spuriously epic claims for itself, and *mémoire involontaire*, which henceforth functions as the legitimate heir of epic memory, even though—or because—it possesses none of its characteristic qualities. For the messianic restoration of the first stage of the triad can, it will repeatedly emerge, come about only through its negation at the second. One day voluntary and involuntary memory will again lose their mutual exclusiveness and the chronicle will fulfill its promise. "Only to a redeemed humanity will its past be fully granted [*zufallen*]." Such a state of grace will no longer be stumbled on exclusively by chance (*Zufall*). But before the messianic age of total recall all chronicles will be necessarily fragmentary. Benjamin's own childhood recollections, *Berliner Kindheit um Neunzehnhundert* and *Berliner Chronik*, are cases in point.

Proust is concerned solely to salvage his own past; its salvation is, he keeps intimating, his "private affair" (*GS*, 1, 2, p. 643). For the author of "Über den Begriff der Geschichte," on the other hand, salvation has come to assume, on the eve of the Second World War, world-historical dimensions. Resituated in a supra-individual context, Proustian memory remains the privileged agency of redemption:

> The historical articulation of the past involves recognizing in the past the elements that come together in the constellation of one and the same moment. Historical cognition is possible only in the historical instant. Cognition at a historical instant is, however, always the cognition of an instant. By contracting into an instant—into a dialectical image—it enters the involuntary memory of mankind. (GS, 1, 3, p. 1233)

But such fleeting instants of involuntary memory represent no more than fragmentary redemptions of the unredeemed past. Their messianic contact takes place in a present (*Jetztzeit*) which, however intense, is no more than "shot through" with "slivers" of "messianic time" (ibid., p. 704). Just as a cup of tea harbors the whole of Marcel's childhood, so, it is true, the isolated historical monad contains "the whole course of history" (ibid., p. 703). But whereas the *mémoire volontaire* of the historicist survey (course) provides a neat overview of the whole preestablished order of history—the obverse side, this, of its short-sightedness, and a far cry from the stark spectacle that meets the angel's eyes—, the hallmark of involuntary memory is a certain "disorder":

> (The image of the past that flares up in the now of its recognizability [*im Jetzt seiner Erkennbarkeit*] . . . resembles the images of one's own past that line up [*antreten*] at a moment of danger. These images come involuntarily. Historiography in the strict sense is thus an image taken from involuntary memory, an image that suddenly presents itself to the subject of history at the moment of danger. . . . What occurs to involuntary memory is—and this distinguishes it from voluntary memory—never a course of events but solely an image. (Hence "disorder" as the visual space [*Bildraum*] of involuntary memory)). (GS, 1, 3, p. 1243)

Involuntary memory is no longer prompted by the chance encounters of an individual biography. It is precipitated by a historical crisis that at once destroys the epic dimension of memory and reestablishes something of its collective function. The emergency also dictates a certain order amidst seeming "disorder;" *antreten* means "to fall in" in the military sense; it is only when measured against the historicist "chain of events" that the compelling logic of involuntary association appears chaotic.

Nowhere, we will see, is the disorder of this *Bildraum* more emphatically evoked than in the final pages of Benjamin's essay on surrealism. It closes by describing the surrealists as "exchanging the play of their features for the dial of an alarm clock that rings for sixty seconds of every minute" (*AN*, p. 215). Only a permanent alarm can rouse history out of its clockwork nightmare. Salvation (*Rettung*) is also to be understood as rescue in the literal sense. And while the historical materialist is, according to the published text of "Über den Begriff der Geschichte," to swim against the stream, Benjamin's notes evoke the possibility of being drowned by the historical deluge. It is the drowning man who proverbially sees the whole of his past flash by his mind's eye—and who grasps at straws. These two motifs are in turn compressed into two telegraphic jottings: "The smallest guarantee, the straw at which the drowning man grasps . . . : *Eingedenken* as the straw" (*GS*, 1, 3, pp. 1243–44). Such is *Eingedenken* in its final spasmodic contraction. The "dialectical image" of the past, the "true" image that "flashes by, never to be seen again" (*GS*, 1, 2, p. 695), is itself the straw:

This concept [of *Jetztzeit*] grounds a relation between historiography and politics that is identical to the theological interrelation between remembrance and redemption. This present crystallizes in images that can be called dialectical. They represent mankind's "saving grace" [*"rettenden Einfall" der Menschheit*]. (*GS*, 1, 2, p. 1248)

If the dialectical images of involuntary memory can themselves offer precarious hope of salvation, this is because the redemption of the past by the present is also a reciprocal process. To rescue the past is also to rediscover the messianic resources with which to seize the present, and vice versa. Just as historiography is inseparable from politics, so involuntary memory coincides with the "presence of mind" (ibid., pp. 1242, 1244) that can arrest time and transform the present into *Jetztzeit*—in short, save the day—only by mobilizing the relevant past. Far from being confined to the passive contemplation of inner images, *Eingedenken* (which was associated with the revolutionary calendar) marks the inauguration of a new present. But the metaphor of the straw also implies that the *nunc stans* of involuntary memory is at best a moment's grace, and can no more avert disaster than, say, prayer—itself a hallowed form of *Eingedenken*.[6] Unlike more pragmatic, "progressive," social-democratic solutions, however, such remembrance does not at least face the wrong way or play into the wrong hands. Such is Benjamin's hope against hope. "Only for the sake of the hopeless is hope given to us" (*GS*, 1, 1, p. 201). At an earlier juncture in the crisis of historical memory, Nietzsche had redefined it as an interaction of contradictory impulses, the monumental, the critical, and the piously antiquarian. In the act of Benjaminian *Eingedenken*, Jewish prayer and the revolutionary calendar, melancholy and action, all converge.

As for the story of his own life, Benjamin knew that Proust could not be emulated:

The towering literary achievement of our time is assigned a place in the heart of the impossible. . . . This great realization of a "life's work" stands as the last for a long time. The image of Proust is the highest physiognomic expression which the relentlessly growing discrepancy between poetry and life could assume. (S, 2, p. 132)

This discrepancy is in no way mitigated—but on the contrary confirmed—by a certain parallelism between private and public history. It marks their synchronization, not their reconciliation. The last paragraph of Benjamin's fragmentary memoir *Berliner Kindheit um Neunzehnhundert* anticipates his last-minute reflections on the collective historical subject *in extremis*:

I imagine that the "whole life," which, one tells oneself [*sich erzählt*], passes before dying men's gaze, is composed of such images as the little man has of us all. They flit quickly past like the pages of those stiff-bound little books that were once the predecessors of the cinema. . . . (S, 1 p,. 652)

The "little man" in question is the hunchback, *das bucklichte Männlein*, who at that time belonged to the folklore of a German childhood. It is he who is responsible for all the mischief of one's life, for broken pots and bruises:

Anyone whom this little man looks at fails to pay attention. To himself and also to the little man. He stands in consternation before a heap of broken pieces. . . . But otherwise he did nothing to me, the grey bailff, except to levy his share of oblivion [*den Halbpart des Vergessens einzutreiben*] for every single thing I happened upon:
        Will ich in mein Stüblein gehn,
        Will mein Müslein essen;
        Steht ein bucklicht Männlein da,
        Hat's schon halber 'gessen.
The little man often stood there. But I never saw him. Only he always looked at me—all the more closely, the less I saw of myself. (ibid., p. 651)

'*Gessen* stands, in this retrospective interpretation of a childhood nursery rhyme, for *vergessen* ("forgotten"), not *gegessen* ("eaten"). The hunchback penalizes us for every act of inattention. He takes away what was "given" to the storyteller—the ability to tell one's own life. All that is left of that gift is a somber counterpart to the "historical time-lapse camera," namely, a dying man's instantaneous recapitulation of his life—unless, that is, even this popular belief in a synoptic last-minute vita is itself no more than a story that "one tells oneself." The "whole life" that flashes past at that instant is, clearly, no longer whole. It is Eliot's "heap of broken images." "He stand in consternation before a heap of broken pieces." The images that the hunchback "has of us all" are those of our collected misfortunes. The past that we finally glimpse would thus resemble the "facies hippocratica of history" as perceived by its angel or allegorist, "history in all its untimeliness, suffering, failure" (S, 1, pp. 289–90). (The little bailiff is himself an allegorical figure, a relative of

Time, Death, and the Devil, the creditors who forever hover invisibly about us.) A dark version, this, of *"Eingedenken* as the straw" and *Le Temps Retrouvé*. The happy Proustian epiphany is replaced by a premonitory sample of the involuntary images that will be belatedly released only by the last misfortune of all. The negativity of the past is, Horkheimer wrote to Benjamin, "irreparable": "This applies in the first instance to the existence of the individual, in which it is not happiness but unhappiness that is sealed by death" (Tiedemann, "Historischer Materialismus," p. 88). Benjamin published his childhood recollections in 1938, the time of the "gathering storm," two years before "Über den Begriff der Geschichte" and the holocaust which sealed his fate.

But the nursery rhyme closes with the dwarf's conversion from spoiler to suppliant, and it is with his prayer that Benjamin's memoir also closes:

The little man also has the images of me.[7] He saw me in my hiding place and in front of the otter's dungeon, on winter mornings and in front of the telephone in the back of the hall. . . . Now he has done his work. Yet his voice . . . whispers to me over the threshold of the century:
Liebes Kindlein, ach ich bitt,
Bet fürs bucklicht Männlein mit. (ibid., p. 652)

To this reversal of the dwarf's role there corresponds an unobtrusive maneuver on the writer's part. For in reviewing the cinematographic sequence of his childhood past in quasi-epic accents—*and* being, he elsewhere shows, the conjunction out of which chronicles are built (*S*, 2, p. 242)—Benjamin demonstrates the opposite of what he says. The narrator shows that he *is*, however partially, a narrator. The images he knows the little man to have he thereby has himself. It seems that he has paid attention after all, at least retrospectively, and his memoir would be an act of literary *Tikkun* that pieces the broken vessel together. *Wo Gefahr ist*, wrote Hölderlin, *wächst das Rettende auch*: such would be the hopeful version of *"Eingedenken* as the straw." But the conclusion of the memoir remains profoundly ambiguous. "Now he has done his work." Is the dwarf now definitively converted, and has he, like Mephisto, been working all along on the side of the good—that is, on behalf of the chronicle, the narrative genre of a redeemed humanity? Or will his harmful work continue, in far less diminutive form, beyond childhood? And is the narrator, in quoting the hunchback's plea to be included in the prayers of the younger generation, also seeking inclusion in ours? Having redeemed what he can of his past, is he now laying claim to our redemptive attention?

It is in the last section of the essay on Kafka that the little hunchback first appears in Benjamin's writings. He figures as "the archetype of distortion":

This little man presides over life's distortions [*der Insasse des entsellten Lebens*]; he will disappear with the coming of the Messiah, who, according to a great Rabbi, does not want to change the world by violence but will merely make slight readjustments to it [*um ein Geringes sie zurechtstellen*]. (*AN*, p. 263)

A hunchback in Kafka's universe is, Benjamin shows, a back bent by a burden of fatigue or guilt that is synonymous with forgetting—and with the penalty which the dwarf comes, in another guise, to collect; the double meaning of *Schuld*, guilt and debt, is here compounded by the interchangeability between debtor and creditor. Distortion (*Entstellung*) is due to the mis-placement of memory. With the coming of the Messiah—whose realignments will be as minimal as the crookednesses they correct ("otherwise he did nothing to me, the grey bailiff") —memories will fall into place; they will "fall in," every one present and correct and in its "particular place" (*bestimmte Stelle, GS*, 1, 3, p. 1234). In slightly straightening (*zurechtstellen*) the world, the Messiah will repair the damage done by obliviousness. The resurrection will be a reawakening, a re-collection; the Messiah will redeem what a dangerously unobtrusive debt collector spirited away. Redemption is remembrance; the present has been invested with "a *weak* Messianic force" with which to "settle" the past's "claim" to "redemption" (ibid., 1, 2, pp. 693–694). Where distortion consists in obliviousness and misfortune in inattention, redemption is coterminous with the attentiveness that the present owes the past and the happiness that is the crowning fulfillment of a past wish. Such attentiveness is, it has emerged, traditionally codified in prayer, secularized in various literary modalities of *Eingedenken*, and exemplified by the storyteller's sympathy with the humblest creatures of God's creation. The closing lines of the Kafka essay interweave these seemingly disparate motifs:

> Wenn ich an mein Bänklein knie
> Will ein bisslein beten,
> Steht ein bucklicht Männlein da,
> Fängt als an zu reden:
> Liebes Kindlein, ach ich bitt,
> Bet fürs bucklicht Männlein mit.

So ends the folk rhyme. In his depth Kafka plumbs . . . German as well as Jewish folklore. We do not know whether Kafka prayed. What at all events he possessed to the highest degree was that attentiveness that Malebranche calls "the natural prayer of the soul." He included all creatures within it, as saints do in their prayers. (ibid.)

In interrupting the child's prayers, the little hunchback would seem to be intent on distracting his attention one last time, but in asking to be remembered in his prayers the little devil comes at the last moment to seek redemption, attention, release from his ugliness. "German as well as

Jewish folklore" coincide with the theodicy of the fairy tale, which characteristically ends with the act of loving attention that transforms monsters back into princes and awakens princesses from their spells. The faith that active remembrance may dispel the mythical forces of evil is also the crux of Benjamin's theology. Leskov's Greek Orthodox conception of the resurrection of all souls in paradise, which Benjamin specifically likens to the *Entzauberung* of the fairy tale, is the doctrinal fulfillment of the prayers which intercede for the humblest, most forgotten creatures. It represents the storyteller's utopia, utopia as the (hi)storyteller's moment: "The chronicler who recites events without distinguishing the large from the small thereby takes into account the following truth: nothing that has ever taken place is to be given up as lost for history." But only in the fullness of messianic time will a redeemed humanity be granted the fullness of its past. The end of history will make it possible to tell the whole story.

The antidote to the hunchback's curse, the curse of inattention, is attentiveness in all its forms. Throughout the runaway thirties variations on this motif recur in Benjamin's writings. The historical danger is, he notes at the very last, the test of the historian's "presence of mind" (*GS*, 1, 3, p. 1242):

Presence of mind as salvation; presence of mind in seizing the fleeting images; presence of mind and stoppage [*Stillstellung*]. Definition of presence of mind to be connected to the question of what it means for the historian to let himself go. (ibid., p. 1244)

The materialist historian does not let himself go; he "remains in control of his faculties—man enough to explode the continuum of history" (*GS*, 1, 2, p. 702). Only split-second timing can make possible that "tiger's leap into the past" whereby historian and revolutionary alike pounce on "the actual, wherever it stirs" (ibid., p. 701)—the "actual" being the much-needed resources with which present history is to be brought to a messianic standstill. The merest inattention is enough to lose the (individual or collective) images prompted by involuntary memory, to miss "the sign of a messianic stoppage of action, in other words of a revolutionary chance in the battle of the oppressed past" (ibid., p. 703). Be it political revolution or individual happiness, redemption is a matter of seizing the opportunity: "To the image of 'salvation' belongs a firm, seemingly brutal grip [*Zugriff*]" (ibid., p. 677). Memory is no less purposive for being involuntary; the drowning man scans the newsreel of his past for straws.

The historical presence of mind that seizes the irretrievably disappearing images of the past is modelled on its Proustian counterpart. The materialist historian is to bring to bear in the arena of history and politics the same presence of mind that enabled Proust to take hold of his individual experience. Even before he translates it from the cork-lined room to the historical battlefield Benjamin detects a revolutionary potential in Proustian memory. *Mémoire involontaire* brings time to a revolutionary halt. The essay on Proust calls it "the rejuvenating force that is a match for the inexorable process of aging" (ibid., p. 143)—an opposition related to that between the Messiah and the hunchback, attentiveness and obliviousness. A "painful shock of rejuvenation pulls together [*zusammenrafft*]" past and present in a "dew-fresh 'now'" (ibid.)—an unscheduled feast not without analogy to the inaugural day of a revolutionary calendar, which functions as an "historical time-lapse camera [*Zeitraffer*]":

> Proust pulled off the enormous feat of letting the whole world age by a lifetime in a single instant. But this very concentration whereby what would normally merely fade and doze is consumed in a flash is called rejuvenation. *A la recherche du temps perdu* is the uninterrupted attempt to charge a whole lifetime with the utmost presence of mind. Actualization [*Vergegenwärtigung*], not reflexion, is Proust's procedure. (ibid.)

This procedure has its historiographical counterpart in Benjamin's "technique of awakening,"[8] which, like Proust's, yields to sleep the better to outwit it, and exemplifies Hegel's dictum that the dialectician "enters the enemy's strength":

> The utilization of dream elements upon awakening is a textbook example of dialectical thinking, which is thus the agency of historical awakening. (S, 1, p. 422)

> And there is no telling what encounters would be destined for us if we were less inclined to sleep. Proust was not thus inclined. And yet—or, rather, precisely for that reason—Jean Cocteau could say . . . that the cadence of his voice obeyed the laws of night and honey. . . . He is dedicated to the insight that we all have no time to live the true dramas of the life that we are destined for. This makes us age. Nothing else. The folds and furrows in our faces are the entries of the great passions, the vices, the insights that called on us—but we, the masters of the house, were not at home. (S, 2, pp. 134, 143)[9]

When (in "Über den Begriff der Geschichte") it is the salvation of the *present* that is the order of the day, Benjamin equates *Rettung* with the Proustian presence of mind that captures the fleeting recurrences of the *past*. His reflections on Proustian memory are, no less disconcertingly, dedicated to the salvation of the *present*. What Benjamin means by presence of mind is, it is beginning to emerge, constituted by a dialectic of past and present. It is perhaps because Proust's *passéisme*, the "elegiac" (ibid., p. 135) nature of his quest for happiness, cannot be overlooked that in the above quotation presence of mind is oriented less to the persisting past than to the call of the present. The Proustian enterprise is no longer understood as mere recuperation.[10] For where the past is recovered at the expense of the present, which then serves only as the occasion for archeological rediscovery, there can be no question of presence of mind, which is nothing if not availability to the actual present. To be *plunged* in memory is to be lost to the present. It is one way of not being at home to visitors. But presence of mind as Benjamin conceives it both collects itself and recollects the past in a flash too instantaneous to be called self-reflexive. To seize the past with a "firm, seemingly brutal grip" is also equivalent to taking hold of the future. In each case it is a matter of seizing the present:

Day and night premonitions, omens, signals pass through our organism in waves. To interpret them or to use them, that is the question. One cannot, however, do both. . . . To change the threat of the future into the fulfilled now—this, the only desirable telepathic miracle, is the work of bodily presence of mind. (S, 1, pp. 574-75)

The images of the past are, likewise, to be *utilized* upon awakening. Their reconstruction is to coincide with the construction of the present. Involuntary memory is not to be the object of antiquarian interpretation. The right interpretation is—or at least coincides with—the right deed: such would be the practical and political dimension of memory, and thence of all literary and historical studies. "Über den Begriff der Geschichte" substitutes "quotation" for "reading," and aims to reconcile the alternative between using and interpreting the past. Benjamin's "interpretation" of Proust is a case in point. It quotes involuntary memory out of its original context and unpolemically drives its presence of mind beyond itself. It applies them, in short, to themselves and uses them in the revolutionary "struggle for the oppressed past." To politicize involuntary memory in this way would thus not be to falsify Proust's resolutely private ambitions but rather to reactivate its revolutionary implications, or, in a different but comparable way, to "fan the spark of hope in the past" (GS, 1, 2, p. 695).

A further, wholly profane, and more problematic model of attentiveness figures among the central motifs of one of Benjamin's last completed writings. "Über einige Motive bei Baudelaire" explores the esthetic consequences of the Freudian proposition that an organism threatened by potentially traumatic shock parries the danger by mobilizing its reserves of hyperconscious "anxiety-preparedness" (*Angstbereitschaft*, GS, 1, 2, p. 613). Consciousness has, on this model, the task of protecting the organism against outside dangers. Its preventive "system" has learned from experience to be prepared for all eventualities. *Angstbereitschaft* represents the attempt not to be caught napping again; memory (*Erinnerung*) likewise enables us, Valéry is quoted as observing (ibid., p. 614), to come to terms with surprises for which we were originally unprepared; Benjamin's warning image of a drowning man belongs to the same complex. Thus seen, presence of mind is a vital function; and in the era of capitalist cities, World Wars, and shocks of all kinds, Freud's biological model, itself prompted by the study of war trauma and accident neurosis, clearly acquires special relevance—all the more so because neutralization is not without negative effects. The price paid for prevention is the impoverishment of experience. Presence of mind does not in this case connote being at home to visitors; it is a sentinel who repels them.[11] Such shockproof vigilance resembles the type of "attentiveness" *against* which Proust defines involuntary memory (ibid., p. 610). It is conducive only to voluntary memory—or, in Theodor Reik's terminology, to *Erinnerung*, which serves to *destroy* impressions, as opposed to *Gedächtnis*, which conserves them—and thus "sterilizes" aesthetic experience. Such a theory of consciousness confirms the mutual exclusiveness of voluntary and involuntary memory.[12] It is against the odds that Baudelaire "holds in his hands the fragmented components of authentic historical experience" (ibid., p. 643).

"Über den Begriff der Geschichte" is grounded in the same historical experience of the fragmentation of historical experience. It is moved, like the powerless angel of history, to piece the fragments together. "We do not know whether [Benjamin] prayed," but the intensity with which scattered messianic energies are gathered together and dispersed motifs interwoven into a text of the utmost concentration imparts to his literary testament the quality of a prayer for their reunification. In summoning up all its presence of mind it marshals the most various resources, past and present, sacred and profane, some overlapping and some contradictory. It musters the "dialectical images" that "fall in" at a moment of danger. It cites the two major components of epic memory that have, since their millennial dissociation, gone separate but crisscrossing ways —*Eingedenken* and *Gedächtnis*. It transposes to the larger sociopolitical context both *mémoire involontaire*—the inspiration of the most significant epic project of modern times—and the type of alertness with which it is in theory least compatible. It undoes the dissociation of voluntary and involuntary memory, pits itself against the mutual exclusiveness of interpretation and praxis, and ignores any antinomy between remembrance and actuality. Presence of mind (*Geistesgegenwart*) thus anticipates something of that inclusive re-presentation (*Vergegenwärtigung*) of the past which will be fully given only to a redeemed humanity. But if "Über den Begriff der Geschichte" holds out the chronicle as a utopian model of such comprehensiveness, then it is only to measure the distance that separates it from its telos. For the fragmentary totalizations of the "dialectical image" are a far cry from the epic totality of more leisurely days. Under the pressure of a global historical crisis[13] epic breadth has been compressed into "a flash of ball-lightning" (*GS*, 1, 3, p. 1233), an S.O.S. message devoted to the reciprocal salvation of past and present, a series of flares and Baudelairean *fusées*, a flurry of involuntary images. Benjamin's last theses and jottings are, in every sense, the *precipitate* of a lifetime's thought—"that 'whole life' which, one tells oneself, passes before a dying man's gaze."

II

Only if epic models are abandoned can they perhaps be one day reinstated. If today's materialist historian has need of the two complementary forms of memory that once coexisted in undivided epic unity, it is no less imperative that he undertake the "liquidation of the epic element in historiography" (*GS*, 1, 3, p. 1243).[14] "He no longer succumbs to the idea that history is something that lets itself be told" (ibid., p. 1252), and eyes tradition, the central category of epic memory, with suspicion. Therein he resembles the "destructive character," who, if he "stands in the front of the traditionalists," hands traditions down only inasmuch as he "makes them handy and liquidates them" (*GS*, 4, 1, p. 398). "Über den Begriff der Geschichte" destroys the modern, "historicist" conception of history, which can be summed up in a word—progress. Here as elsewhere the destructive character's effacement of traces is a response to prior destruction. The quasi-scientific, positivist historian has already seen to the "total eradication of everything that recalls [history's] original definition [*Bestimmung*] as *Eingedenken*" (*GS*, 1, 3, p. 1231). Modern historiography is without real memory, a mere pile of souvenirs; it substitutes "false liveliness" (ibid.), artifical resuscitation, voluntary memory, for authentic remembrance; in removing "every reverberation of 'lament' " (ibid.) from history, it replaces melancholy with spleen, "the inertia of the heart, the acedia, which despairs of taking possession of the authentic historical image that fleetingly flares up" (*GS*, 1, 2, p. 696).[15] The angel of history sees a single catastrophe "where a chain of events appears before *us*." We thereby share the historicist perspective, which is no less myopic for laying claim to a bird's eye view. Historicism establishes "a causal nexus between various moments of history . . . lets the sequence of events run through its fingers like the beads of a rosary" (ibid., p. 704). It is as the perception of a chain that historical consciousness both begins and ends. Epic memory, the oldest form of historiography, "establishes the chain of tradition which hands events down from generation to generation," and the historian's insight into the *enchaînement* of events ends as the "telling" of beads. Historicism lets history run its course; its discourse imitates that course. It both liquidates *Eingedenken* and yet conserves, in decayed, anachronistic form, elements of the epic, the story, the chronicle. If the full chronicle of mankind cannot be told before it has been redeemed, today's alternative lies between the phony "universal-historical panorama" that historicism "unrolls" (*AN*, p. 451) before us and highly particular, arresting interactions between past and present.

The historicist chronicler of world history perpetrates a confusion between the present and the age of its messianic redemption. In identifying the utopian telos with the present, historicism betrays it. The identification comes too early or too late: the present can *no longer* be written as an epic and *not yet* as "universal history." In the modern age epic historiography, the oldest kind, is tantamount to ideology. Epic diversity now functions as a distraction, and pseudoconcrete facts conceal an absence of "theoretical armature" (*GS*, 1, 2, p. 702). The patient, pre-industrial rhythm of the storyteller becomes a treacherous "leisureliness" (*GS*, 1, 3, p. 1250) and epic panoramas a false "comfort" (*AN*, p. 451) in the face of a permanent historical emergency. Epic continuity is enlisted in the service of a catastrophic historical continuum:

> In materialist investigations epic continuity will go by the board in favor of constructive rigor. Marx recognized that it is with the steel scaffolding, the wide span of theory that the "history" of capital is to be represented. (*GS*, 1, 3, p. 1252)

Such construction strips from history-writing any vestiges of epic "immanence of meaning" or the chronicle's embeddedness in theology. The medieval chroniclers were "the precursors of modern historians" (*S*, 2, p. 243); the chronicle is by the end of the process reduced to chronology, and chronology to the ideology of progress, which, like Chronos, murders its own children; narration [*Erzählung*] is reduced to enumeration [*Aufzählung*], recounting to counting. The societal dynamic that destroys all forms of the epic, while itself (as certain paragraphs of Marx's *Communist Manifesto* also indicate) not without epic dimensions, cannot be narrated in epic form. Only where it serves to disrupt the flow of history does historical narrative still escape ideology. Brecht's "epic theater" is calculated to *interrupt* continuity. The historical materialist likewise "leaves it to others to dally with the whore 'Once upon a time' and dissipate themselves in the brothel of historicism. He remains in control of his powers, man enough to blast open the continuum of history" (*GS*, 1, 2, p. 702). The act of *Eingedenken* is synonymous with a concentration of revolutionary energies, a "tiger's leap" into the "thickets of the once [*des Einst*]" (ibid., p. 701). Between that single "once" and the eternal "once upon a time" lies the decisive difference. It is no longer a question of the "many scattered events" but of an experience of history "that stands alone" (ibid., p. 702). At this juncture of history diversions are fatal; the drowning man has no time for fairy tales. The historical materialist cannot let history, or any of its straws, slip through his fingers. He "holds fast" (ibid., p. 695) to its fleeting images. He cannot afford to dissipate his energies but must bend all his presence of mind to a single urgent task. He enters into a particular, not an indiscriminate, relation with the past. The indiscriminateness of the chronicle may have a messianic potential, but here and now it amounts to prostitution.

"A constructive principle underlies materialist historiography" (ibid., pp. 701–702). Such construction involves destruction; the materialist historian is one version of the "destructive character." The latter follows the Brechtian injunction to "efface the traces," and it is the traces of the epic narrative that the destructive historian effaces. For, according to "Der Erzähler," it belongs to the definition of the storyteller's craft that, like a potter, he leaves "traces" of his hands on his handiwork (S, 2, p. 233). Once again it is not the destructive character who initiates the destruction, and here too it is a question of "entering the enemy's strength" in order both to resist and to utilize his destructions. Just as the destruction of historical memory derives from the hurricane we call progress (and historicist memory knows no better than to play in ruins it does not recognize as such), so the story is, according to "Der Erzähler," gradually undermined by the dynamic of the bourgeois economy, to be all silenced by the press (S, 1, p. 235) and the First World War (ibid., p. 230). Benjamin's essay on the storyteller knows itself to be the product of a rendezvous between two specific historical moments. It is devoted to a genre that, as it disappears, acquires a "new beauty" (ibid., p. 233). But Benjamin does not simply linger over the aura of the storytelling past. "Über den Begriff der Geschichte" rescues its messianic potential, while such essays as "Der Autor als Produzent" and "Das Kunstwerk im Zeitalter seiner technischen Reproduzierbarkeit" place their historical faith in what look like the least promising products of the forces that destroyed it. Thus the press not merely undermines literature but, once emancipated from the bourgeois relations of production in which it originated, extends and renews it. Here too slavation and destruction are "dialectically" related:

But herein is concealed a dialectical moment: the ruination of the written word in the bourgeois press proves the formula of its renewal in Soviet Russia. . . . It is where language is being utterly degraded—that is, in the newspaper—that its salvation is under way. (VüB, pp. 100–101)

Benjamin variously conceives revolution (with Marx) as accelerating the dialectic of historical progress and (against Marx) as pulling its emergency cord (GS, 1, 3, p. 1232).

Does such dialectical destruction insert itself within the triadic scheme as its second, negative phase? Or is "dialectics at a standstill" more ambiguously located outside or against the movement of the dialectical triad? Inside or outside, it is this destructive moment that most clearly distinguishes Benjamin's scheme from the one to which it is most immediately indebted. We noted earlier a certain *dédoublement* that *Die Theorie des Romans* and "Der Erzähler" share in common: the faith that the (Lukàcsian) novel keeps with the epic, and the (Benjaminian) story with the naïve age, repeats itself in the critic's relation to his chosen epic genre. The naïve age, when, in Leskov's words, nature "speaks to man," (S, 2, p. 244) is the world of Baudelaire's *Correspondances*. The poem belongs to the opening cycle of the *Fleurs du Mal*, a cycle "devoted to something that is irretrievably lost" (GS, 1, 2, p. 638). But Baudelaire does not only shed "tears of homesickness" (ibid., p. 640) in memory of the prelapsarian *époques nues*. Baudelaire, like Benjamin, obeys a double pull. They both resurrect lost aura and assent to its destruction, especially when it is artifically resuscitated. In that destruction lies the modernism that separates them from Lukács, who could only conceive it as a modernist aberration. His later formula for modern art, "the distortion of distortion," conceives it as the heightened repetition, the tautological worsening, of the evils of modern society; it makes an instructive contrast with the Benjaminian destruction of destruction. Among Lukács's writings *Die Theorie des Romans* is often singled out in the name of aesthetic modernism, but in defining the novel as "the epic of the god-forsaken world" and centering it on the loss of the epic cosmos, it exhibits the same conservatism that will characterize Lukács' later Marxist writing. Like Engels, Lukács will consider Marxism the rightful heir to German Idealism. With the corresponding shift of emphasis from a quest for meaningful epic totality (conceived as a harmonious countermodel to the alienation and contradictions of modern society) to the no less normative demand for the *intelligible* representation of the existing, contradictory totality—that is, representation in the implicit perspective of a new noncontradictory totality not dissimilar from the Greek status quo ante—, the epic will come to function as the model for that imperishable "realism" which is bequeathed, by way of the bourgeois novel's "critical realism," to its socialist heirs. And while the accompanying attack on naturalism rejects positivism in the same terms as Benjamin's denunciation of historicism, the positive alternative that Lukács holds out, in a well-known essay,[16] to such fact-mongering "description," is nothing other than . . . "narration." "Efface the traces" could never have been a Lukácsian motto.

A comparison with the "destructive character" will, indeed, clinch the difference. "Der Erzähler" bases its interpretation of the novel on *Die Theorie des Romans*: "The 'meaning of life' is the center around which the novel revolves" (S, 2, p. 247). Seen thus, the novel's relation to epic immanence anticipates the existentialist's negative fixation on metaphysical transcendence. Sartrian *délaissement* echoes Lukácsian god-forsakenness. In each case the isolated bourgeois subject is haunted by the loss of objectively given meaning and seeks by way of compensation to become a metaphysically self-made man. To make (up) one's meanings as one goes along—such is the compulsive post-Kantian imperative for a Sisyphean subject who is "condemned to freedom." As for relinquishing meaning itself, or at least relaxing its hold, this is left to the destructive character, who, while defined by his deeds, is no existentialist:

Not for one moment is the destructive character inclined to search for a "meaning" to life. If he could give it meaning for a moment, and were it only in the destruction of whatever needs destroying, more would already have been accomplished than he ever hoped for. (*GS*, 4, 2, pp. 1000–1001)

One way or another triadic thinking is committed to the quest for ultimate meaning. Even where it locates the very category of meaning (along with the search for it) at its second stage, the triadic dream is governed by the quest for a meaningfulness beyond meaning or a fullness beyond meaningfulness.[17] In all but dropping the quest for meaning, the destructive character comes to scrapping the triadic scheme altogether. But the destructive radicalization of the second stage can, on the other hand, itself function as the necessary condition for bringing about triadic fulfillment. Such, in crude paraphrase, is the gesture of Benjamin's "Theologisch-politisches Fragment" (*S*, 1, pp. 511–12). The dialectic of the press cited above describes a similar movement at a secular but no less messianic level. The printing press signals the end of collective oral forms and the beginning of solitary written ones, but, pushed to its most relentless consequences—that of the "press" *tout court*—it is transformed into an agency of collective renewal, a productive force that presses for transformed relations of production. Such examples could be multiplied.

III

If the epic and the chronicle represent originary points of "creative indifference" roughly equivalent to the first stage of a triad, and both the historical present and the historiography it calls for are characterized by the destruction of the epic, then the hope for messianic redemption, with its concomitant reinstatement of the chronicle, looks forward, however precariously, to the consummation of the triad, to paradise regained. This third phase is, according to *Die Theorie des Romans*, already being prefigured in Russia—not, that is, in Soviet Russia but in the recovery of the epic dimension in the Russian novel. In "Über den Begriff der

Geschichte" the triadic prospect is not, strictly speaking, a prospect at all—"Jews are known for having been forbidden to investigate the future"—but rather a name, an imageless image,[18] a straw, perhaps, at which to clutch. For the Jews "every second was the strait gait through which the Messiah might enter" (GS, 1, 2, p. 704), writes Benjamin in the closing lines of this last-minute message. The angel of history who is being blown away from paradise would "willingly return" (ibid., p. 697). Such messianism—indeed, all messianism—is clearly triadic by definition; it is predicated on a second coming, a return from exile.

It is in this triadic perspective that the critique of historicism is made. Historicism is premature inasmuch as it takes it for granted that history can already be told in its totality. It thereby confuses the exile with the return. In presuming to write history "as it actually happened"— *wie es denn eigentlich gewesen ist* (ibid., p. 695)—Ranke usurps a God's-eye view and considers history sub specie aeternitatis, as if he had the whole of world history before him and all the time in the world in which to contemplate it: " 'The truth won't run away from us'—this *mot* coined by Gottfried Keller marks the precise place in the historicist conception of history which historical materialism breaks through" (ibid.). But the "destructive moments" of materialist history-writing— namely, the "dismantling of universal history [*Universalgeschichte*], elimination of the epic element, no empathy with the victor" (GS, 1, 3, p. 1240)—are in turn oriented toward a "messianic notion of universal history" (ibid., p. 1235). "Historicism culminates by rights in universal history" (GS, 1, 2, p. 702)—yet at the same time

(Not every universal history has to be reactionary. Universal history *without* a constructive principle *is*. The constructive principle of universal history makes possible the representation of the universal in the partial. It is, in other words, monadological. It exists in religious doctrines of redemption [*Heilsgeschichte*]). (GS, 1, 3, p. 1234)

The double implication of this passage parallels the two complementary meanings contained in Lukács's concept of totality. The totality of a given historical present, we argued, distinguishes itself from the totality of a past cosmos or future utopia, but also presupposes or anticipates it. Here likewise the highly partial historical constellation that is constructed according to the dictates of involuntary memory preserves, in the form of *Aufhebung*, "the life-work *in* the work, the epoch *in* the lifework, the whole course of history *in* the epoch" (GS, 1, 2, p. 703). This totality is also a double one. Like Blake's grain of sand, the "monad" contains the universe and simultaneously represents a "sliver" (ibid., p. 704) that prefigures the universal history that will be fully available only to a redeemed humanity. Is this possible except on the basis of a *Heilsgeschichte* whose third, redemptive phase is already at work in the second? Benjamin's conception of *Rettung*, which is neither theological nor atheological, does not clearly decide the issue either way. What is clear, however, is that the partial wholes it is given to the present to glimpse presuppose and anticipate their ultimate totalization. Only when redemption is complete will the local quotations that have been exploded out of their historical context be reinserted within it. Only then will it no longer be a historicist vice to let the sequence of events run through one's fingers "like the beads of a rosary":

> Only where the course of history glides smoothly as a thread through the historian's hands may one speak of progress. But if it is a frayed rope with a thousand loose ends that hang down like unravelled braids, none of them has its appointed place until all of them have been taken up and braided into a headdress. (*GS*, 1, 3, pp. 1233–34)

Only when history comes to its head, its capital moment, can the text that is its headdress be woven. Only from the summit can the *summa* be written. Even the metaphor of braiding hair has a triadic resonance. It recalls the spinning and weaving that define the world of the storyteller.

Another series of jottings brings the ambiguity of a universal history, at once ideological reality and utopian promise, into conjunction with that of a universal language:

> (The multiplicity of "histories" is closely related, if not identical, to the multiplicity of languages. Universal history as conceived nowadays is always merely a kind of esperanto. . . .) (ibid., p. 1235)

> (The idea of a universal history hinges on the idea of a universal language. As long as the latter was grounded either in theology, as in the Middle Ages, or in logic, most recently by Leibniz, universal history was not unthinkable. As practised since the nineteenth century, however, universal history can never be anything but a kind of esperanto.) . . . It can have no objective basis until the confusion that stems from the tower of Babel has been settled. It presupposes the language into which every text, be its language living or dead, is to be translated undiminished. Or rather it is that language itself. (ibid., pp. 1239–40).

If in the parable of the dwarf and the automat that opens "Über den Begriff der Geschichte" Benjamin openly plays a covert game of hide-and-seek with his theological premises, here in the privacy of his unpublished notes he lays his theological cards on the table. In grounding a universal history on a universal language, Benjamin's very last speculations revert to the philosophy of language set forth in his early essays "Über Sprache überhaupt und über die Sprache des Menschen" and "Die Aufgabe des Übersetzers." The interpretation to which he there subjects the Biblical story of Genesis in terms of a heterodox theology of language that integrates the "task of the translator" and the multiplicity of languages into the movement of the Divine Word cannot be gone into here. Suffice it for our purposes to note that this movement enacts the triadic scheme in pure and massive form—an original unity of language in paradise, followed by the Fall (". . . as many translations as languages once man has fallen from paradise, which knew only one language" [S, 2, p. 414]), thereafter by the tower of Babel (ibid., pp. 416–17), and ever since by the "yearning" (S, 1, pp. 49, 51) for the "integration of the many languages into the one true one" (ibid., p. 48); and that it becomes the translator's task to make the languages in which he works "recognizable, like shards, as fragments of a vessel, fragments of a larger language" (ibid., p. 50). But if an authentic translation is animated by the yearning to restore the universal language, it must necessarily remain as fragmentary and temporary as authentic historiography will later be said to be:

. . . all translation is only a somewhat provisional way of coming to terms with the foreignness of languages. An instantaneous and definitive solution of this foreignness, as opposed to a temporal and provisional one, remains denied to mankind, or cannot at any rate be immediately attempted. (ibid., p. 46)

Such a direct attempt would, in Benjamin's later metaphor, result not in the final synthesis but in "esperanto," the false kind of "synthetic" language. The late Benjamin's critique of historicism is thus already implied in the early Benjamin's philosophy of language, and his "materialist" theory of quotation reformulate his theology of translation.

Translation is, by this theory, a translucent medium that enables pure language to shine all the more fully on the original (ibid., p. 51). Languages are likewise distinguished according to their varying degrees of "density," the higher languages being the translation of the lower, more opaque ones, all of them finding their fulfillment in the ultimate clarity of God's word (S, 2, pp. 407, 412, 419). These optical metaphors anticipate that of the "spectrum" of epic forms which refract the pure colorless light of historiography. Such unrefracted light is, one is tempted to say, light which contains its own translation, light from before (or after) the fall into multiplicity; it is the *terminus a quo*, logical or chronological, and the *terminus ad quem*; it is, in Benjamin's recurrent phrase, an originary point of "creative indifference," a point, it is beginning to emerge, of triadic return. The occupants of this privileged position were, according to "Der Erzähler," the epic (in relation to its subgenres), great prose (in relation to the various metric forms), and the chronicle (in relation to forms of storytelling). The latter, we saw, is to come back into its own at the third, messianic stage of the triad. And it is in turn to the spectrum of prose forms that the notes to "Über den Begriff der Geschichte" keep returning in order to characterize more closely the universal language of universal history (and thus rule out any confusion with "esperanto"):

(The idea of prose coincides with the messianic idea of universal history. Cf. "The Storyteller": the types of literary prose [*Kunstprosa*] as historiographical spectrum.) (*GS*, 1, 3, p. 1235. Cf. also pp. 1234, 1238)

If the various forms of esthetic prose represent so many ways of writing history, and "great prose" is the "creative indifference between the various metric forms," in what kind of prose will the final historical summation, the Last Judgment, be couched?

The messianic world is the world of all-sided [*allseitig*] and integral actuality. Only then will there be universal history. Not, however, as writing, but as festive celebration [*die festlich begangene*]. This feast is cleansed of all ceremony [*Feier*]. It knows no festive songs. Its language is integral prose, which has burst the fetters of the written word and is understood by all men (like the language of birds by Sunday's children). (ibid., p. 1238. Cf. also pp. 1235, 1239)

In the beginning had been the epic, universal historiography in a collective, metrical genre not unrelated to "festive song"; and later came the story and the chronicle, prose forms, but, like the epic, oral (and in the former case collective) in spirit even where committed to paper. Then occurred the fall, the loss of universality and collectivity, the age of the printed word, of literature and historiography produced and consumed in isolation (*S*, pp. 233–34). The language of a messianic, no longer premature universal history is in turn neither festive song nor written prose. Or rather the relation of the triadic synthesis to its thesis and antithesis is one *both* of neither/nor *and* of both/and. On the one hand, its prose, like "great prose," doubtless represents the white light which contains a prismatic spectrum of verse forms within it. On the other hand, it is emancipated from both song and the written word. The negation of the second stage, which was the negation of the first, is not a simple reaffirmation. A feast without ceremony or festive songs, it does not celebrate a return to the ritual origins from which already the second stage was divorced.

There can be no question of restoring the calendar, the institutional precondition for actual, ceremonial festivals as well as for "experience in the strict sense," and it is not on a "holy day" (*Feiertag*) that the messianic feast, a feast without "ceremony" (*Feier*), is celebrated: the reference to "Sunday's children" has merely metaphorical value. The secular epiphany of Proustian *mémoire involontaire*, which occurs outside the framework of "rituals, with their ceremonies and feasts," constitutes one model of such a nonceremonial feast. Surrealist experience enacts another, and it in turn leaves no room for *die "gute Stube"* (*AN*, p. 215), the "Sunday best" room that is used only for such special occasions as, say, receiving the vicar. The *gute Stube* is to the others what Sunday is to the rest of the week; both are defined by absence, boredom, official piety. To "clean out" the *gute Stube* as the destructive character would, or to cancel all Sundays as the Russians have done, is in each case to evacuate what has already been emptied but left standing:

The future will be characterized by transparency—not merely that of space but, if we are to believe the Russians, who are now planning to abolish Sunday in favor of moveable shifts [*bewegliche Feierschichten*] even of the week. (*GS*, 3, p. 197)

We recall Benjamin's account of Baudelairean spleen as the sensation of having been dropped from the calendar, the response to a Sunday that is no longer a day of public worship, a holy day, but only a nominally "public" holiday. The communist answer is to drop Sunday from its calendar, a radically secular calendar in which the moveable shift replaces the moveable feast.

Not even the nostalgic author of *Die Theorie des Romans* seeks to set back the world-historical clock to the age that did not yet tell time by the clock. But whereas even the Marxist Lukács of *Geschichte und Klassenbewusstsein* considers the quantification of time symptomatic of the capitalist rationalization and bourgeois alienation that socialism will have to overcome, Benjamin identifies socialist transformation as the *radicalization* of quantity. If Benjamin might to that extent seem the better Marxist of the two, his materialism is nevertheless neither dialectical nor orthodox. Revolution as he conceives it is the movement, at once mystical and profane, whereby the historical dialectic leaps beyond itself and thus suspends its own movement. Benjamin's writings variously combine dialectical movement with "dialectics at a standstill." Whereas Lukács's esthetic consistently seeks in effect to slow down the historical dialectic, Benjamin's aim of bringing it to a standstill nowhere precludes a radical faith in its technological momentum. It is, in this latter perspective, only in and through its "mechanical reproduction" that what has traditionally been called art can be superseded, politicized, resocialized, and the unstructured "public" transformed into a collective subject no longer defined by the bourgeois antinomy between production and consumption. But the considerable difference between the esthetic conservatism of a Lukács and the modernism of a Benjamin is, to some extent, that between two variations on the triadic theme. And insofar as it is only in and through the negativity and alienation of its second stage that, according to one recurrent variant of the scheme, the triadic movement is to be completed, Benjamin's modernism would hark back to motifs at least as old as Jewish mysticism. We will, according to Kleist's essay "Über das Marionettentheater," regain paradise only if we go all the way round the world and reenter it from the back. Paradise regained will doubtless be all the more complete for encompassing the intervening alienation. Indeed, German idealism in general makes the fall, the self-alienation of a unitary origin, the motor of its theology. In short, the fall is in many contexts not without its advantages. Who would want to return to *Gemeinschaft* after having tasted the forbidden fruits of *Gesellschaft*? "Closed cultures" inspire a certain claustrophobia even in their most eloquent eulogist: "The metaphysical circle in which the Greeks live is smaller than ours . . . we can no longer live in a closed world"; "our going on [*Weitergehen*] (no matter whether rise or fall)" is, in any case, irreversible.[19] Triadic myths characteristically situate their first stage "outside all properly historical categories" (S, 2, p. 244) and equate history with the second. History thereby becomes synonymous with the fall, and, conversely, the fall becomes the precondition for all historical movement, be it progress, regress, or both. No one is more convinced of the negativity of "ongoing" progress than Benjamin: "That it 'goes on like that' ['*so weiter*' *geht*] *is* the catastrophe" (GS, 1, 2, p. 683). But the destructive character's profound mistrust of progress is not its abstract negation; he is closer to being a technician than a Luddite. The angel of history is carried away from paradise by a storm called progress, but it is only by harnessing its force that paradise could be brought back within reach.

The historical process of secularization goes by various names: demythologization (Bultmann), rationalization, *die Entzauberung der Welt* (Max Weber), prose (Hegel).[20] It is with another version of prose that Benjamin identifies the messianic future. The messianic prose that is "cleansed of all ceremony" bears the destructive marks of a certain demythologization.[21] It unreservedly identifies itself with the irreversible movement of history, the better to be able to reverse it. That movement is the storm called progress, not Hegel's "progress in the consciousness of freedom." The notion that prose is the creative indifference of the various metrical forms can, it is true, be accommodated under the capacious rubric of Hegelian *Aufhebung*. Not merely, however, are wholly different types of prose involved, but the messianic élan of Benjamin's "integral prose" carries it beyond the whole genre of the written: it has "burst the fetters of the written word." If prose in general can be seen as an emancipation from the constraints of meter,[22] messianic prose in turn enacts a violent liberation from *Kunstprosa* itself, a liberation from literature that, unlike its Hegelian *Aufhebung*, no longer takes place in the name of philosophy. Messianic prose would thus make the first emancipation the object of a second. If reality is, according to the superimposition of the *Surrealist* on the *Communist Manifesto*, to "exceed" itself (AN, p. 215), demythologization is likewise to outleap its own limits. The release from metrical limitations connotes dithyrambic excess, unruly, unbounded energy. Demythologization does not only signify the "disenchantment of the world;" it also means that all and nothing is holy. The universality of prose is also a general lifting of taboos,[23] and the liberation from writing, from pre-scribed forms, will inaugurate the informal performance of a free feast. A "feast" without "festive songs," it combines the preservation of the festive spirit with the destruction of the letter—a destruction which in turn appears to partake equally of messianic purification and enlightenment rationality, of both myth and demythologization. The relation of this third stage to the first two is, we claimed, one both of both/and and of neither/nor. Neither oral nor written, it retains features of both foregoing stages; the celebration is, after all, synonymous with commemoration. As *prose* it participates in a process of demythologization. As *messianic* prose, the demythologization of demythologization, it no more coincides with the second stage than with the first. Even though this double liberation does not cancel itself out into a simple reaffirmation of the first stage, the third moment of the triad does, in conjugating the first two, entertain a special relationship with the originary point of creative indifferecce. The prose that is "understood by all men" is the restoration of the universal language that preceded the Fall, the word that was in the beginning. "Über die Sprache überhaupt und über die Sprache des Menschen" had stated that in naming nature in accordance with God's word man redeems it. A "continuum" of vertical "translations" relays the mute language of nature in an ascending movement of cosmic communication that begins and ends with the universal language of divine creation (S, f2, pp. 412–419). Higher languages are thus translations of lower ones; the example Benjamin cites is the affinity between song and the language of birds (ibid., p. 418). It is in this sense that messianic prose is "the language into which every text . . . is to be translated," a language which "is understood by all men (like the language of birds by Sunday's children)" (GS, 1, 3, p. 1239).[24] The Logos clearly exceeds the bounds of the written word. Such an extended notion of language is necessarily accompanied by a reduced estimation of the paradigmatic role of art. And yet it was, we recall, in terms of the spectrum of *Kunstprosa* that messiance prose is defined. In an idealist esthetics categories and their worldly referents can mutually presuppose one another because both proceed from the same all-creating Logos. Like the Logos, festive prose is pitched in the performative mode.

The world of messianic prose both invites and repels comparisons with corresponding Hegelian motifs. The analogies between the two logocentric systems, Benjamin's early idealist theology (and its recurrence in his late speculations on history) and Hegel's theological idealism extend even to their choice of metaphors.[25] Is not the messianic triad structurally bound to culminate in the total recall of "absolute knowledge"? Does not the messianic feast which preserves the festive spirit while destroying its literal forms enact the two meanings of Hegelian *Aufhebung*? The universal language into which all others can be rendered without anything getting lost in translation, the universal history which gathers up all the loose ends of the past into a crowning headdress; a text in which every strand finally finds its "appointed place";[26] the world-historical chronicle, which, like the storyteller, has the whole of its past at its disposal; the Last Judgment as the integral resurrection and understanding of the past—these and other formulations suggest certain equivalences between the "integral prose" of the messianic era and the encyclopedic format of the Hegelian system.[27] The major difference can provisionally be called a matter of timing. In passing final judgment before the messianic age has dawned, Hegel would be a false (because premature, "historicist") Messiah.

The point may also be made as follows. The category of imperfection does not, as Descartes argued it did, logically entail the existence of God. But the description of the present in terms of fragmentation does presuppose some concept of wholeness as the criterion, postulate, or perspective by which it may be thus privatively defined, the light by which it may be seen.[28] Transposed into the categories of a messianic Marxism,

Marx's idea of a classless society secularized the idea of messianic time. And this was as it should be. (*GS*, 1, 3, p. 1231)

A classless society cannot be conceived as existing in the same time as the struggle for it. The concept of the present to which the historian is committed is, however, necessarily defined by both these temporal orders. The historian who does not in some way measure the past by the touchstone of a classless society cannot but falsify it. To that extent every concept of the present partakes in that of the Last Judgment. (ibid., p. 1245)

The secularization of messianic time,[29] which Benjamin here associates with Marx, does not weaken the duality between the profane present and the messianic hereafter. The idea of a classless society is both sharply separate from class history and yet essential to its definition. The present is neither identical with the messianic age nor entirely cut off from it. Not only does the proper definition of the present rest on a notion of the messianic that is plainly intended to function as more than a heuristic fiction or narrative device, but the fleeting moments of authentic memory that grace the unredeemed present are themselves sparks of redeemed time. To seize the historical constellation of past and present is to possess a "concept of the present as 'now time' interspersed with splinters of the messianic" (*GS*, 1, 2, p. 704).[30] But these epiphanies are fleeting moments. Only the messianic world will, it would seem, see its past steadily and see it whole. The light cast by the messianic age would no longer be the lightning flash of an intermittent "dialectical image" but the unending illumination of an "eternal lamp" (*GS*, 1, 3, p. 1245). Historiography would no longer be a matter of snatched glimpses; total recall would no longer be occasioned solely by life-or-death crises, truth would no longer be precarious and fugitive, but rather, as in Lukács's Greece, "adventurous and yet possession" (*Die Theorie des Romans*, p. 22). It would, it seems, be couched in epic language—which is, in Thomas Greene's words, characterized not by the "partial, fragmentary images," the brief "flickers," "abrupt" impressions, "compressed, suggestive, unfulfilled," the "unknowability" of the *tragic* (or—according to Erich Auerbach's earlier comparative description of epic immanence—the *Biblical*) mode, but by the "leisurely" simile, the "stabilizing concreteness," the "even" "continuity" and "expansiveness" of a "well-lit" world capable of "panoramic" or "scenic" portrayal from an "Olympian" vantage point.[31]

Such, at least, would seem to be the built-in logical consequences if the triadic scheme were allowed to run its preordained course. But would not such a course suspiciously resemble the easy, inert momentum of progress against which the alert historian mobilizes his messianic resources—which amount in turn to another, but disruptive, version of the triad? The messianic realm "is not the goal but the end" (*S*, 1, p. 511). To assume that historicism is simply premature is to wait for time to ripen, to postulate an organic, evolutionary, "social-democratic" conception of history, and, by postponing historicism till the right time, to perpetuate it indefinitely. It is this temporal continuum, along with the temporizing that (merely) accompanies it, that the revolutionary insistence on a messianic *Jetztzeit* is calculated to explode. More closely examined, Benjamin's quotations from triadic schemes contain alternative possibilities and immanent complications. One jotting, for example, defines the dialectical image—which, though an epiphany, occurs to an *unredeemed* present that is no more than *interspersed* with messianic splinters—as "the involuntary memory of a *redeemed* humanity" (*GS*, 1, 3, p. 1233, italics mine). This is presumably the same redeemed humanity as the one that is "fully granted its past." Why, then, would such remembrance *still* take the erratic form of involuntary memory? Is Benjamin saying that even final redemption is a matter of short-lived Proustian epiphanies? If so, is this compatible with the architectonics of the triadic scheme? If historicism confuses the second stage of the triad with the third, Benjamin's jotting would seem to have conflated the third with the second. Even if the reference to a redeemed humanity merely varies the claim that, as splinters of messianic time, the punctual redemptions of the past effected by involuntary memory themselves already partake of the larger salvation, the further question remains as to the nature of the difference—which seems neither nonexistent nor merely quantitative —between the parts and the whole, the pieces and the vessel, the lightning flashes and the full light of messianic revelation. In partaking, how far do they coincide and how far do they differ? Insofar as such flashes represent the mesianic *in actu*, and messianism exists only as the actuality of a present, it brooks no postponement. (Or rather waiting can be either waiting for Godot or waiting for the Messiah, the intense expectancy of a "profane illumination" (*AN*, p. 213) or the passive socialdemocratic posture of sitting back in an anteroom expecting the revolutionary situation to materialize (*GS*, 1, 3, p. 1231).) On the other hand, the secularization of messianic time does not reduce its differentness: "a classless society cannot be conceived as existing in the same time as the struggle for it." Where, within this distinction between unredeemed and redeemed stages, are the redeemed moments of the unredeemed stage to be accommodated? Are privileged moments of involuntary memory the good fortune *of* the privileged, already classless, or only the last supper of the condemned?

It would be a mistake to see in such alternatives no more than logical confusion. Rather they point to the inherent problem of visualizing the messianic era. Not merely does there exist a tension between the Jewish taboo on "delving into the future" (*GS*, 1, 2, p. 704) and the impossibility of leaving the third stage of the triad, the fulfillment of all its expectations, a blank. There is a further, related contradiction between the impulse to visualize it as being radically, discontinuously other—in short, as unvisualizable—and the urge to imagine the new world in terms of the known, be it the lost past or the prefigurative present.[32] There are, at all events, several further indications that the messianic splinters, which by rights represent no more than the isolated premonitions of better things to come, nevertheless furnish privileged examples of the way in which the integral resurrection of the world is to be conceived. Preliminary, fragmentary, and idiosyncratic though they are, the profane modalities of the messianic are, in any case, its only visible and accesssible, but also its only desirable, forms; they are, indeed, the modalities of desire itself. The universal language into which all others are translatable cannot be "directly aspired to" because the only translations available to humankind are "temporal and provisional" ways of coming to terms with the mutual foreignness of languages. This already indicates that in practice the temporary solutions will, despite their lesser ontological status, function as privileged modalities. Does such privileging of its second stage further imply that the whole triadic scheme does, after all, represent a heuristic fiction built around a founding experience allotted to its middle slot? That the triad should be a narrative in three parts based on one part of experience would perhaps not in itself be proof of its fictionality. But that experience is in turn a partly fictive one, an experience of lack and longing, an experience of the insufficiency of experience, an experience which straddles the limits of experience. And it is in turn to an "image" that the lack turns for fulfillment, an image that refers us back, but in the subjunctive mood, to our experience, our past and what it might have been:

> The kind of happiness that could arouse envy in us exists only in the air we have breathed, with people to whom we might have spoken, with women who might have given themselves to us. (*GS*, 1, 2, p. 693)

Under these circumstances it is, at all events,[33] not surprising that the modalities of the second stage should become models of the third.

The theory and practice of quotation is a case in point. "Quotations in my work are like armed highway robbers who loom up and relieve the idler of his convictions" (*S*, 1, p. 571). Quotations are to hold up "'the spoiled idler in the garden of knowledge'" (*GS*, 1, 2, p. 700) in the same way that revolutions are to "arrest" (ibid., p. 702) the course of time. They thus practice the convergence of literary and revolutionary action: "The French Revolution conceived itself as the return of Rome. It quoted ancient Rome . . ." (ibid., p. 701). In the unredeemed world quotation stands more generally for a kind of guerilla warfare with the ruling culture, a quasi-anarchistic technique which explodes, and in every sense arrests, the continuity of texts, biographies, and periods—a continuity which merely reflects the inherited continuity of accumulated power relations and thereby serves as an ideological justification for "progress" and the status quo (ibid., pp. 701–03).[34] The function of quotation is to break up the unified, totalitarian blocks that conformist historiography passes out as history and thereby to isolate the elective affinities between the present and specific moments of the past. To grasp such correspondences is to seize the chance of the moment. The right quotation is a matter of the right opportunity. It is closely related to involuntary memory, which may indeed be called a form of quotation. Benjamin himself identifies it with fashion:

> [The French Revolution] quoted ancient Rome the way fashion quotes a past costume. Fashion has a flair for the actual wherever it stirs in the thickets of long ago. It is a tiger's leap into the past. Only it takes place in an arena commanded by the ruling class. The same leap under the open sky of history is the dialectical one with which Marx identified the revolution. (ibid.)

Quotation, like prose, emerges as the coincidence of literary and non-literary, interpretative and revolutionary impulses. Thus conceived, it is hardly a matter of repeating the immortal words of the bard. It is, in every sense, *citation*, summons, act rather than word, the fashion rather than eternity, or word as act and fashion as eternity—the eternal being "at all events the ruche of a dress rather than an idea" (Tiedemann, *Studien*, p. 130). It takes a quintessentially temporal, partial mode to prefigure the integral redemption of the past. Quotation is, like criticism for Baudelaire, "partial, passionate, political." Not merely does it pounce on particular moments of the past, but, like the historiography it opposes, it does so on behalf of particular interests. The difference is that these are ultimately in the universal interest. The universal resurrection of the past can be reconciled with the necessary and irreducible partiality of present-day quotation only if the act of disintegrating false continuities is conceived as the fragmentary anticipation of an authentic reintegration.

But here too quotation, like involuntary memory, enjoys a special status. Born of an unredeemed age, it does not disappear with its redemption. It becomes rather the positive medium *of* redemption. Not merely do the momentary illuminations of the past that light up the unredeemed world have the fragmentariness of quotations. Even their steady, totalizing counterpart, the "perpetual lamp," is fueled by quotation:

(The perpetual lamp is an image of authentic historical existence. It quotes the past—the flame that was once lit—by constantly furnishing it with new nourishment.) (*GS*, 1, 2, 703)

It is, indeed, in a redeemed world that quotation comes into its own:

... only for a redeemed humanity has its past become quotable in every one of its moments. Each of its lived moments becomes a *citation à l'ordre du jour*—that day being, precisely, the Day of Judgment. (ibid.)

On the Day of Judgment the *whole* of the past could be cited to appear, but it will still be *cited*. The difference between a redeemed and an unredeemed humanity would thus be that between fragmentary quotation and more integral citation. But to blur the distinction still further, the unredeemed world itself already has its moments of illumination, those moments when, precisely, it cites the past. Quotations bring to bear on the past the *"weak* messianic power" with which the otherwise unredeemed present is to redeem the past. Only on the Day of Judgment will the whole past be "quotable in each of its moments." But present-day quotation already draws on that final re(-)source. For the present "partakes of ... the Day of Judgment," "every moment" being one of "judgment over certain moments which preceded it" (*GS*, 1, 3, p. 1245). Which raises the possibility that "the Day of Judgment would not ... distinguish itself from the others" (ibid.). But what, in that case, of the distinction between the two temporal orders, the profane and the messianic? What *essential* difference is there between the messianic epiphanies of the present and the steadier illuminations of the messianic era, *Jetz-*

tzeit now and *Jetztzeit* then? The secularization of messianic time would seem, after all, to have the effect of reducing the ontological dualism to almost quantitative—but still decisive—questions of parts and wholes, more or less ("a *weak* messianic force," "quotable in *every one* of its momoments," "voluntary and involuntary memory thus *lose their mutual exclusiveness*," etc.). But if the modalities of the second stage are transformed rather than superseded by those of the third, it becomes difficult to tell which is modelled on which, the prefiguration on its fulfillment or the fulfillment on its prefiguration.

It is not merely that the binary oppositions of triadic thinking, being logically simultaneous and yet *at the same time* spread out into a successive narrative, presuppose one another. The specific tensions of the Benjaminian scheme, notably the unstable relation between its last two phases, perhaps mark a certain resistance to whatever glibness might be programmed into the triadic patterns his thinking cannot do without.[35] It is the resistance of lived experience to prospects, programs, and perspectives too vague to be adequate to its own utterly particular fulfillment. Even certain of Benjamin's own more programmatic formulations seem to suggest that redemption is merely to be visualized as historicism come true. But whereas historicism claims to survey "the 'eternal' image of the past" (*GS* 1, 2, p. 702) with Olympian impartiality, as if history were an open book which may be *idly* quoted at the beck and call of voluntary memory,[36] "Über den Begriff der Geschichte" has no time for the "idler." Even a redeemed humanity will not randomly skim its prehistory or chew its world-historical cud. The claim that "only for a redeemed humanity has its past become quotable in every one of its moments" is symptomatic of the tension between the momentum of the scheme and the pull of experience. The emphasis can be made to rest on "every one of its moments" or on "quotable"; or, in the subsequent phrase "each of its lived moments," on "each" or on "lived." Will, then, the past, even in the promised land, still be quotable rather than legible? Voluntary memory, which is all that historicism has at its disposal, is incapable of reliving it. The "lived moment" of the past re-presents itself most authentically in involuntary memory. Voluntary and involuntary memory will, it is true, have ideally lost "their mutual exclusiveness"; the latter will, in a redeemed world, acquire something of the availability of the former. Redeemed time can, however, hardly be conceived as homogeneous. It is *against* the "homogeneous and empty time" of present-day history and historiography that the concept of messianic time is invoked. Opportunity, attentiveness, and presence of mind will not have been anachronistic categories, and the need for the particular, local, motivated quotation, the *citation à l'ordre du jour*, will remain. A new continuity will have emerged out of the destruction of the old, but insofar as it remains a continuity of *quotations* it can hardly be conceived as an unbroken *chronicle*. The breaks in the vessel will, as it were, still be visible. But the past will now be quotable in *every* one of its moments. What then distinguishes such quotation from reading? And would not the final Day of Judgment, on which everything will have been summoned to its proper place,[37] logically be the occasion to end all occasions, all modalities of contingency—including appropriate quotations?

Even though triadic myths almost invariably contain the end of history as their telos, the messianic era as Benjamin conceives it is not some timeless, static, unhistorical space.[38] The perpetual lamp is, on the contrary, an image of "authentic historical experience." In quoting the past, it finds "new nourishment" in the old; it both opens and burns ever more of it up. Traditional theological distinctions between time and eternity, the profane and the messianic, are secularized (in accordance with, say, Marx's opposition between history and prehistory) and internally displaced. "Über einige Motive bei Baudelaire" quotes the following *pensée* of Joubert's: "Time is also to be found in eternity; but it is not earthly, worldly time. . . . This time does not destroy, it merely completes" (ibid., p. 635). Not merely is the distinction between time and eternity to be understood in temporal terms, but it is the time of lived experience in all its irreducible contingency—"the time to which the course of our own existence happens to have referred us" (ibid., p. 693)—that provides the most opportune model for such an eternity. The time that completes is the time that structures "experience in the strict sense" (ibid., p. 611). Joubert's distinction between such time and the time that destroys parallels Reik's earlier quoted opposition between destructive *Erinnerung* and conservative *Gedächtnis*, which is in turn correlative to that between voluntary and involuntary memory. "Experience in the strict sense" is always a matter of memory (*Gedächtnis*, *Eingedenken*), be it the coincidence of the collective and the individual past on certain festive days of the calendar or the fulfillment of an early wish:

The wish . . . belongs to the order of experience. . . . The earlier in life one makes a wish, the greater the prospects of its being fulfilled. The further a wish reaches back in time, the more one may expect from its fulfillment. But what accompanies one back into the far reaches of time is experience, which fulfills and structures it. Thus a wish fulfilled is the crowning of experience. (ibid., p. 635)

The category of fulfillment, which in the essay on translation stood for the ultimate completion and reconciliation of languages in a single universal "language of truth," here connotes a significantly profane, experiential model of messianic redemption. And inasmuch as experience ideally culminates in its own redemption, the messianic and the profane are not merely inextricable but practically indistinguishable. The connection between the individual wish that will or might have been fulfilled and the collective redemption of history's outstanding debts and unredeemed promise is explicitly made in "Über den Begriff der Geschichte": "The idea of happiness is . . . inextricably bound up with that of redemption. The same holds for the image of the past to which history gives its allegiance" (*GS*, 1, 2, p. 693). Happiness is synonymous with redemption, just as melancholy governs a world bereft of redemption (*S*, 1, pp. 289–90). Such happiness would appear to be neither "hymnic" nor "elegiac," neither wholly unprecedented nor merely repetitive. Therein Benjaminian redemption differs from its Proustian model, which it quotes—and thereby completes—against its context. Unlike *mémoire involontaire*, which finds its fulfillment in the pure repetition of the past (and which has, however, been steeping meanwhile in the unconscious and accreting further associations [ibid., p. 637]), the recuperation of the past that Benjamin intends is its restructuring completion, the fulfillment of its wishes. The wish is the precondition of its fulfillment, but the movement is not a unilinear one. Just as the weak, brave forces of historical redemption "act on the distant past [*wirken in die Ferne der Zeit zurück*]" (ibid., p. 694), so experience "accompanies one into the distant past [*in die Ferne der Zeit zurückgeleitet*]." In each case, individual and collective, the messianic light of redemption has the effect of retroactively articulating the past. Only with its fulfillment does the past fall into place; its completion coincides with its final reinterpretation. "Only the Messiah himself completes all historical activity . . ." (*S*, 1, p. 511). The historian's "construction" (*GS*, 1, 2, p. 701) of the past parallels its autobiographical articulation, and the fulfilled wish that "crowns" experience recalls the "headdress" that unifies the disparate strands of human history. Both metaphors of culmination also intimate the royal, "festive" atmosphere of messianic resurrection. And the rhythm of fulfillment is that of messianic actuality, the split second of the "fulfilled now" (*S*, 1, p. 575):

In folk symbolism distance in space can stand for distance in time; the shooting star which plunges into the endless distance of space thus became the symbol of a fulfilled wish. . . . The time contained in the moment that the light of the shooting star flashes before one is of the kind that Joubert outlined with his characteristic assurance. "Time," he says, "is also to be found in eternity. . . ." (*GS*, 1, 2, p. 635)

Such an equivalence of time and space reverses the endless time-space of historicist progress. The fulness of time is not, as one might have expected, long drawn out. The time of completion—the eternity that is to be visualized as the *ruche* of a dress—is as fugitive a flash as the time of incompletion, and the conditional tense, that of Baudelaire's encounter with the *passante* (*O toi que j'eusse aimée, ô toi qui le savais!*), one of the "women who might have given themselves to us" (*GS*, 1, 2, p. 693). The time that is "also to be found in eternity" is indistinguishable from that of the *trouvaille*, the partial completion, the apt quotation, the happy memory, the haphazard *correspondence* with an "earlier life."[39] Not merely is time to be found in eternity, it is *quintessentially* temporal. Far from having been filtered out of eternity, contingency—"the time to which the course of our own existence happens to have referred us" (ibid., p. 693)—remains of its essence.

Benjamin's triadic scheme returns at its third stage to the epic motifs of the first by way of their negation of the second. But the persistence into the messianic era of contrary motifs associated with the "liquidation" of epic continuity, its spacious time and leisurely breadth, introduces a considerable complication, one of several, into the temporal scheme. Not that triadic logic requires the total effacement of the second stage by the third. On the contrary, the fulfilling synthesis in which it culminates provides for a return to the first stage, which, far from falling behind the second, has meanwhile profited from its negativity. The headdress that crowns history *capitalizes* on it. While all triadic schemes come full circle—the full circle being the very figure of fulfillment—the closing of the circle no longer fits into the original charmed circle. The reconciliation of thesis and antithesis is the squaring of the line with the circle, and it is as a "spiral"[40] that the double movement of Hegelian *Aufhebung*, which appropriates the best of both worlds, may best be represented. The messianic world as Benjamin at times visualizes it seems, it is true, to encompass all previous history as its *Aufhebung*. For it is only within some quasi-Hegelian perspective that terms like *Universalgeschichte* have their place. Categories such as quotation and involuntary memory, on the other hand, remain obstinately fragmentary, and while they can be defined *as* fragmentary only in the messianic light of redemption, they also appear to extend into the age of their anticipated totalization. To that extent even the messianic world would remain one of splinters and flashes. True, the "dialectical image" is a flash of "ball lightning" that momentarily "traverses the whole horizon of the past" (ibid., p. 1233); and the quotation that fragments the historicist continuum is also a monadological microcosm in which the greater whole is explicitly said to be *aufgehoben* (*GS*, 1, 2, p. 703). But they are no less at odds with the all-inclusiveness of historicist eclecticism and Hegelian *Aufhebung* for being *extended* fragments. As for Benjamin's more programmatic, Hegelian, totalizing formulations, the headdress is no less partial a glimpse than the *ruche*. The drowning man who *sees* his "whole life" pass before him also fleetingly *envisions another* wholeness.[41] Home(land) is a dream, and totality a mirage, born of the intolerable, contrary experience of fragmentation: "The magnitude of the Messianic idea," writes Scholem," corresponds to the endless powerlessness in Jewish history during all the centuries of exile . . ." (*Messianic Idea*, p. 35). To claim that there will be universal history "only" in the messianic world, or that the eternal is "at all events" the *ruche* of a dress rather than a Platonic idea, is, furthermore, to make a polemical gesture rather than a doctrinal statement. Removed from their original, ideological context, "eternal" and "universal history" are, precisely, quoted against it, resituated, fitted to "the order of the day."

Instead of being *aufgehoben* in obedience to the "official" pressures of the triadic scheme, the messianic splinters of *Jetztzeit* are, as moments of messianic actuality, closer to messianic fulfillment than any future prospects ever could be. Ideas of future fulfillment are perhaps always in danger of coinciding with doctrines of progress. But Scholem has stressed the "catastrophic," antiprogressive tendencies especially characteristic of left-wing messianism, which dreams of "entirely new aspects of free fulfillment" (*Messianic Idea*, p. 21); and it is likewise *against* progress that, despite its necessarily triadic structure, Benjamin's messianism pits all its energies. Not in theological perspectives and teleological prospects but, according to the "Theologisch-politisches Fragment," in the "rhythm of messianic nature," the transient intensity of the moment, in *Glück*, *Vergängnis*, and *Untergang*, is fulfillment "destined" (*S*, 1, pp. 511–12) to be found. Or, alternatively, the fulfillment of a wish does not end it the way food and drink satisfy hunger and thirst, but, like a work of art or the smell of a flower, it keeps nourishing a desire that can never have its fill of it (*GS*, 1, 2, p. 645). Either way fulfillment is no cause for smug satisfaction, no durable plenitude. It is not as if, with the advent of the messianic age, mankind will enter into a fat "inheritance" (*GS*, 1, 3, p. 1242), a parousia of absolute knowledge, a historicist eternity in which truth will be finally incapable of running off. The coming of the Messiah is not, first appearances to the contrary, to be equated with the postponement of the historicist *Weltanschauung* until the right moment—the moment to end all right moments. For merely to delay the historicist (or, synonymously, the social-democratic[42]) vision of things until some future date is to perpetuate both it and the intervening waiting period, to project ideology onto utopia. Its categories are doubtless too compromised by the ideological function they occupy in the unredeemed present to deserve to be held over for later reinstatement. The eternity that is *not* the *ruche* of a dress will for the foreseeable future continue to help eternalize the continuity of class rule.

Epic categories are, likewise, too contaminated by the vices of historicist historiography to retain much of their utopian promise, and the motif of the chronicle enters Benjamin's conception of the messianic world as only one motif among many. If his description of messianic "prose" refers to "Der Erzähler," it is from the essay on surrealism that it actually quotes (ibid., pp. 1234–35). And it is the note that predicates historical insight on "the liquidation of the epic element in historiography" that supplies the link between the two accounts of messianic and surrealist prose:

> It is the convergence of past and present in a constellation that produces an image [*Bild*]. . . . The historian's credentials are the result of his sharpened awareness of the crisis into which the subject of history has entered at any given time. This subject is by no means a transcendental subject but the embattled, oppressed class in its most exposed situation. Historical insight exists only for it, and for it only in the historical moment. Therein the liquidation of the epic moment in historiography finds confirmation. What occurs to involuntary memory is—and this distinguishes it from voluntary memory— never a course of events but solely an image. (Hence "disorder" as the visual space [*Bildraum*] of involuntary memory.) (ibid., pp. 1242–43)

Nowhere is the difference between Benjamin's and Hegel's conception of historical remembrance more apparent than here. In both cases it is a question of remembered *images*, but there the resemblance stops. At the moment of final synthesis and "absolute knowledge" the Hegelian *Weltgeist* also contemplates its own past, which

> represents the sluggish [*träge*] movement and succession of spirits [*Geister*], a gallery of images each of which is provided with the complete wealth of the spirit [*Geist*], and hence moves so slugglishly because the self has to penetrate and digest this whole wealth of its substance.[43]

"Raising itself again" "as if everything that preceded it were lost for it" (ibid., p. 564), the *Geist* methodically works its way through its prehistory. It assimilates itself. Nothing, in other words, is finally lost, the past cannot run away, and the present is a time of digestion, not drowning. One has indeed to be the *Weltgeist* for the past to reappear in the atemporal copresence of a "gallery of images." Here too, "succession and movement" exist in spatial simultaneity. It is once again the Olympian, historicist perspective on the past "as it actually was," "the 'eternal' image of the past." The sluggish tempo at which the *Weltgeist* reappropriates its past is the diametrical opposite of the Benjaminian lightning flash. On the one hand, "the labor of the negative," the sluggish [*träge*] rhythm of a philosophico-digestive system, the laws of digestion, inertia, and gravity; on the other hand, their messianic, momentary suspension. On the one hand, "epic leisureliness"; on the other, the pressures of a crisis which compresses the past into an instant too transient and discontinuous to permit the equation of messianic illumination with the casting of light, let alone the workings of a system.

On the one hand, the orderly "progress" of "reason in history," calmly reviewed by its moving spirit; on the other, the "storm" called "progress" in which even the appalled "angel of history," who surveys only wreckage, is helplessly caught up. On the one hand, partisans—"the embattled, oppressed class in its most exposed situation"—as the authentic subject of history; on the other hand, the leisureliness of the leisure class, the seamless continuity of the unfolding *Weltgeist*, whose divine impartiality stands revealed under the alien gaze of the angel of history as the "triumphal procession" of all the ruling classes that ever were: "Whoever to this day has carried off the victories participates in the triumphal procession which leads today's rulers over those who nowadays lie prostrate. The spoils are as usual paraded in the procession. They are called culture [*die Kulturgüter*]" (*GS*, 1, 2, p. 696). From the vantage point of the *Weltgeist* history is estheticized into the history of great men, into culture, "the complete wealth of the spirit," a well-endowed gallery. When the historical materialist permits himself an overview, his response is that of the angel: "For whatever culture he surveys [*überblickt*] has . . . origins which he cannot contemplate without horror" (ibid.).

Where Hegel considers the process of disgestive remembrance to be the interiorization of the past [*Er-Innerung*], Benjamin associates involuntary memory with a contrary exteriorization of the self that explodes the confines of its private interiority. The "disorder" of this anarchic *Bildraum* (which, if spatial, is anything but homogeneous) dislocates the orderly "gallery of images." The *Weltgeist* passes in review the procession of its "moments," the *Geister*, which successively "relieve" one another after their respective turns of duty. If involuntary memories are said to "fall in" before the subject of history, the order amidst their disorder—a "true" order that appears "distorted" (*S*, 2, p. 136) only in the eyes of a distorted order—is neither military nor organic, and the historical subject *in extremis* has no time to take their salute. Only the victors can afford to be contemplative. Unlike a gallery, the *Bildraum* is, according to the essay on surrealism, no longer accessible to contemplation. It is the space of collective political action (*AN*, p. 214). Benjamin distinguishes sharply in this context between two forms of political language, the surrealist image and the social-democratic comparison (ibid., p. 213). Images are born of an interaction between the present and the past, a historical "constellation." Comparisons are oriented towards the future. Rosy comparisons, optimistic comparatives, evasive similes, and disembodied figures of speech—such is the stock-in-trade, the tell-tale poetry of social-democratic party programs, a rhetoric of visions, vistas, and ideals, of progress and postponement, which reveals its utopia for what it is—a vague never-never land contemplated for all too far away. The best energies of the working class are, however, "nourished on the image of their oppressed forefathers, not on the ideal of their liberated grandchildren" (*GS*, 1, 2, p. 700). Unlike the future-oriented ideal or "poetic" comparison, the image is a matter of literal prose, spatial proximity, temporal actuality, of a "reality" that "has exceeded itself as much as the Communist Manifesto demands" (*AN*, p. 215). It is in the actual practice of his surrealist contemporaries that Benjamin sees enacted here and now the messianic world of "universal and integral actuality," the "feast" that is "cleansed of all ceremony"[44] and "has burst the fetters of the written word":

... wherever action itself is and throws off images, seizes them back and devours them, where proximity looks itself in the face, this sought-for visual space [*Bildraum*] opens up, the world of all-sided and integral actuality in which the "Sunday best" ["*die gute Stube*"] falls away, the space, in a word, where political materialism and the physical creature share between them the inner itself, the psyche, the individual, or whatever else we wish to throw before them, with such dialectical justice that no limb remains untorn. (ibid.)

"All-sided and integral" though such a *Bildraum* is, it is clearly not to be confused with Hegel's picture gallery. Its all-sidedness is not all-inclusiveness; its wholeness is synonymous with dismemberment; it is not a synthesis but an explosive force field. "Integral actuality" connotes an unreserved commitment to the moment, an affirmation of the transient which suspends the transitional, "a present which is not transition but in which time is answerable [*einsteht*]" (*GS*, 1, 2, p. 702). It is diametrically opposed to the Hegelian temporality of narcissistic retention and self-digestion. It does not accumulate temporal capital. For the author of "Über den Begriff der Geschichte" what world history accumulates is precisely a mounting heap of rubble, and what it consolidates is a stock of domination which the powers that be inherit from their predecessors (ibid., pp. 696–97); the world still lives under an ancestral curse; capital is mythical. "For the essence of mythical events is repetition" (*GS*, 1, 3, p. 1234). The messianic instant disrupts the closed immanence of the eternal return, the fateful clock. Only when the subject opens himself, without Hegelian cover but not without hope of redemption, to truths that can run away does the *Bildraum* "open up" the way that in Baudelaire's poetry "a few rare days," which "stand out from time," are likewise said by Proust to "open up" (*GS*, 1, 2, p. 637). But in this case it is no longer a matter of completion, fulfillment, and the gradual Baudelairean *vaporisation du moi*. The experience of integral actuality coincides with the surrealist disruption of bodily integrity, a festive rupturing of the self. The difference between this almost Dionysian celebration "in which no limb remains untorn" and Hegel's "Bacchantic ecstasy [*Taumel*] in which no limb is not drunk" (*Phänomenologie des Geistes*, p. 39) is a significant one. The latter is immediately qualified as "transparent and simple repose." The self-intoxication of the Hegelian system causes no disorderliness in its serried ranks. But what Benjamin apostrophizes is a revolutionary *dérèglement* of the bourgeois subject, of his inwardness and isolation, in the name of bodily communication and a political collective. Dialectics as Benjamin here understands it is synonymous with "annihilation" rather than *Aufhebung*, with abandon rather than conservation. Destruction would, however, be dialectical, even Hegelian, to the extent that its negativity was productive—in this case, of the third phase of the triad. It would be in and through such "dialectical annihilation" that the *restitutio in integrum* (S, 1, p. 511) of the past, the resurrection of the body and the reestablishment of a social community, would be brought about. Involuntary re-membrance, which "articulates" (*GS*, 1, 2, p. 695) the past, is the product of dismemberment, not of *Er-Innerung*. But such intensive moments recover the past more integrally than any other (more epic) form of memory. To that extent the historicist panorama is, *as* view, itself a very partial view. Disintegration would thus prove to be the medium of reintegration. The motif has many antecedents in the messianic tradition. According to its more apocalyptic versions, Scholem points out (*Messianic Idea*, pp. 12–13), the final order in which everything will have its proper place is heralded by anarchy. If intimations are to be had of the messianic aftermath that Jews are forbidden to visualize (*Bilderverbot*), then they are only in the disarry of the *Bildraum*. The glimpses it affords of messianic fulfillment never amount to a Hegelian plenitude of meaning.

Already Benjamin's early theology of language rested on its idealist extension far beyond the realm of what is spóken and written: in the beginning was the Word. The materialist *Bildraum* and the world of messianic prose likewise exceed the confines of the book. Surrealism seeks to overcome the oppositions between life and literature, word and deed, the individual and the collective, and the language of "integral actuality" is the "liberated prose which has burst the chains of writing." Persistently literary though its models remain, they are not confined to literature. To quote is to leap and to summon(s); involuntary memory is ball-lightning; cultural interpretation is inseparable from political praxis, and *vice versa*. Only in the messianic age will universal history exist, but it will not be limited to historiography. Not that the oral is here played off against the written: messianic prose is "not written but . . . festively performed." Actuality demands action; its form is performance. But the suspicion arises that such heightened immediacy is all the more indebted to the "metaphysics of presence" that in the Western tradition attaches to all "phallogocentric" activity.[45] Benjamin himself was the first to point to the theological dwarf hidden under the table, and his concept of presence alludes no less undisguisedly to the mystical *nunc stans*. But it is not with some undivided presence of voice or action that Benjamin equates the messianic instant. Integrity consists in being rent asunder. Far from being a unitary moment of metaphysical presence pure and simple, the mystical actuality of *Jetztzeit* is a *split* second predicated on an assent to rupture and mortality, and its agency is an immediate but mediated presence of mind constituted by the shifting constellations of past, present, and future. The present is a forcefield of tensions. Messianic prose, we argued, enacts a double liberation, an emancipation from ritual forms and an emancipation from that emancipation—a tension between myth and demythologization within which each acts to free the other. Myth and demythologization are not only contraries. At once accelerated and arrested, demythologization coincides with a new mutation of myth: such would be the *messianic* "dialectic of the enlightenment."[46] Inasmuch as the forces of messianic annihilation tap apocalyptic sources, myth is at once the agent and the object of demythologization. The relation between the two is as intense and difficult as that established between the profane and messianic orders in the "Theologisch-politisches Fragment"; they further each other not by a process of convergence and reconciliation but by going their separate ways. Benjamin calls the epiphanies generated by their tangential interaction moments of "profane illumination" (*AN*, pp. 202, 215). The expression is itself the scene of a "dialectical annihilation." It yokes together the same contrary, but noncontradictory, tensions that are at work in the world of messianic prose. "Festively performed" yet without "festive song," that world is itself profane illumination, a feast which survives the elimination of traditional festivities. And it is precisely in the "proximity" of the *Bildraum* that something in the order of "aura"—a category that originates in the context of religious ritual, is defined by inviolable distance ("however close it may be"), and is liquidated by the contemporary need to "bring things humanly and spatially closer" (*GS*, 1, 2, p. 479)—reemerges out of its very destruction. The bourgeoisie has, according to Marx, stripped the "halo" away from men's perception of their relations, which they can henceforth "consider with sober eyes";[47] Benjamin derives from the selfsame *Communist Manifesto* the demand that reality "exceed" itself; only both impulses together produce profane illumination. "Thanks to a dialectical optic which recognizes the everyday as impenetrable and the impenetrable as everyday" (*AN*, p. 213), the "creative overcoming of religious illumination" (ibid., p. 202) neither eradicates the mystical nor preserves it intact, but plunges it into the heart of the profane world. Despite Benjamin's references to dialectics,[48] this movement of double negation is not strictly comparable to Hegelian *Aufhebung*, which never exceeds the bounds of philosophical prose, the immanence of conceptual assimilation.[49] (Rather it resembles certain aspects of the German Romantics' alternative concept of prose as elaborated in Benjamin's dissertation.) But it is the profane illuminations of Benjamin's own writing that perhaps best enact what it means to burst the fetters of the written word. Messianic *Jetztzeit* is festively enacted at those instants of "hymnic" climax when, half prose and half dithyrambic incantation, Benjamin's own language is governed by the free messianic rhythms it invokes. Nowhere is it less prosaic than where it invokes messianic prose:

... und der Rhythmus dieses ewig vergehenden, in seiner Totalität vergehenden, in seiner räumlichen, aber auch zeitlichen Totalität vergehenden Weltlichen, der Rhythmus der messianischen Natur, is Glück. (*S*, 1, p. 512)

... überall, wo ein Handeln selber das Bild aus sich herausstellt und ist, in sich hineinreisst und frisst, wo die Nähe sich selbst aus den Augen sieht ... (*AN*, p. 215)

For if the record kept by memory—historiography—constitutes the creative indifference of the various epic forms (as great prose is the creative indifference of the various metrical forms) ... (*S*, 2, p. 245)

Epics arise, according to Hegel, in "poetic" periods before the world has become "prose." They are "absolutely first books," "Bibles," which would, put together, form a "gallery of *Volksgeister*."[50] But historiography proper begins where poetry ends (ibid., pp. 352–53), and it is only from the vantage point of "absolute knowledge" that the picture gallery of world history may be contemplated. To that extent the Hegelian system supersedes the novel as the prose epic of the "bourgeois" world (ibid., p. 452). Benjamin for his part raises the question

whether historiography does not represent the point of creative indifference between all forms of the epic. Then written history would relate to the epic forms as white light to the colors of the spectrum. (*S*, 2, p. 243)

Messianic historiography is the final point of creative indifference. Universal history come true, the restoration of a universal language, it too represents the *Aufhebung* of epic categories. Benjamin both rejects and retains them. The historicist assumption that history is "something that can be told" is ideology, but the chronicler, the "history-teller" who tells events great and small and weaves the strands of the past into a crowning headdress, is a utopian version of the historian. The great messianic prose that is the creative indifference of the various metrical forms differs markedly, however, from the grey prose of Hegelian philosophy, the owl of Minerva that takes flight only at dusk. It is rather the white light of revelation, which contains all the colors of the spectrum.

The fragmented present knows only discontinuous illuminations. But even at present there is method to the surrealist disorder of the

Bildraum, and the interweaving of the loose ends has already begun. Nothing reveals the continuity of Benjamin's own development more than his late, apparently discontinuous jottings. Too heterogeneous to be harmonized, they are nevertheless interconnected by an overarching messianic aspiration. They are best described by the concepts they themselves invoke and the metaphors they coin. A drowning, shipwrecked[51] writer's instantaneous recollection of his past production, so many Baudelairean *fusées* that link widely separate moments of his past, they apply Benjamin's theory and practice of quotation to his own already fissured corpus. At such a moment distinctions between the early and the late Benjamin lose their relevance. Under and against the ungodly pressures of the actual moment, Benjamin's theology of language, his theory of the baroque *Trauerspiel*, the dissertation on the German Romantics' theory of criticism, the essays on Baudelaire, Proust, surrealism, and Brecht disclose covert correspondences and enter into unforeseen constellations. Time is, however, too short for anything but short circuits. The angel of history, Hannah Arendt argues (*Illuminations*, pp. 12–13), recalls the Baudelairean *flâneur*. It is not, however, the man who swims in the crowd as in his element but the stranded dandy of *Le monde va finir*, "lost in this miserable world, elbowed by the crowds" (ibid., p. 54), the author who is precisely "no *flâneur*" (*GS*, 1, 2, p. 652), that she has in mind. Benjamin's late jottings are written by an *homme de lettres* cruelly jostled by world history. Benjamin's version of the materialist historian further recalls Baudelaire's account of the hectic activity of the "painter of modern life," the *homme du monde* and "perfect *flâneur*," "hurried, violent, active, as if he were afraid that the images would escape him," images that need to be subjected to "forced idealization." The *idéal* of euphoric memory has its counterpart in the spleen of *L'Ennemi*. Memory as reclamation of the past from a flood, re-collection with rake and shovel in the premature "autumn of ideas," a decimated harvest of unripe fruit—such is allegorical *Eingedenken*, bereft of *fusées*. There can be no question of a definitive summation ripended in the fullness of time.

If Benjamin's late notes insistently return to motifs from his early theological writings, this is perhaps because now more than ever he needs to cling to the saving straw of salvation itself, to hold fast his original faith in the "consistency of truth," the ultimate unity of a "language of truth" in which the "ultimate secrets" are "preserved" "without tension [*spannungslos*]" (*S*, 1, p. 49). But by now such unity can be aspired to only in and through its impossibility. Theology, not unlike historicism, its vulgar secularization, is at once ideology and utopia. All would-be universal languages are so many forms of "esperanto," and the urge to unity is programmatic at best, "lewd" (*AN*, p. 452) at worst.

Already in the "Theologisch-politisches Fragment" it was by persevering in opposite directions that the profane and the messianic were to intersect and combine forces. The dream of a single, tensionless truth is both preserved and negated by the intensity of Benjamin's commitment to the tension between truths. Is it perhaps because he is never without a sense of the ultimate order of things that he can entrust himself to the gravitation of centrifugal pulls, opposing influences, and different languages? Such would be the enabling faith behind his intellectual experimentation. In the process he discovers connections inaccessible to common sense. Not middle ways—the *via media* is the only way, said Schönberg, that does not lead to Rome—but lines between the (battle-)lines, intersections that are the scene neither of compromise nor paralysis: "Where others come up against walls or mountains, there too he sees a way. . . . Because he sees ways everywhere, he himself always stands at the crossroads" (*GS*, 4, 1, p. 398). When Brecht objects that the "depth" of a Kafka leads nowhere, Benjamin rejoins that "going deep" is his way of "proceeding to the antipodes" (*VüB*, p. 122). It is in the "border area" (ibid.) where such extremes—depth and surface, literature and politics—intersect, and "the strange interaction between reactionary theory and revolutionary practice" (*S*, 2, p. 167) takes place, that the right line emerges:

. . . the tendency of a literary work can be politically right only if it is also literarily right. This means that a politically correct tendency includes a literary tendency. . . . The correct political tendency of a work includes its literary quality for the good reason that it includes its literary tendency. (*VüB*, pp. 96–97)

It is because Benjamin's later writings take an increasingly direct political line that Adorno will be prompted in effect to cite against him a variation of the type of argument—"depth" revalued—with which Benjamin had countered Brecht's attack on Kafka. Fidelity to his "innermost being" will, Adorno argues, do the cause more good than a damaging outer conformity:

. . . you have done yourself violence . . . in order to pay tributes to Marxism which profit neither it nor yourself. . . . You have done your innermost being [*Ihrer eigensten Substanz*] a disservice by imposing a kind of materialist self-censorship on your boldest, most fruitful thoughts. . . . There is, in God's name, only one truth, and if your insights into this one truth are gained in categories that seem apocryphal when confronted with materialism as you conceive it, you will nevertheless bring home more of this one truth that way than if you avail yourself of the conceptual machinery you must ceaselessly balk at setting in motion. (*BR*, 2, p. 787)

Truth has a center, a capital. There is a "home" at which all truths can come to rest (*spannungslos*). "There is, in God's name, only one truth."

There can, on the basis of this monotheistic faith,[52] *ultimately* exist no conflict between materialism and metaphysics. Which *ultimately* implies that Benjamin would be all the better a Marxist for remaining true to the metaphysician within him. Such convergence within divergence is, it is true, a Benjaminian motif. Benjamin never abandons the aspiration to unity, nor does he indefinitely postpone it. But while Adorno's position echoes that of the "Theologisch-politisches Fragment," it also reverses its profane thrust. And while the tensions may be *ultimately* reconcilable, what if, here and now, there are priorities? The unity of truth is no panacea for the tensions of the present. In his reply to Adorno Benjamin invokes "solidarity with the experiences we have all been through in the last fifteen years" (ibid., p. 793), a difficult union of the personal and the political which, moreover, he equates with his "innermost [*eigenste*] productive interests." Adorno had urged Benjamin's own interests against him; his reply quotes them back. Whether or not the intellectual's mind can be spared some kind of civil war, it further claims, is a historical matter beyond individual control. Benjamin does not seek to deny that his present interests "may occasionally seek to do violence" to his original ones. But the author of "Der destruktive Charakter" does not shirk such violence: "An antagonism is at work from which I would not dream of wanting to be exempted" (ibid.). Rather than let himself be protected against himself, Benjamin urges politics against Adorno, metaphysics against Brecht, and exposes his innermost being to their tension. In so doing he posts himself at the limits of theology, but this side of its "deconstruction." For both sides of the "antagonism" remain committed to the productivity of antagonism, the reversibility of extremes, to truth through contradiction. The story of the dwarf and the automat indicates that metaphysics and materialism can, after all, indeed must, work in tandem. In the end the two have, despite the continuing tension and occasional violence between them, become inextricable. What underlies them both are the binary oppositions of a triadic scheme. Benjamin's last, fragmentary notes are structured by a series of erratic, idiosyncratic, displaced quotations from a millennial narrative. And what, indeed, is fragmentation, according to that narrative, if not the definition of its second stage—the stage at which, the story says, the story originates, the broken mirror image of Truth?

NOTES

1. The later foreword (1962) names Goethe, Schiller, Hegel, Friedrich Schlegel, and Solger as antecedents (*Die Theorie des Romans* [Neuwied: Luchterhand, 1965], p. 10). Cf. also Schelling on the epic as "a state of innocence where everything that will later exist only in a dispersed state, or will be reunited out of such dispersal, is still one and together [*beisammen*

und eins]" (in *Philosophie der Kunst, Werke* [Stuttgart: J. G. Cotta, 1856–61], 1. Abteilung, Bd. 5). Marx's celebrated "difficulty" (*Grundrisse*, tr. D. McLellan [London: Vintage Books, 1971], p. 45) in understanding why "Greek art and epos" still constitute a "standard and model beyond attainment" had found a repeated answer in the esthetics of German Idealism, notably in Hegel's version of the Greek epic as a "poetic" world-historical home, a *vie antérieure* prior to the classic antinomies of bourgeois society. The epic holds out the Marxist image of utopia, and the "eternal charm" exerted by the "childhood of human society" (ibid.) derives from its capacity to accommodate the contradictory desire simultaneously to outgrow and recapture one's childhood, to embody Baudelaire's definition of genius. Like Odysseus, Marxism seeks, through detours and battles, to return home. Its concept of liberation bears witness to what E. M. Butler called "the tyranny of Greece over Germany." In "The Idealist Embarrassment: Observations on Marxist Aesthetics" (*New Literary History* 7, no. 1 [1975]: 208), H. R. Jauss cites Marx on the epic as one indication among many that a materialist esthetic cannot do without "a central core of idealism," and correctly locates triadic thinking in the *Ōekonomisch-philosophische Manuskripte* (p. 196) and Herbert Marcuse's esthetics (p. 208).

2. *Gesammelte Schriften* (Frankfurt: Suhrkamp, 1974–   ), Bd. 1, 2, pp. 695–704. Quotations will, where possible, refer to this new complete edition. The following abbreviations will be used: GS for *Gesammelte Schriften*; S for *Schriften* (Frankfurt: Suhrkamp, 1955); AN for *Angelus Novus* (Frankfurt: Suhrkamp, 1966); VüB for *Versuche über Brecht* (Frankfurt: Suhrkamp, 1966); BR for *Briefe* (Frankfurt: Suhrkamp, 1966). Translations from the German are my own.

3. In Lukács's scheme, on the other hand, the story represents, qua "epic form without totality," a fall from true epic "grace" (*Die Theorie des Romans*, pp. 45–49). "With the merest trembling of its transcendental points of reference" (ibid., p. 35) the epic cosmos crumbles.

4. *Gedächtnis*, which establishes the narrative "chain" and "network" common to epic and story alike, represents memory as a noun, a substantial, quasi-spatial, "extensive" entity. *Eingedenken*, though not itself a verb, derives, more directly than *Gedächtnis*, from the verb *gedenken* and connotes a correspondingly greater degree of activity—"intensive" memory as recollection, remembrance. Such remembrance is focused, not digressive; the preposition *eingedenk* ("mindful of") refers to specific acts of memory. *Gedächtnis*, by contrast, is a matter of less active, plural memories; diverse, scattered (*zerstreut*) occurrences occur (*einfallen*) to it. *Zerstreut* is cognate with *Zerstreuung* ("diversion"), and thus connects with *kurzweilig* ("diverting," whiling away the time and thereby shortening it). As the antithesis of *verewigend* it connotes not so much a short memory—the storyteller can, on the contrary, tell stories indefinitely—as the type of attention that epic memory devotes to any one of its objects: unlike *Eingedenken*, *Gedächtnis* does not dwell on single events but weaves them together.

5. *Eingedenken* represents, according to one of Benjamin's notes, the "quintessence" of the Jews' "theological conception of history" (*GS*, 1, 3, p. 1252); and, according to another, epitomizes "an experience which forbids us to conceive history in fundamentally atheological terms, however little one ought to try to write it in theological categories" (ibid., p. 1235). Like prayer, the *Eingedenken* practised by the *angelus novus* would symbolically enact that restoration of the broken whole known in the Kabbalist tradition as

Tikkun. Just as *Ursprung des deutschen Trauerspiels* freezes history at the moment of baroque allegory, which itself freezes history, so "Über den Begriff der Geschichte" represents the *Eingedenken* of *Eingedenken*. That Benjamin should on the eve of the holocaust accentuate its Jewish component needs no explanation. He both seeks to save *Eingedenken* and already speaks of it in the past tense ("an idea of how past time *was experienced* in remembrance," italics mine). Its salvation could not, even if it wanted, be synonymous with preservation. It must be differently saved, like salvation itself.

6. Benjamin's differing estimates of the (in)efficacy of *Eingedenken* are indicative of a tension that found its most explicit formulation in a recently published exchange with Max Horkheimer over the question of whether the past is ever "over and done with (*abgeschlossen*)." Benjamin's claim that it is *not* rests, Horkheimer argues, on a theological belief in the Last Judgment and the resurrection of the dead. But, he adds, positive and negative aspects of the issue are perhaps to be distinguished: happiness is "negated," but unhappiness "sealed," by death. A manuscript of Benjamin's quotes Horkheimer's letter and adds the following "corrective": ". . . history is not only a science but equally a form of *Eingedenken*. What science 'establishes,' *Eingedenken* can modify. *Eingedenken* can close the open (happiness) and open up the closed (suffering). This is theology; but the experience of *Eingedenken* forbids us to conceive history in fundamentally atheological terms. . . ." (quoted by Rolf Tiedemann, "Historischer Materialismus und der politische Materialismus," in *Materialien zu Benjamins Thesen "Über den Begriff der Geschichte,"* ed. P. Bulthaup [Frankfurt: Suhrkamp, 1975], pp. 87–88). This tension will be enacted in the text and notes of "Über den Begriff der Geschichte." The equation of *Eingedenken* with a straw—with the inefficacy of magic hope or the efficacy of a *"weak* messianic force"—incorporates something of Horkheimer's scepticism.

7. Hannah Arendt interprets Benjamin's "whole" life as having been lived under the baleful influence of *das bucklicht Männlein.* Cf. her introduction to the English volume *Illuminations* (New York: Schocken, 1968, notably pp. 1–18).

8. Rolf Tiedemann, *Studien zur Philosophie Walter Benjamins* (Frankfurt: Suhrkamp, 1965), p. 96.

9. The greatest dramas are thus quite undramatically, unwittingly, missed: we were not at home. The resultant distortion is, as the word *Entstellung* indicates, synonymous with such "displacement" or "misplacement" of the self. The most insidious distortions of all are the folds left by the passing of time that should have been seized—inscriptions that are made in our absence, like the forgotten "sentence" that is engraved on the back of the guilty in Kafka's penal colony (*AN*, p. 262). It is not, as common sense has it, experience, but its blanks and absences that leave the worst marks. It is as if the stories we cannot *tell* thereupon *write* themselves into our bodies. These distortions are then chalked up to a distorted version of "experience." *Genuine* experience will then itself appear distorted, "the world distorted in the condition of resemblance, in which the true surrealist face of existence breaks through" (*S*, 2, p. 136). This face is a face without "folds and furrows." It thus requires no magical rejuvenation to resist aging: it is enough to be fully present. It requires no transfiguration to be resurrected: it is enough that the spell be lifted. Nor does messianic redemption require violent change: minimal readjustments suffice.

10. Benjamin's reading of Proust defines itself against misreadings that

take *Le temps retrouvé* at its idealist word (*S*, 2, pp. 142–43). Such a misreading partially invalidates Peter Szondi's discussion of the difference between Proust's and Benjamin's search for lost time (in his essay "Hoffnung im Vergangenen. Walter Benjamin und die Suche nach der verlorenen Zeit," in *Theodor W. Adorno zum sechzigsten Geburtstag*, Max Horkheimer, ed. [Frankfurt: Europäische Verlagsanstalt, 1963], pp. 241–56). In the coincidence of past and present, Szondi argues, Proust seeks liberation from time, death and the future; what Benjamin seeks in the past is, on the contrary, the anticipation, positive or negative, of the future.

11. In "Der destruktive Charakter" Benjamin describes the socio-political counterpart to such physiological alertness—"the consciousness of the historical individual whose basic emotion is an invincible mistrust of the course of events" (*GS*, 4, 1, p. 398). The destructive character's sole activity, like that of consciousness, consists in "effacing traces," and consequently he does not age: "For destruction rejuvenates, because it clears away the traces of our own age" (ibid., p. 397). The nonexperience that in the Proust essay is said to leave the marks of age on our faces here functions, conversely, as the agency of all-effacing rejuvenation. There would thus exist two antithetical forms of presence of mind and, correlatively, two opposite types of rejuvenation—the involuntary recuperation of traces and their evacuation, writing and erasing, the text of memory and the *tabula rasa* of consciousness, "spiritual exercises" (*S*, 2, p. 143) and "training" (*GS*, 1, 1, p. 614). But the opposites are opposite ends of the same spectrum. Each enacts a dialectic between past and present. Proustian memory, as Benjamin conceives it, is no more lost to the present than is destructive action to the past. The notes to "Über den Begriff der Geschichte" refer to both.

12. The Freudian hypothesis according to which "becoming conscious and leaving behind a memory-trace are mutually incompatible within one and the same system," and in consequence memories are "often most powerful and enduring when the incident that left them behind never came to consciousness" (*GS*, 1, 2, pp. 612–13), means that only what has not been consciously experienced can become an involuntary memory. Judged by criteria of alert punctuality, it is, rather, a form of absent-mindedness, a belated reversal of inattention, a presence of mind predicated on its original absence and an intervening time-lag during which memories interact in the unconscious. This interweaving of remembrance (*die Penelopearbeit des Eingendenkens*) is—compared to the *Erinnerung* that usually passes for memory—"a Penelope work of forgetting," and involuntary memory is a presence of mind "much closer to forgetting than what is usually called memory": "For here the day unravels what the night has woven. Every morning upon awakening we hold in our hands, usually weakly and loosely, only a few fringes of the tapestry of lived life that has been woven in us by forgetting" (*S*, 2, p. 133). The goal-bound consciousness that accompanies daylight activities undoes "the text" the night has woven. Of this text forgetting is the woof and remembrance the warp; and the *other* forgetting, which unravels (unwrites) it simultaneously inscribes a contrary text, the text of age, into our features. Forgetting and remembering are doubly synonymous: to remember the day is to forget the night, and vice versa. In "Der Erzähler," likewise, the art of storytelling is linked to the ability to remember stories and thence to rhythms of physical relaxation that have more in common with sleep than with concentrated attention. Storytelling is dying "because there is no more weaving and spinning to go on while one

listens. The more self-forgetful the listener, the more deeply what he hears is impressed on his memory" (S, 2, p. 236). But self-forgetfulness may, conversely, give *das bucklicht Männlein* his chance and *cost* us half our memory.

13. Such pressure also generates and renews tripartite schemes. The triads of apocalyptic messianism characteristically grow out of crises they locate at their second stage. Closer to home, the number three, Paul Fussell points out in *The Great War and Modern Memory* (New York: Oxford Univ. Press, 1975, pp. 125–31), structures the "myth, ritual and romance" of modern war memoirs. (The triadic vision is, he notes, an immemorial one; the reader is referred to J. Brough's "The Tripartite Ideology of the Indo-Europeans: An Experiment in Method," *Bulletin of the School of Oriental and African Studies* 22 [1959]: 69–85.) Not merely, then, do Northrop Frye's archetypal structures survive modern warfare strikingly intact, but they organize its narrative assimilation. Such an analysis stands in stark contrast to Benjamin's account of the speechlessness which afflicted soldiers returning from the front, unable to tell the unspeakable (S, 2, pp. 6–7, 230). The image of the *angelus novus* faced with the endless, mounting rubble of history is born of this "experience." The angel is transfixed in *mute* horror. Yet he is also the emblem of an apocalyptic triad, one which may, however, never know the return to paradise.

14. In his essay "Geschichte der Kunst und Historie" (in *Literaturgeschichte als Provokation* [Frankfurt: Suhrkamp, 1970]), Hans Robert Jauss elaborates on Droysen's critique of historicism and shows that what historicism took to be its objective, god-like account of historical reality in fact rests on unrecognized esthetic categories. Not merely is its model of history that of the (itself highly stylized) history of style (*Stilgeschichte*) (pp. 222–26), but Ranke's representation of history "as it actually was" resorts to "epic fictions" and conventions of literary narration. Its illusion of a closed chain of events without missing links is nothing but a narrative effect (p. 219); its illusion of organic completeness, of a beginning, a middle, and an end, remains faithful to the Aristotelian definition of the poetic fable (pp. 219–20); and its poetics of quasi-scientific objectivity, with its concomitant self-effacement of the teller in order to let history tell itself, strictly parallels that of the contemporaneous historical novel (pp. 220–21). Narration being, in Jauss's view, intrinsic to the very nature of historical perception and representation (p. 228), the only way of opening up the closed horizon of classical narration is to oppose to it the poetics of post-Flaubertian literary narrative, which dismantles omniscience, totality, teleology, and the intelligibility of the whole (p. 230). The history of historiography is characterized by "phases of progressive literarization, but also of contrary de-literarization" (p. 228); and insofar as modern poetics serves as its paradigm even de-literarization does not transcend literature. But to what extent do the modern works that undo traditional narrative still narrate? For Jauss all historical interpretation of the past in the light of the present ineluctably involves narrative continuity, whereas for Benjamin historical insight, whether in the form of messianic "illumination" or Marx's "theoretical armature," is predicated on a break with narrative and continuity, which henceforth amount to ideology. In their differing ways both Jauss and Benjamin argue for a new conception of (literary) history that will emerge out of the "destruction" of its "epic" versions (p. 244). There is, however, little actual indication that Jauss's historiography is itself indebted to modernist esthetics. On the other hand, Benjamin's version of historical materialism, though contained within the epic model of a beginning, a middle,

and an end, *is*. His projected history of the nineteenth century would have owed much to surrealist technique; and Proustian memory is one of the materialist historian's models.

15. Spleen breeds a false, alienated type of memory, *Andenken* ("memory," "memento"), wholly different from *Eingedenken*. It assembles souvenirs of its own past. In Baudelaire's poetry "*Erinnerung* wholly recedes in favor of *Andenken*. . . . The 'memento' epitomizes the transformation of the commodity into the collector's item. . . . It crystallizes man's increasing self-alienation; he catalogues his past as so many dead belongings" (*GS*, 1, 2, pp. 690, 689, 681). "Cataloguing the past is for Benjamin the personal correlative to the standard view of history against which his theses on the philosophy of history rebel" (Szondi, "Hoffnung im Vergangenen," p. 255).

16. "Erzählen oder Beschreiben?," in *Essays über Realismus* (Neuwied, 1971). In Lukács's theory of realism his earlier opposition between the epic and the novel is replaced by their continuity; it is almost as if the nostalgia that from the outset governed the novel's relation to the epic thereby finds alternative gratification. Lukács here interprets Marx's celebrated remark that "Greek art and epic" continue to be "in certain respects . . . a norm and unattainable model" (ibid., p. 207) to mean that the epic still represents a touchstone of realism by which—"mutatis mutandis" (p. 224), given the greater complexity of modern society—the novel should still measure itself. (As Jauss has pointed out ("Geschichte der Kunst und Historie," p. 159), Lukács thereby disregards the problem of the "unequal relation between the development of material production and that of art" to which it was the point of Marx's observation to draw attention). He can consequently quote Lessing's well-known account of the Homeric portrayal of the origins and history of Agamemnon's scepter (ibid., pp. 223–24) as an exemplary analysis of an undimmed model of narrative realism. (In so doing he seemingly ignores the esthetic consequences of Hegel's world-historical distinction between the living poetry of handmade epic objects such as Achilles's shield and the dead prose of factory products (*Ästhetik*, ed. Friedrich Bassenge [Frankfurt: Europäischer Verlagsanstalt], Bd 2, pp. 414–17); and yet it had been to the elaboration of these consequences that his earlier theory of the novel as the quest for epic concretion under nonepic, abstract conditions had been devoted). The defense of realism as the only adequate literary modality for representing *history* thus rests on certain *quasi-eternal* verities that Lukács holds to be self-evident—namely, that the "inner poetry" (p. 212) of the world is elicited through a principle of epic selection based on the criterion of its relation to historical praxis; that human praxis thus invariably contains an inner poetry which can to some extent resist "the domination of capitalist prose" (p. 213); and that "epic art—and self-evidently also the art of the novel—consists in discovering the characteristic humanly significant features of societal praxis" (ibid.). Lukács opposes such a permanently available possibility of epic *construction* oriented to human *praxis* to the modern positivist aberration of passive, cumulative, naturalist description. But it is the criteria of praxis and construction that motivate Benjamin's *rejection* of the epic as a viable historiographic model. And the historicism to which, on Benjamin's argument, epic narration has been reduced is itself (as the author of *Der historische Roman* would not have needed telling) equivalent to the naturalism against which Lukács's whole defense of realism is directed. There are, indeed, moments when his positive account of epic realism sounds suspiciously like Benjamin's negative characterization of historicism:

"Only the connection with praxis, only the complex chain [*Verkettung*] of the various deeds and sufferings of men can prove what things, institutions, etc. decisively influenced their fate. . . . All this can be surveyed [*überblicken*] only from the end. The necessarily contemporaneous observer must lose himself in the tangle of equivalent details. . . . The omniscience of the author gives the reader security, makes him at home in the world of art" (pp. 214–15). Gone, then, is the transcendental "homelessness" that defined the world of the novel in *Die Theorie des Romans*. It is, we noted, to the antithetical poetics of the modern *post-realist* novel (to which *Die Theorie des Romans* was indeed a major early contribution) that Jauss, who places a positively Lukácsian value on the role of narrative in historical representation, looks for models of how to write history today. And as for hindsight, retrospective omniscience, epic distance, chains of events, and overviews, all these signal, in Benjamin's scheme of things, a *disconnection* from *actual* praxis, Cf., on the normative value attached to epic narrative throughout Lukács's writings, Frederic Jameson's chapter on Lukács in *Marxism and Form* (Princeton: Princeton Univ. Press, 1971), especially pp. 163, 171–73, 179, 189–90, 204–05. Jameson's argument combines two somewhat contradictory theses. *Firstly*, that Lukács's analyses of the novel in *Die Theorie des Romans*, all of which "depend on what is a kind of literary nostalgia, on the notion of a golden age or lost Utopia of narration in Greek epic" (p. 179), establish the premises of his later theory of realism. (Jameson refers here to Hegel's abovementioned account of epic concretion and totality [pp. 165–66]. The contradiction he then claims to exist between the "purely formal Hegelian conceptual framework" of Lukács's account of the novel as "a process in which no guidelines are given in advance" and the "preconceived psychology" of the hero in terms of "the primal homesickness of being" [p. 179] is, however, nothing but the immanent opposition between the antithesis and the other two moments of the triad: primal homesickness is built into the by no means "formal" or "neutral" scheme, the absence of guidelines being the homesick disorientation of its second stage). *Secondly*, that this continuity is nevertheless modified, or materialized, by the impact of *Geschichte und Klassenbewusstsein* on Lukács's later theory of realism: ". . . the ultimate realization of a reconciled future will now be projected into the future, and with such a shift in perspective we are already well within a Marxist theory of history" (pp. 179–80). But it is not at all clear whether what Marx called the substitution of "the poetry of the future" for feudal nostalgia, the "removal" of the golden age from past to future, makes the difference between materialist and idealist historiography or whether it merely rearranges the idealist triad. "Now indeed that nostalgic vision of some golden age in which an epic wholeness was still possible gives place to a view of history which sees men as already implicitly reconciled to the world around them, in the sense in which that world is itself necessarily the result of human labor and human action" (p. 190). Such a view of history—namely, realism—does not, Jameson claims on Lukács's behalf, emerge before the nineteenth century. But novelistic realism being, on our earlier argument, based on an epic norm, the continuity between the two is perhaps even more unbroken than Jameson's first thesis implies. Whatever the intervening impact of *Geschichte und Klassenbewusstsein*, it too is grounded in much the same triadic scheme, and *Marxism and Form* follows suit. Cf., in this respect, the closing pages of Jameson's preface, pp. xvi–xix. To quote its last sentence against him, it ignores the nonneutrality of Hegelian categories only at the price of reinventing them.

17. This emerges most powerfully from Benjamin's essay on translation, "Die Aufgabe des Übersetzers." "For the great motif of an integration of the many languages into the one true one fills [*erfüllt*]" the translator's work, which is to intimate "the predestined, denied realm of the reconciliation and fulfillment [*Erfüllungsbereich*] of languages" (*S*, 1, p. 47). But to this end languages must be released from their burden of "heavy and alien meaning": "In this pure language, which no longer means or expresses anything, . . . all communication, all meaning and all intention finally reaches the point at which it is destined to be extinguished" (ibid., p. 52). That "the word should communicate *something* (beyond itself)" is indeed the "fall" of language (*S*, 2, p. 415).

18. Cf., for mystcal solutions to the problem of imagining God without taking his image in vain, Gershom Scholem, *Von der mystischen Gestalt der Gottheit* (Zürich: Rhein-Verlag, 1962). This tension between the Jewish taboo on graven idols of God or images of the future and the teleology intrinsic to all messianism informs the opening lines of the "Theologisch-politisches Fragment" (*S*, 1, p. 511), Benjamin's most extended venture into messianic theology. A heterodox variant on its triadic patterns, it constitutes a theological model for later less overtly theological motifs. The movement of its central argument (according to which the profane order is never closer to the messianic than when it goes its own separate, indeed opposite, way) will, *mutatis mutandis*, recur in various materialist guises.

19. *Die Theorie des Romans*, pp. 27, 31.

20. Cf., on Hegel's concept of prose, Peter Szondi, *Gattungspoetik und Geschichtsphilosophie* I, Bd 2 (Frankfurt: Suhrkamp, 1974), pp. 333, 488–90. In Hegel's *Ästhetik* "prose" and "contemporary prosaic conditions" refer interchangeably to the literary medium and the extra-literary essence of the modern bourgeois phase of world history. Its symmetrical counterpart, "the general epic condition of the world," has the same double connotation, and the double genitive of Lukács's "age of the epic" likewise closes the circle which makes each the other's frame of reference. This metaphorical extension of literary categories beyond the confines of the esthetic finds its way into Benjamin's thinking by way of the German Romantics' conception of prose, which occupies a central position in his dissertation, *Der Bergriff der Kunstkritik in der deutschen Romantik*.

21. To point out the messianic dimension of Marxism is, as a rule, to want to demythologize it. In Benjamin's writings, on the other hand, demythologizing and messianic impulses coexist and combine. Remembrance, according to "Über den Begriff der Geschichte," "demystified [*entzauberte*] the future to which those succumbed who sought knowledge from soothsayers. For the Jews the future did not on that account become empty, homogeneous time" (*GS*, 1, 3, p. 704); and in "Der Erzähler" Leskov is said to "interpret resurrection less as transfiguration than as the breaking of a spell [*Entzauberung*]" (*S*, 2, p. 251). The two impulses nevertheless project distinct models. Messianism necessarily presupposes a positive origin, a golden age, which is to be in some sense recreated. To break the mythical spell, on the other hand, is to free oneself from more negative origins. Whereas paradise lost belong to a positive, irrevocable past, myth extends, for better and mainly for worse, into the present. It is from this fateful continuum that its utopian potential must be released. Positively resolved, this movement would thus amount to another, "dialectical" version of the triad. Each of its terms, myth and demythologization, contains the other, and only by way of a productive interaction with each other could they progress to triadic fulfillment. Adorno's

critique of Benjamin's "Paris, die Hauptstadt des XIX Jahrhunderts" would thus represent the "dialectical" critique of one triad by another. Measured against such a "dialectic of the enlightenment," Benjamin's messianic (positive-negative-positive) triad looks "undialectical." It misses the negativity of the first stage (which is not merely a "golden age" but, above all, "hell" and "catastrophe") and the positivity of the second, capitalist phase (which is not merely hell but its potential liberation): this double omission, Adorno argues, brings Benjamin perilously close to the "regressive" myth-making of Jung and Klages (*BR*, Bd 2, pp. 671–83). (As our earlier comparison between Benjamin and the Lukács of *Die Theorie des Romans* indicated, Adorno's critique would apply still better to the latter.) That he need merely cite Benjamin against himself is an indication that the two models are as compatible as they are divergent. Once again the theoretical differences between Marxist estheticians amount to differing versions of the triadic scheme. But to call them "mere" variations would be to minimize their differences.

22. "Flaubert presumably had the profoundest mistrust of all the fashionable concepts of history that were current in the nineteenth century. As a theorist of history he was, if anything, a nihilist" (*GS*, 1, 3, p. 1244). But even as implacable a critic of progress as Flaubert saw in the liberation of prose from formal constraints the esthetic expression of more general historical developments: "La forme en devenant habile, s'atténue; elle quitte toute liturgie, toute règle, toute mesure; elle abandonne l'épique pour le roman, le vers pour la prose; elle ne se connaît plus d'orthodoxie et est libre comme chaque volonté qui la produit. Cet affranchissement de la matérialité se retrouve en tout et les gouvernements l'ont suivi, depuis les despotismes orientaux jusqu'aux socialismes futurs. C'est pour cela qu'il y a ni beaux ni vilains sujets . . . , le style étant . . . une manière absolue de voir les choses" (*Extraits de la correspondance, ou Préface à la vie d'ecrivain*, ed. G. Bollème [Paris: Editions du Seuil, 1963], pp. 62–63). "L'idéal n'est fécond que lorsqu'on y fait *tout* rentrer. C'est un travail d'amour et non d'exclusion" (ibid., p. 164). What Flaubert's conception of prose shares with Benjamin's is the subversive assumption that the effacement of formal restraints is correlative to the abolition of hierarchical standards. From the absolute standpoint of style no discriminations can be made between beautiful and ugly subjects, just as the chronicler, who occupies the similarly absolute vantage point of the Last Judgment, makes no distinction between large and small events. Such indiscriminateness is ambiguously poised between historicist ideology and the messianc utopia. "C'est trop vrai," Flaubert observed of *L'Education sentimentale*, "et esthétiquement parlant, il y manque: *la fausseté de la perspective*. . . . Toute oeuvre d'art doit avoir un point, un sommet, faire la pyramide, ou bien la lumière doit frapper sur un point le la boule. Or rien de tout cela dans la vie" (ibid., p. 288). Lukács quotes this statement as a perfect example of naturalist ideology, and in *Der historische Roman* he analyses *Salammbô* as an instance of the type of positivist accumulation that Benjamin denounces as historicism. Benjamin, however, finds a messianic dimension in the novel: "Witiko and Salambo [sic] present historical periods as self-contained, 'directly accessible to God's gaze' [*'unmittelbar zu Gott'*]. Historiography must emulate these novels' capacity to explode the temporal continuum" (*GS*, 1, 3, p. 1244). The quotation is from Ranke, one of the historicist villains of "Über den Begriff der Geschichte," and, in accordance with Benjamin's conception of quotation, it explodes the motif out of its context and quotes it against itself. Such disruption is, moreover, its theme.

The God's eye view is no longer to enable the historicist viewer to range over the historical continuum; it is, on the contrary, to make possible its disruption, the isolation of a monadological segment.

23. Cf., in this context, Gershom Scholem's account of the *Zohar*, "the masterpiece of Spanish Kabbalism" (*The Messianic Idea in Judaism* [New York: Schocken, 1971], p. 39). "Since the Fall of Adam, the world is no longer ruled by the Tree of Life as it had been in the beginning, but by the Tree of Knowledge.... Under the rule of this Tree, the world contains differentiated spheres: the holy and the profane, the pure and the impure, the permitted and the forbidden, the living and the dead, the divine and the demonic.... In a world in which the power of evil has been broken, all those differentiations also disappear which had been derived from it.... Where everything is holy there will no longer be need of restrictions and prohibitions ..." (ibid., pp. 23–24). Is it perhaps this return to the prelapsarian Life which preceded our fallen epistemological oppositions that explains the apparent contradiction whereby Benjamin's world of messianic prose is defined both as the culmination of universal history-writing and as a final liberation from the written word, as both Knowledge and Life? Such is the all-inclusiveness of triadic fulfillment, that the third stage is more than the first two put together: "In the redemption lights shine forth from within the universe which until then had remained hidden inside their source. There are locked-up realms of the divine which will not be opened until that time, and they make the state of redemption infinitely richer and more fulfilled than any initial state" (ibid., p. 34). Benjamin translates this motif of the "locked-up realms of the divine" into a theory of revolutionary memory according to which each present has the power to open up a "quite definite, hitherto locked chamber of the past" (*GS*, 1, 3, p. 1231). The taboos that are thereby lifted are the inhibitions of men's historical memory.

24. Cf. Baudelaire's *Elévation* ("Heureux celui ... / Quie plane sur la vie, et comprend sans effort / Le langage des fleurs et des choses muettes") and *Correspondances* ("La Nature est un temple où de vivants piliers / Laissent parfois sortir de confuses paroles"). The first stage of the triad, man's ontogenetic or phylogentic childhood, is variously identified as that of Baudelaire's *correspondances* (*GS*, 1, 2, p. 638) and Leskov's "olden times" when "nature cared about man's fate" (*S*, 2, p. 244) and its "voice" was clearly audible (ibid., pp. 253–54). (But Baudelaire's paradises are lost from the outset. The subject of *La Vie Antérieure* is already in mourning. And in *Correspondances* it is not Man who interprets oracular Nature but, if anything, Nature that recognizes him; the effect is not one of original unity but of alienation, not of home but of *das Unheimliche*).

25. "The language of nature is comparable to a secret password that each sentry hands on to the next in his own language ..." (*S*, 2, p. 419). "The realm of spirits [*Geisterreich*] ... constitutes a succession in which one relieved the other, and each took ... over from his forerunner" (*Phänomenologie des Geistes*, [Hamburg: F. Meiner, 1952], p. 564). Cf., in this context, Jacques Derrida's proposal to translate *Aufhebung* by *relève*.

26. "The reestablishment of all things in their proper place, which constitutes the redemption, produces a totality which knows nothing of ... a division between inwardness and outwardness" (Scholem, *Messianic Idea*, p. 17. Cf. also pp. 45–47). The messianic dream of totality converges with the Hegelian-Lukácsian version of the epic. Benjamin draws on both traditions.

27. Such motifs of course derive more directly from messianic theology

than from German Idealism. But in his essay "Der deutsche Idealismus der jüdischen Philosophen" (in *Philosophisch-politische Profile* [Frankfurt: Suhrkamp, 1971], pp. 37–66) Jürgen Habermas has documented the inextricability of the two traditions.

28. Such light is, however, itself too fragmented to be a source of uniform global illumination: "It is not as if the past casts its light on the present, or the present its light on the past, but the image is the coincidence of past and present in a constellation" (*GS*, 1, 3, p. 1242). Cf., by contrast, the closing section of T. W. Adorno's *Minima Moralia* (Frankfurt: Suhrkamp, 1969): "The only form of philosophy for which responsibility can be taken in the face of present despair would be the attempt to consider everything as it would look from the standpoint of redemption. Knowledge has no light but that shed on the world by redemption: all else is mere technical duplication. Perspectives must be devised that displace and estrange the world, reveal it to be, with its rifts and cracks, as indigent and distorted as it will appear one day in the messianic light" (pp. 333–34). Adorno's messianic light is that much steadier and more "philosophical" than Benjamin's. The problem of its epistemological status immediately arises. While the world cries out for such messianic perspectives, they in turn presuppose an impossibly exterior standpoint undistorted by the existent; and in the face of the exertions involved in reconciling the impossible with the indispensable, "the question of the reality or unreality of redemption is itself almost inconsequential" (ibid.). Adorno here comes close to equating the messianic idea with a theological postulate which is then absorbed by the philosophical argument it generates. Cf., on obsorption and its limits, note 49 below.

29. Jewish messianism, Scholem has shown, both resists and lends itself to secularization. Cf. *Messianic Idea*, pp. 10, 26, 37.

30. These splinters of messianic time recall the languages which the translator is to make "recognizable, like shards, as fragments of a vessel, fragments of a larger language," which in turn seem related to the heaps of debris with which both the angel of history and the little hunchback's victim find themselves confronted, the ruins of a world that is, in every sense, fallen. Such metaphors are so many variations on a central motif of the Lurianic Kabbalah, the "breaking of the vessels": "The divine light entered these vessels in order to take forms appropriate to their function in creation, but the vessels could not contain the light and thus were broken. . . . The light was dispersed. Much of it returned to its source; some portions, or 'sparks,' fell downward and were scattered, some rose upward. . . . The divine light which should have subsisted in specific forms and in places appointed for it from the beginning is no longer in its proper place because the vessels were broken, and thereafter all things went awry. . . . Next comes reparation, the third juncture in the great process: the breaking can be healed. The primal flaw must be mended so that all things can return to their proper place, to their original posture" (Scholem, *Messianic Idea*, pp. 45–46). Benjamin translates these sparks of light into splinters of messianic time and implicitly conceives the "task" of translator and historian alike, and the angel's longing, in terms of the Kabbalistic *Tikkun* (ibid., pp. 13, 109) or *restitutio in integrum* (*S*, 1, p. 511), whereby all the broken pieces and loose ends are to be restored to their "appointed place" (*GS*, 1, 3, p. 1234). As the rubble outside piles up, this Kabbalistic myth, which structures Benjamin's early philosophy of language and translation, is itself dispersed and buried in the later writings, the last of which then gathers up some of the pieces. And it is precisely in

the oddest, lowest places that Benjamin lights upon the divine sparks, which, by association with the shards of the broken vessels, he calls "splinters."

31. Cf. *The Descent from Heaven, A Study of Epic Continuity* (New Haven: Yale Univ. Press 1963), pp. 10–11, 16, 20, 49.

32. It emerges from Scholem's work on Jewish messianism that the messianic idea is never reducible to what Mircea Eliade has called "the myth of the eternal return." It is, rather, a mesh, "deeply intertwined, and yet . . . of a contradictory nature," of "conservative," "restorative," and "utopian" forces (*Messianic Idea*, pp. 3, 4, 13–14, 34). An analogous tension is at work, according to Benjamin, in the "will to happiness"—and the "Theologischpolitisches Fragment" defines happiness as *the* profane modality of the messianic. There is, according to the essay on Proust, "a double will to happiness, a dialectic of happiness: a hymnic and an elegiac form. The one: the unheard-of, the unprecedented, the height of bliss. The other: the first happiness" (*S*, 2, p. 135). In Benjamin's hands Proust's "elegiac" will to happiness becomes, it has emerged, the interaction of restorative and utopian impulses. His recurrent emblem for "hymic" happiness is the talmudic legend, according to which innumerable angels are created anew every minute in order to sing their "hymn" of praise before God and then vanish into nothingness (*S*, 2, pp. 195, 279). Such happiness, "the rhythm of messianic nature" (*S*, 1, p. 512), is the "hymnic" rhythm of messianic "prose."

33. A great divide separates those who are driven by the messianic impulse in one or another of its forms (e.g., Ernst Bloch's *Prinzip Hoffnung*) and those who—hoping *beyond* rather than *against* hope and seeking a *different* awakening—deconstruct it as a millennial dream which generates narrative fictions. The present essay sits on the fence. It is torn between the impulse to have done with the ubiquitous triad as a figure of thought and admiration for the thinking that Benjamin could not have done without it.

34. The "continuity" of the past is *both* historicist ideology *and* historical reality. Each cements the other. To the negative continuity of ruling class *historiography* Benjamin opposes the damaged traditions of the oppressed. To seek to repair the damage—that is, to lend continuity to their discontinuity—is to combat one form of self-fulfilling prophecy with another: "(Basic contradiction: 'Tradition as the discontinuum of the past versus history-writing as the continuum of events.'—'It may be that the continuity of tradition is illusory. But in that case the very persistence of this illusion of persistence establishes its continuity')" (*GS*, 1, 3, p. 1236).

35. Benjamin had himself diagnosed a similar problem in his dissertation on the German Romantics. Friedrich Schlegel was, he approvingly notes, intent on imparting the upmost definition and particularity to his notion of the universal "idea" of art. In order to avoid giving the impression that it was an abstraction, Schlegel proceeded to posit a contrary equation between the universal and the individual. As valid as the underlying impulse was, Benjamin concludes, this could only result in strained concepts and forced paradoxes (*GS*, 1, 1, pp. 88–90). In seeking to invest the messianic idea with maximum concretion, Benjamin is also forced to resort to fragments and conceptual twists.

36. In taking a God's-eye view (Ranke's *alles gleich unmittelbar zu Gott*), historicism transforms historical succession into simultaneity. Indeed, the divine suspension of historical time—which is not to be confused with messianic *Jetztzeit*—ultimately negates even the process of reading: God "saw" that it was good. It is this spatialization of time that reduces history to

homogeneous "progress" and empties it of both "lamentation" and "messianic force." It belongs to the ideology of those who (would) command history from above, possess it as far as the eye can see. The dense, involved, voluminous text is flattened into an open page, unfolded, unbound, unrolled, a flat, one-dimensional version of epic breadth. Something similar could be said of the triadic scheme itself—a present experience that projects its genesis and telos into past and future and expands the atemporal simultaneity of its logical oppositions into the successivity of a triadic narrative, one that, however, would merely repeat that simultaneity in seemingly more temporal form. As the unfolding of a present, the temporal structure of the idealist triad could thus contribute to the dissipation of revolutionary energy. Whence Benjamin's contrary emphasis on the compression and narrowness of messianic actuality as a bounded present, "strait gate" (*GS*, 1, 2, p. 704), and "Caudine yoke" (*S*, 1, p. 575). Just as historicism drains history of its energy (and is, correlatively, a "brothel" [*GS*, 1, 2, p. 702] that drains the historicist of *his*), so for the same reason, Jacques Derrida has shown, the structuralist reading of literature deprives it of its (temporal) "force." (Cf. his essay "Force et Signification," in *L'Ecriture et la Différence* [Paris: Editions du Seuil, 1967]). In both cases the inert flatness of the reading would be a certain impotence. Structuralism would thus rejoin the historicism it is forever denouncing. It would be its "specular opposite." And so would even the Bergsonian vitalism that makes the spatialization of time its primary target: "The *durée* from which death has been eliminated has the bad infinity [*schlechte Unendlichkeit*] of an ornament" (*GS*, 1, 2, p. 643).

37. There would seem to be some contradiction between the two conceptions of the messianic era as the Last Judgment and as a festive world of prose. In one case everything is visualized as having been finally restored to its *proper*, appointed place. The other recalls more anarchic visions of Jewish messianism according to which the new age is defined as a *release* from the proprieties and taboos imposed on a sinful world. "A positive commandment or a prohibition could scarcely still be the same when it no longer had for its object the separation of good and evil to which man was called, but rather arose from the Messianic spontaneity of human freedom purely flowing forth. . . . At this point there arises the possibility of a turning from the restorative conception of the final reestablishment of the reign of law to a utopian view in which restrictive traits will no longer be determinative and decisive, but be replaced by certain as yet totally unpredictable traits which will reveal entirely new aspects of free fulfillment" (Scholem, *Messianic Ideas*, pp. 20–21). The two motifs, both topoi of the messianic tradition, are less incompatible than it first appears. For if the world of anarchic prose marks a liberation from law, order, and propriety, it is also another triadic version of the reestablishment of everything in its proper place. The taboos from which it has released itself are themselves symptomatic of a fall from grace, the loss of an original propriety which is a point of "creative indifference," a positivity prior to the distinction between positive and negative, a state (of goodness?) prior to the separation of good from evil, the Tree of Life that precedes the Tree of Knowledge (ibid., p. 23). The Fall ought not to have happened. It both *was* improper and inaugurated the distinction between the proper and the improper, that distinction ultimately being, *as* distinction, an improper one. The final stage of the triad reestablishes the original creative nondistinction—propriety before (and now after) propriety. Now that everything is, in this sense, in its place, law and order can be dispensed with.

The first and third stages of the triad thus represent a *coincidentia oppositorum*. The law of contradiction, another taboo that has its proper place only in a fallen world, did not yet hold or will do so no longer. In an unredeemed world redemption would thus be formulable only in paradoxical terms. Everything and nothing will be holy, proper, etc. Seen thus, the contradiction between a feast and a judgment would be without objective foundation; it would be attributable to the limits of fallen, second-stage reason. Such a messianic world could also be seen as the impossible dream of enjoying the best of both worlds, orderly judgment and the transgression of order.

38. On the one hand, the "end" of history that Jewish messianism envisages is not a final telos but an abrupt stop, "not a goal but an end" (*S*, 1, p. 511). Cf. Scholem, *Messianic Idea*, p. 7. At the same time, Jewish messianism, unlike its more spiritual Christian counterpart, "has always maintained a concept of redemption as an event which takes place publicly, on the stage of history and within the community" (ibid., p. 1). Both impulses —to break with the continuum, the cumulative evil, of previous history and to make the historical world the "arena" of its redemption—inform Benjamin's thinking. The tension relates to that between the actuality and the inconceivability of the redeemed world.

39. "'Time,' writes Proust, 'is peculiarly chopped up in Baudelaire; only a few rare days open up; they are significant ones. . . .' These significant days are, in Joubert's terms, days of completion. They are days of recollection [*Eingedenken*]. . . . Baudelaire defines their content in the notion of *correspondances*. . . . What makes the festive days great and significant is the encounter with an earlier life." (*GS*, 1, 2, pp. 637–39). In "collecting" the "festive" "days of recollection" into a "spiritual year" (ibid., p. 641), Baudelaire compounds the act of *recueillement*. It is the reverse of the "grey bailiff's" tax collection. It also serves as an antidote to spleen, the feeling of "having been expelled from the calendar" (ibid., p. 643). Recreating an equivalent to the calendar of yesteryear out of the festive epiphanies of the present, Baudelaire also anticipates the messianic feast day, which will gather up the "fragmented components of authentic historical experience" (*GS*, 1, 2, p. 643) into a crowning totality.

40. Cf. Szondi, "Hoffnung im Vergangenen," pp. 499–500.

41. Where vision is *substituted* for perception, the utopian response to the present can, however, become an ideological reaction-formation: "[Bergson] rejects any historical determination of experience. He thus manages above all to avoid coming any closer to that experience out of which his own philosophy originated or, rather, against which it was pitted. It is the inhospitable, blinding experience of the era of heavy industrialization. To the eye that closes itself to this experience there presents itself an experience of a complementary kind as its spontaneous after-image. Bergson's philosophy is an attempt to flesh out and retain this after-image" (*GS*, 1, 2, p. 609). But how distinguish the after-image that spontaneously "presents itself" from the "dialectical image" which "suddenly presents itself to the subject of history at the moment of danger" (*GS*, 1, 3, p. 1243)? *Can* historical and wishful images be cleanly disentangled? Benjamin's own "historical determination of experience," which provides the basis for his significantly respectful critique of Bergson and *Lebensphilosophie*, itself remains caught within this problematic. By what authority does he two pages later define "experience in the strict sense" (!?) as resting on the preestablished harmony of individual and collective experience? Is not this conjunction itself *in part* a spontaneous

after-image prompted by the present-day disjunction he is with its help seeking to describe?

42. "The past seemed to [social democracy] to have been gathered into the barns of the present once and for all; if the future held out the prospect of work, it also had in store the certainty of a rich harvest" (*AN*, p. 310).

43. *Phänomenologie des Geistes*, p. 563.

44. One such "ceremony" (*Feier*) is the celebration of the famous at the expense of the anonymous, unknown soldiers who people history: "It is more difficult to honor the memory of the nameless than that of the famous, the celebrated [*Gefeierte*], not excluding the poets and thinkers" (*GS*, 1, 3, p. 1241. Cf. ibid., p. 1237). "Great books" thus celebrated are the spoils of the "colossal triumphal procession of ideal German figures," "eternal values celebrated according to a syncretistic ritual" (*AN*, pp. 451–52).

45. Cf., on the classic "onto-theological" interrelationships of logos, phallus, voice, presence, life, etc., the works of Jacques Derrida.

46. Both myth and demythologization each carry a double connotation, at once positive and negative; each is, in its respective way, mythical and more than mythical; each could be the other's corrective; only their reconciliation could bring about their emancipation from myth—such is the dialectical model of demythologization elaborated in T. W. Adorno's and Max Horkheimer's *Dialektik der Aufklärung* (Frankfurt: Fischer, 1969). But in that work, which responds to Benjamin's call for "a theory of history from which fascism can be sighted" (*GS*, 1, 3, p. 1244), the authors trace the *negative* dialectic between myth and demythologization that has obtained throughout human history. Myth has acquired a scientific appearance and totalitarian dimensions. Bereft of the hopeless hope he placed in "dialectics at a standstill," their theory is at once more dialectical and more pessimistic than Benjamin's. But, hopeful or hopeless, both diagnoses agree: only the abrupt intervention of the Messiah could stop the locomotive of history. Whereas Adorno's no less dialectical critique of "Paris, die Hauptstadt des XIX Jahrhunderts" (cited in note 21) argued the dialectical potential of capitalism, *Dialektik der Aufklärung* considers fascism as the end towards which the fateful dialectic of history has been gravitating, a satanic parody of utopian reconciliation. It is the refracted difference between the mid-thirties and the mid-forties.

47. *Die Frühschriften*, ed. Landshut (Stuttgart: Kröner, 1953), p. 528.

48. Benjamin's passing allusions to dialectics are often idiosyncratic and sometimes subversive of its classical assumptions. They may be said to "quote" dialectics. Quotation is in turn called a dialectical leap (*Sprung*), that of the tiger; Benjamin equates "dialectical" with *sprunghaft* (*GS*, 1, 3, p. 1243), "abrupt," "discontinuous." The tiger's abrupt departure would be, if that were possible, a leap out of the Hegelian dialectic, which contains all discontinuity within its philosophical continuum. Is "dialectics at a standstill" —the standstill of a leap suspended in mid-air—still dialectics? Whatever the answer, it is, given Benjamin's sense of the continuum, only the leap within and against it that can even hope to break its spell, its momentum: "Salvation attaches itself to the small leap in the continuous catastrophe" (*GS*, 1, 2, p. 683). Cf., for an important account of Georges Bataille's quite different— but comparably minimal and equally decisive—displacement of Hegelian terminology, his "hegelianisme sans réserves," Jacques Derrida's essay "De l'économie restreinte à l'économie générale" (in *L'Ecriture et la Différence*, pp. 369–407). To the "restricted economy" of speculative logic, which is

predicated on work, self-preservation, and the accumulation of capital, Bataille opposes a "general economy" which is characterized by such (non)concepts as "excess," "dissipation [*dépense*]," "communication," "heterogeneity," the erotic "affirmation of life unto death," etc. Such "poetry" is, *mutatis mutandis*, nourished by some of the same impulses as Benjamin's conception of messianic prose. Both, for example, equate revolution with bodily transgression, that of the potlatch or the feast; the "Theologisch-politisches Fragment" has something in common with "De l'Erotisme"; and in their respective ways Bataille's dualistic oppositions and Benjamin's triadic reintegrations necessarily compromise with the Hegelianism they transgress. But it is what they are against that they share in common. And it is with certain motifs that originate with the German Romantics, the regular objects of Hegel's polemical asides, that Benjamin's attack on historicism (itself a diluted form of Hegelianism) has the most explicit affinities.

49. The *Weltgeist* is guaranteed to assimilate anything—and thereby the Hegelian encyclopedia is in return assimilated to the model of a theological *summa*. Benjamin, for his part, knows that his powers of assimilation have their limits: "My thought is to theology as blotting paper is to ink. It is completely saturated with it. But if the blotting paper had is way, nothing of what is written would remain" (*GS*, 1, 3, p. 1235). At which point the fetters of the written word—namely, holy writ—would be burst and, instead of returning to itself (as in Benjamin's early theological writings), the divine word would be absorbed into the human element, *aufgehoben*, preserved and negated, "blotted out." Theological *Aufhebung* would be more or less theologically *aufgehoben*. But the desire for *Aufhebung* that knows itself to be desire is already that much freer of theology than the one that takes its answering mirage for reality. And *Aufhebung* is not Benjamin's only desire.

50. *Ästhetik*, Bd. 2, p. 407.

51. ". . . like one who keeps afloat on a shipwreck by climbing to the top of the mast that is already crumbling. But from there he has a chance to give a signal leading to his rescue" (*BR*, Bd. 2, p. 532).

52. In *Der Begriff der Kunstkritik in der deutschen Romantik* Benjamin had shown that the intellectual activity of the German Romantics rested on an equivalent "metaphysical credo" (*GS*, 1, 1, p. 62), an axiomatic belief in a unitary absolute which takes the form of an unfolding system, a "reflexive medium" to whose continuity and coherence—*Zusammenhang* is the recurrent term—Benjamin repeatedly draws attention. Thus the Romantic conception of criticism as the dissolution of particular literary works is grounded in the conviction that there exists an underlying continuum, a capital(ized) unity, of which they constitute so many moments (ibid., p. 77): "Criticism wholly sacrifices the individual work for the sake of all-encompassing unity [*um des Einen Zusammenhanges willen*]" (ibid., p. 86). The givenness of this *Zusammenhang* functions as an a priori guarantee that even the seemingly disparate hangs together, and that, thanks to two closely interrelated modes, "mystical terminology" and "wit," there can be an intuitive apprehension of the whole: "What is presupposed is a continuous, mediating *Zusammenhang*, a reflexive medium of concepts. In wit, as in the mystical term, that conceptual medium appears in a flash [*blitzartig*]" (ibid., p. 49). If *Witz* does not belong to Benjamin's own terminology, its correlative, *Blitz*, does; and their activity parallels that of involuntary memory and quotation. "Romantic messianism," which, according to Benjamin, supplies the "viewpoint" (ibid., p. 12) of early Romantic esthetics, is clearly one of the sources of his

own. Philosophy is, according to Novalis, "a mystical . . . penetrating [*durchdringend*] idea which ceaselessly drives us in all directions" (ibid., p. 47). At the same time reflexion is defined as "the beginning of a true self-penetration [*Selbstdurchdringung*] of the mind, which never ends" and the future as the "chaos that penetrated itself" (ibid., p. 38). The centrifugal directions thus have a secret center. Such is also the mystical conviction implicit in Benjamin's metaphor of a movement that "penetrates" downwards but ends up at the "antipodes." More generally, Benjamin's extensive characterization of Romantic thinking as being "systematically oriented" without being "systematically developed" (p. 47 passim) is highly relevant to his own, not only where it cites Romantic motifs. In his late notes such motifs represent one source among others for a nucleus of terms which, like the Romantics' "mystical terminology," form a constellation which is neither a system nor a non-system. But, given the gap between, on the one hand, Romantic prose as the last phase of an esthetic continuum notable for its "integrity and unity" (ibid., p. 64) and, on the other, "integral" surrealist prose, which, if it can be called a medium at all, is a medium of division, Benjamin's later quotation of Romantic motifs cannot but alter them by introducing them into a still more fragmented context of continuums that have to be broken and discontinuities that are to be pieced together.

NOTES ON CONTRIBUTORS

BARBARA HARLOW is a visiting assistant professor at the American Unisity in Cairo in the Department of English and Comparative Literature. She has published articles on Nietzsche, and Ruskin and Proust, and is currently preparing a monograph on Proust and translation.

CAROL JACOBS is an associate professor of German at The Johns Hopkins University. Her book, *The Dissimulating Harmony*, appeared this spring from The Johns Hopkins University Press. Her essays have appeared in *Diacritics*, *Sub-Stance*, and *Modern Language Notes*.

RICHARD JACOBSON teaches semiotics and the literature of antiquity in the Department of Comparative Literature of the University of Wisconsin–Madison. He has published extensively on Biblical semiotics and is preparing a monograph on the semiotics of legal discourse.

LOUIS MARIN studied at the Ecole Normale Supérieure in Paris, where he received his academic degrees: Licence-ès-lettres, Agrégation (philosophy), and Doctorat d'Etat (philosophy); his thesis, *La critique du discours: Etudes sur la logique de Port-Royal et les "Pensées" de Pascal*, was published in 1975. Now a professor of Romance languages at The Johns Hopkins University, he has taught at the Sorbonne, the Ecole Pratique des Hautes Etudes, and the University of California at San Diego. He is also the author of *Etudes sémiologiques* and *Utopiques*, and his article, "Disneyland: A Degenerate Utopia," appeared in *Glyph I*.

Contributors

PIERO PUCCI is a professor of classics at Cornell University. His book, *Hesoid and the Language of Poetry*, was recently published by The Johns Hopkins University Press.

RICHARD RAND is an assistant professor of English at the State University of New York at Stony Brook. He is currently at work on a book entitled *Reading Portraits*, which will include his essay in the present volume of *Glyph*.

JAMES SIEGEL is an associate professor of anthropology and Asian studies at Cornell University. He is the author of *The Rope of God*, and his essay, "Pramoedya's 'Things Vanished,' with a Commentary," appeared in *Glyph I*. In his current work he is examining Sumatran epics.

IRVING WOHLFARTH is an associate professor of comparative literature at the University of Oregon. He has published essays on Laclos, Baudelaire, and Benjamin, on whom he is currently completing two book-length studies.

ANDRZEJ WARMINSKI is a Ph.D. candidate in comparative literature at Yale University. He has published essays on Hölderlin in *Modern Language Notes* and Rilke in *Rilke Centennial Studies*.